beginner's
japanese
helen gilhooly

For over 60 years, more than
50 million people have learnt over
750 subjects the **teach yourself**
way, with impressive results.

be where you want to be
with **teach yourself**

For UK order enquiries: please contact Bookpoint Ltd, 130 Milton Park, Abingdon, Oxon, OX14 4SB. Telephone: +44 (0) 1235 827720. Fax: +44 (0) 1235 400454. Lines are open 09.00–17.00, Monday to Saturday, with a 24-hour message answering service. Details about our titles and how to order are available at www.teachyourself.co.uk

For USA order enquiries: please contact McGraw-Hill Customer Services, PO Box 545, Blacklick, OH 43004-0545, USA. Telephone: 1-800-722-4726. Fax: 1-614-755-5645.

For Canada order enquiries: please contact McGraw-Hill Ryerson Ltd, 300 Water St, Whitby, Ontario, L1N 9B6, Canada. Telephone: 905 430 5000. Fax: 905 430 5020.

Long renowned as the authoritative source for self-guided learning – with more than 50 million copies sold worldwide – the **teach yourself** series includes over 500 titles in the fields of languages, crafts, hobbies, business, computing and education.

British Library Cataloguing in Publication Data: a catalogue record for this title is available from the British Library.

Library of Congress Catalog Card Number: on file.

First published in UK 1996 by Hodder Education, 338 Euston Road, London, NW1 3BH.

First published in US 1996 by The McGraw-Hill Companies, Inc.

This edition published 2003.

The **teach yourself** name is a registered trade mark of Hodder Headline.

Typeset by Transet Limited, Coventry, England.
Printed in Great Britain for Hodder Education, a division of Hodder Headline, 338 Euston Road, London, NW1 3BH, by Cox & Wyman Ltd, Reading, Berkshire.

The publisher has used its best endeavours to ensure that the URLs for external websites referred to in this book are correct and active at the time of going to press. However, the publisher and the author have no responsibility for the websites and can make no guarantee that a site will remain live or that the content will remain relevant, decent or appropriate.

Hodder Headline's policy is to use papers that are natural, renewable and recyclable products and made from wood grown in sustainable forests. The logging and manufacturing processes are expected to conform to the environmental regulations of the country of origin.

Impression number 10 9
Year   2010 2009 2008 2007 2006

iii

contents

• introducing yourself in a business or
formal situation • exchanging business cards
• making a phone call to a Japanese home
and office

About the author

Helen Gilhooly has lived and worked in Japan, and has extensive experience of teaching Japanese and writing teaching materials at secondary school and adult level. She has an MA and a PGCE in Japanese and is the Language College Director of Aldercar Community Language College in Derbyshire. She is also a teacher trainer of Japanese at Nottingham University.

Acknowledgements

Many thanks to all those people who have supported me in the writing of this book. In particular, thanks to Chizumi Fallon for her patient work in checking the drafts and contributing to the dialogues; to Mavis Pilbeam for her invaluable help with proof-reading and input into the text; to Masae Sugahara for her advice; to Robert Gilhooly for his help in seeking out authentic materials; to Martin Hodge for composing the Japanese music for the recording; and to Kate Jarratt and Sarah Mitchell for reading and commenting on the lessons and audio-script. But most of all, to John Rogers for his untiring support and encouragement.

Language adviser: Chizumi Fallon

The publishers and author would like to thank the following for the use of material in this book: Japan National Tourist Office, UK; NTT Europe; the Japanese Inn Group; East Group Japan Rail; Ministry of Post and Telecommunications; Shibuya Seibu department store; Domino's pizza, Tokyo; and Tama City International Center.

introduction

About the course

Japanese has become increasingly popular as a language to learn in recent years, and a growing awareness of Japan has been created through industry, television, newspaper articles, Japanese events and exhibitions. However, Japanese is still regarded as an 'exotic' language by many people and believed to be 'too difficult to learn'. Nothing could be further from the truth – Japanese is a very accessible language and can be a great deal of fun to learn. The language itself can teach you many interesting things about Japanese life and culture, and this book seeks to give you an understanding both of the language and the culture behind that language, and so demystify something of the 'exotic' in order to give you a clearer view.

Teach Yourself Beginner's Japanese is the right course for you if you are a complete beginner or want to make a fresh start. It is a self-study course which will help you to understand and speak Japanese and apply what you have learnt to business and social situations both in Japan and in this country. There is even an opportunity for you to learn some of the basics of reading Japanese.

Two key elements

This book has two main parts. Units 1–12 introduce you to the basic structures and grammatical points you'll need in everyday situations. These units should be done in order as each builds on the previous ones.

Units 14–20 involve you in everyday situations such as shopping, eating out, travelling, meeting a Japanese business person and entertaining a Japanese person in your home. In these units you have the opportunity to put into practice the language you have learnt in the first 12 units. You can do these units in any order.

The course is best used together with the accompanying recording, but is not dependent upon them. You are recommended to obtain the recording if possible because it will help you to pronounce Japanese correctly and to acquire an authentic accent. The recorded dialogues and activities will also give you plenty of practice in understanding and responding to spoken Japanese. The **Pronunciation guide** and the new words in the first few units are also recorded to help you speak Japanese correctly in the important early stages of your study.

The headings on the recording are in Japanese and in English, but in case you want to see them written, here they are:

Tango-hyō	Vocabulary list
Kaiwa	Conversation
Kiku-renshū	Listening practice
Hanashimashō	Let's talk

Readers without the recording will find that there are some units which contain an activity that cannot be done with the book alone, but in such cases the material is always covered by other activities in that unit.

Introducing the main characters

There is a storyline running throughout the book, which involves the following characters.

The Yamaguchi family:

- Reiko Yamaguchi, mother and housewife. She works part-time;
- Masaki Yamaguchi, father and company employee at the Tokyo Bank. He does business with foreign companies;
- Emi Yamaguchi, daughter, aged 19 and a student at Tokyo University. She is planning a trip to England during the university holidays;
- Takeshi Yamaguchi, son, aged 14 and at junior high school;
- Anne Jenkins (pronounced **An Jenkinsu** in Japanese), aged 22. She is coming to Tokyo to stay with the Yamaguchi family and learn Japanese at a local foreign language school.

Language school characters:

- Han is from China;
- Scott (pronounced **Sukotto** in Japanese) is from America;
- Tani is from France;
- Heidi (pronounced **Haidi**) is from Germany;
- Satō-sensei, the teacher.

You'll learn more about these characters as you progress through the book.

About Units 1–12

The first page of each unit tells you what you are going to learn in that unit. Then there is an **Introduction**. There is then an easy activity **Let's talk** to get you speaking straight away.

Vocabulary list. This section contains the most important words and phrases from the unit. Try to learn them by heart. They will be used in that unit and in later units. There are various tips throughout the book to help you with learning new words.

Conversation. Progress to the conversation once you are at least familiar with the new words. The conversations will show you how the words are used and will reinforce the new words in your memory. If you have the recording listen to the conversation once or twice without stopping; if not, read through it without looking anything up. This will help you to develop the skill of listening or reading for gist or general meaning. You don't have to understand every word to understand the overall meaning. There are also extra words (**Vocabulary list**) under each conversation to aid your understanding.

Next, use the pause button to divide the conversation into smaller chunks and try repeating each phrase out loud. This will help you gain a more authentic accent. If you don't have the recording, use a piece of paper or book marker to cover part of the dialogue so that you can concentrate on a small part at a time. The important thing in either case is to *speak out loud* because this will help you to gain confidence in speaking Japanese. If possible, try recording yourself sometimes. If you have the recording, you could compare your recording with the native speakers to help you improve your pronunciation. Or if you have Japanese friends, practise on them!

Sections marked **ℹ** give you two sorts of advice: (1) hints on developing techniques to improve your learning skills; hints on mastering a particular structure or grammar point; hints on remembering vocabulary; hints for developing your confidence, and so on; and (2) about Japan: short notes, in English, offering you an insight into different aspects of Japanese society and culture, and usually linked to the situations you are learning about in each unit.

Explanations. This section concentrates on the main grammar and structures for that unit and gives you lots of examples. You can either read the examples first and see if you can work out the rule for yourself, or read the **Explanation** first. Once you feel confident with the explanations try making up your own examples.

Practice. This section consists of various activities and exercises to help you practise what you have learnt in the unit. Some activities are marked with the **▶** symbol. For these you will need to listen to the recording. It is not essential to have the recording in order to complete the course and most activities are not dependent on it. However, listening to Japanese will make your learning much easier and more varied.

Test. At the end of each unit you can test yourself on what you have learnt up to that point. At the end of Unit 6 there is a **Review** section which gives you the opportunity to look back at the first six units before proceeding further. At the end of Unit 10 there is a **Revision test** which challenges you to test yourself on everything you have learnt in Units 1–10. And finally, at the end of Unit 12 the **Revision test** tests you on points from all the units in the learning section.

About Units 14–20

These units give you the opportunity to practise what you have learnt in meaningful and useful situations.

The first page tells you what you are going to learn, and under **Review** there is a checklist and page number for the structures you have already learnt which you will need in that unit. This gives you the opportunity to refer back to them and so feel fully confident before beginning the unit.

Vocabulary lists give you the basic vocabulary that you will need when dealing, in real life, with practical situations such as introducing yourself to a Japanese person, booking a room, making a phone call, ordering a meal, buying a train ticket.

There are several different **Conversations**, sometimes with **Vocabulary**, each dealing with different aspects of a topic. Remember to listen to the dialogues first and use the pause button to practise new phrases out loud (or read the dialogue out loud).

Practice. These are based on real Japanese situations and sometimes use authentic material, so you can develop a real feel for how things work in Japan.

Test and **Revision test.** As in Units 1–12.

Answers. The answers to all the **Let's talk**, **Practice** and **Tests** can be found at the back of the book.

Unit 13 – an introduction to reading Japanese

Contrary to popular opinion, Japanese is not a difficult language to speak, particularly at beginner's level. Pronunciation is fairly straightforward without any complicated rules, and the grammar is fairly simple and easy to grasp. Where Japanese does offer a more serious challenge to the learner is in reading and writing. However, that can be fun to learn too, and is very interesting. This book is written in our script (known as **rōmaji** or roman letters, in Japanese) so that the learner can get straight down to speaking Japanese without the barrier of an unknown form of writing. However, Unit 13 is a special unit. It gives the learner the opportunity to find out something about reading Japanese, and in the **Let's read** sections in this unit, you will find yourself actually reading some Japanese, including an authentic menu! This unit is designed as a one-off so that learners who would rather concentrate solely on listening and speaking skills can miss it out without it affecting their understanding of other units. However, in Unit 15 there is a menu written both in Japanese writing and **rōmaji** so that those who have read Unit 13 can have the chance to revise and practise what they learnt.

A note on using the recording

If you have obtained the recording which accompanies this book here are some tips for getting the best possible use out of it.

- Try to use in a quiet room or environment so that you can concentrate and listen to what is being said. Using a Walkman or headphones is ideal for this.
- When you first listen to a dialogue or activity, give yourself

an overall picture by listening to it all the way through once or twice. You won't get all the information the first time but it will help you to develop the skill of picking out the essential points and processing them in your brain more quickly. This in turn will help you to increase the speed of your listening and understanding.

- Once you have listened to a whole activity once or twice, break it down into manageable chunks if necessary, using the pause button, so that you can complete the information required. Also, use the pause button when you are practising chunks of dialogue. This will help you to focus on accurate pronunciation and thus to develop your Japanese accent. Use it too when memorizing new words or dialogue – you will get better results if you work on small chunks at a time.

How to be successful at learning Japanese

- A little, often, is far more effective than a long session every now and then. So try and put in about 20–30 minutes' study each day, if possible, or two or three times per week. If you study at a regular time, for example, before you go to bed, or during lunchtime, it will be easier to get into the habit of studying a little, often.

- Find a balance between moving through the book and revising what you have already learnt. If you move forward too quickly, you will find later units difficult because you haven't built effectively on your learning. Equally, however, if you keep going over the points you have learnt, you will feel frustrated at not moving forward. Set aside one session every now and again (maybe once every five sessions) to look back at previous units and remind yourself of what you have learnt. A good place to start is with the test at the end of the unit – if you have difficulties with a certain structure, refer back to its explanations and examples.

- Study in a quiet room where you can speak out loud. People develop different studying habits – some people like to study with music in the background, for example, while others need complete silence. The difference with learning a language is that you need to build up your speaking and listening skills, and so you need somewhere where you can concentrate and, literally, hear yourself speak.

- Don't be too harsh on yourself! Learning a language is a gradual and cumulative process, and everyone makes mistakes. You mustn't expect to be perfect straight away, and you can't be expected to remember every item of vocabulary and every new structure. Learn slowly and surely, and don't be impatient with yourself.

• Seek out opportunities to use your Japanese. You don't have to go to Japan to do this. There are many opportunities these days to experience Japan in this country, and there are quite a number of Japanese people living here. Find out about Japanese societies, join a Japanese class, go to a Japanese restaurant and practise ordering in Japanese (but be careful – people working in Japanese restaurants are not always Japanese) or visit a nearby Japanese department store, bookshop or supermarket, if there is one, where you will hear Japanese being spoken all around you.

There are many tips to help you learn throughout the book in the ![i] sections. They often repeat this advice and add to it – take heed of it, and most of all remember that learning and using a foreign language is *fun*!

At the back of the book

At the back of the book is a reference section which contains:

• **Taking it further**
• a **Key to the exercises;**
• a **Japanese–English vocabulary** list containing all the words in the course;
• a complete list of numbers in Japanese;
• an index to enable you to look things up in the book.

Symbols and abbreviations

▶ This indicates that the recording is needed for the following section. (But often there is an alternative way of completing the section if you don't have the recording.)

![i] This indicates that the following section is about Japan or contains hints with advice on improving your language learning skills.

(Lit.) = literally

Pronunciation guide

The Japanese 'alphabet' is made up of a number of sounds created by combining the five vowels (**a, e, i, o, u**) with a consonant (letters which are not vowels). These vowel sounds are always pronounced in the same way. So whereas in English, for example, the sound **a** can vary as follows:

man   mate   mayor (etc.)

The sound **a** in Japanese is always pronounced as in *man*.

The five Japanese vowels in order are:

a   as in *man*
i   as in *hit*
u   as in *blue*
e   as in *end*
o   as in *hot*

This bizarre 'headline' will help you to remember these sounds:

Man hits two extra shots!
  a   i   u e   o

▶ How to pronounce syllables

Below is a sound chart of the Japanese syllables. If you have the recording, switch it on at the beginning, and you will hear some of the sounds below being spoken. Listen to a line at a time, starting with *a, i, u, e, o*, then pause the recording and say these sounds yourself. Continue like this until you reach Exercise 6, then switch it off (or repeat the process for extra practice). The recording will now be in the right place for the pronunciation exercise on the next page. If you don't have the recording, bear in mind the pronunciation of the five vowels as explained above and work through the chart line by line, saying the sounds out loud. Pronunciation of Japanese is very straightforward, and there are pointers at the side of the chart to help you.

Sound chart

a	i	u	e	o
ka	ki	ku	ke	ko
sa	shi	su	se	so
ta	chi	tsu	te	to

tsu is an unfamiliar sound for English speakers; it is only one syllable (or beat); squash the **t** and **s** together as you say them.

| na | ni | nu | ne | no |
| ha | hi | fu | he | ho |

fu is a soft sound, between **f** and **h**. Your front teeth don't touch your lips as you say it; air is let out between your teeth and lips.

ma	mi	mu	me	mo
ya		yu		yo
ra	ri	ru	re	ro

r is a soft sound, somewhere between **r** and **l**, and not like the French **r** sound.

| wa | | | | n |

n has a full beat. There are examples in **How to pronounce words** on page xvi.

| ga | gi | gu | ge | go |

g as in *get* not *gin*.

| za | ji | zu | ze | zo |
| ba | bi | bu | be | bo |

There is no **v** sound in Japanese, and **b** is substituted for foreign words. For example, *Valerie* becomes *Ba-ra-ri-i*.

| pa | pi | pu | pe | po |
| da | | | de | do |

The final set of sounds in the **Sound chart** consist of a consonant plus **ya**, **yu**, or **yo**. These also have a single beat (i.e. they are one syllable), although English-speaking people sometimes mistakenly pronounce these sounds with two beats. For example, the first sound of the city name **Kyoto** is sometimes wrongly pronounced **ki-yo** instead of **kyō**.

Practise saying these sounds carefully.

kya	kyu	kyo
sha	shu	sho
cha	chu	cho

ch as in *chance* not *character*

nya	nyu	nyo
hya	hyu	hyo
mya	myu	myo
rya	ryu	ryo
gya	gyu	gyo
ja	ju	jo

ja as in *jam* (not the German *ja*)

| bya | byu | byo |
| pya | pyu | pyo |

▶ How to pronounce words

- Every syllable in Japanese is given equal stress, whereas in English we give more stress to some parts of the words than others. Look at this example:

  English   A-<u>me</u>-ri-ca   The stress is on **me**.

  Japanese   A-me-ri-ka   Each syllable has equal stress.

  English-speaking people often add stress to Japanese words. For example:

  Hi-ro-<u>shi</u>-ma   The stress is on **shi** whereas it should sound like this: Hi-ro-shi-ma. (Listen to it on the recording.)

  To make your accent sound more authentic, try not to stress parts of words as you do in English; instead give equal stress to each syllable.

- **Long syllables**

  In this book, when a macron is used over a vowel it indicates that the sound is a long sound. Here is an example to illustrate this:

  Tōkyō   You hold the sounds with macrons for twice the normal length: To-o-kyo-o. (Listen to it on the recording.) The word should be spoken smoothly.

  However, macrons are not used in the case of place names when the name appears as part of an English text, only as part of a Japanese dialogue.

- **N** is a syllable by itself. Look at this example of *hello* in Japanese.

  ko-n-ni-chi-wa   (Listen to it on the recording.)

  When **n** is followed by **p**, **b** or **m** its sound softens to **m**:

  gambatte   *good luck*

  sampaku   *three nights* (Listen to these examples.)

  Where **n** is followed by a vowel, an apostrophe is inserted between them to distinguish the sound n from the sounds **na, ni, nu, ne, no**, as in this example: **ten'in** (*shopkeeper*) has four syllables **te-n-i-n**; it is not pronounced **te-ni-n**.

- **Double consonants**

  A double consonant indicates that you should pause slightly before saying it, as you would in these English examples (say them out loud):

  headdress (pause after *hea* – not *head dress*)
  bookcase (pause after *boo*)

  You will come across these double consonants in Japanese – **kk, ss, tt, tc, pp.** Here are some examples:

  gamba**tt**e   *good luck*

  Ho**kk**aidō   North island of Japan
  Sa**pp**oro   capital of Hokkaidō
  ma**ss**ugu   *straight on* (Listen to these examples.)

  You *always* add this pause in the case of Japanese double consonants.

- **Silent vowels**

  Sometimes **i** and **u** become almost unvoiced. This is indicated below by bracketing the vowel. Read (and listen to) these examples:

  des(u)   *it is*
  s(u)ki   *I like*
  ikimas(u)   *I go*
  hajimemash(i)te   *How do you do?*

  This will be pointed out to you as you come across such words in the units.

- **Pronunciation of non-Japanese words**

  Foreign words have to be adapted to the Japanese sound system. You have already seen one example of this above (the name *Valerie*). Here are some more examples of names:

  Sukotto   *Scott*
  Sumisu   *Smith*
  Furansu   *France*
  Satchā   *Thatcher* (Listen to these on the recording.)

  There is no *th* sound in Japanese and *s* is used instead.

▶ Practice

Below is a map of Japan with the four main islands and some of the main cities marked on it. Moving from north to south (1–12) say each place out loud, then check with the recording or pronunciation guide before moving on to the next one. Particular points to look out for are underlined.

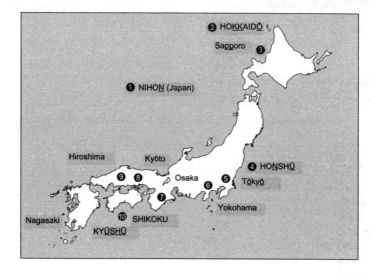

01

hajimemashite
how do you do?

In this unit you will learn
- how to introduce yourself
- how to say *hello* and *goodbye*
- how to say *excuse* me and *thank you*
- how to introduce a friend or business colleague

Introduction

You have already met the main characters in the book in the **Introduction**. You will be following their stories throughout the 20 units. Before you start this unit, look back over the pronunciation guide and practise it with the recording.

Also look at the **Study guide** on page xii. Learning by yourself requires discipline but can be very rewarding and means that you can progress at your own pace.

Try to set aside a regular time when you can put in half an hour's study rather than trying to do too much less regularly. You will progress more smoothly, and you will be able to build more quickly on your learning.

▶ Let's talk

Do you know any Japanese greetings already? People often know the word for *goodbye* – **sayōnara**, and sometimes *hello* – **konnichiwa**. Read out loud the words in the **Vocabulary list** below. If you have the recording, listen to one word at a time, pause, say the word out loud, then go on to the next word.

When you have completed this, you can test your pronunciation by going back to the beginning of the **Vocabulary**, this time saying the word before playing it on the recording.

Follow this routine each time you are introduced to new vocabulary, to develop a really authentic accent and a feel for the pronunciation of Japanese words. If you don't have the recording, there are some pronunciation tips after the new words.

Vocabulary list

Greetings

ohayō gozaimas(u)	*good morning*
konnichiwa	*hello; good afternoon (late morning onwards)*
konbanwa	*good evening*
oyasumi nasai	*good night*
sayōnara	*goodbye* (Lit. *If it must be so –* a fairly formal expression)

bai bai	*goodbye* (from the English *bye bye* – can sound childish)
ja mata ne!	*see you!* (casual)
mata ash(i)ta	*see you tomorrow*

Introductions

hajimemash(i)te	*how do you do?*
dōzo yorosh(i)ku	*pleased to meet you*
kochira wa ...	*this person is ...*
san	*Mr/Mrs/Miss/Ms* (addressing someone else)
dōmo arigatō (gozaimas(u))	*thank you (very much)*
arigatō	*thanks*
sumimasen	*excuse me; sorry*
hai	*yes*
Iie	*no*
desu	*am, is, are*

ℹ️ Pronunciation tips

- The **u** in **gozaimasu** and **desu** is usually not voiced (see the **Pronunciation guide**, page xvii) or appears only as a whispered sound. This also applies to the second **i** in **hajimemashite** and **dōzo yoroshiku**.
- Give the vowels with a macron (**ohayō**, **sayōnara**, **dōzo**, **dōmo**, **arigatō**) an extra beat, but make it sound smooth (see the **Pronunciation guide**, page xvi)
- Make sure the **n** syllable lasts for one beat. For example: **ko-n-ni-chi-wa**, **ko-n-ba-n-wa**.

▶ Conversation

Reiko Yamaguchi and her son Takeshi are meeting Anne Jenkins at Narita International airport near Tokyo. Reiko sees an English girl standing on her own. If you have the recording, switch it on and listen to the whole conversation once or twice. Then play it back line by line, pause, and say the conversation out loud.

Words in **bold** in the dialogues are given in the **Vocabulary lists**. If you don't have the recording, read through the dialogue below once or twice, then practise saying it out loud, remembering what you learnt in the **Vocabulary list** section.

Reiko	Ano … An Jenkins(u)-san desu **ka**.
Girl	Iie …
Reiko	(*embarrassed*) A! Sumimasen.
Takeshi	(*also embarrassed*) **Okāsan!**

Anne is waiting nearby and sees Reiko's sign with her name on it.

Anne	Sumimasen, Yamaguchi-san desu ka.
Reiko	Hai, **sō desu!**
Anne	Hajimemashite, An Jenkinsu desu. Dōzo yoroshiku. (*she bows*)
Reiko	(*bowing*) Hajimemashite, Yamaguchi Reiko desu. Dōzo yoroshiku.

Reiko then introduces her son to Anne.

Reiko	Kore wa Takeshi desu. **Musuko** desu.
Takeshi	(*bowing*) Dōzo yoroshiku.
Anne	(*bowing*) Dōzo yoroshiku.

On the journey back to the Yamaguchi home everyone is quiet: Anne is tired and only knows a few phrases in Japanese; Takeshi is a little shy about practising his English; Reiko is rather hoping that Anne will teach her some English during her stay.

On the train Takeshi bumps into a schoolfriend, Jun, and although Anne doesn't understand a lot of what they say, she's pleased to catch at least one expression that she knows.

| Takeshi | Konnichiwa! |
| Friend | Konnichiwa! |

Takeshi introduces Anne to his friend.

| Takeshi | Kochira wa An Jenkinsu-san desu. |
| Friend | Hajimemashite. Suzuki Jun desu. Dōzo yoroshiku. (*bows*) |

Later as they arrive at their station:

| Takeshi | Ja mata ne! |
| Jun | Mata ashita! |

ano …	*a hesitation word*, like *er, erm*
ka	*indicates a question*
okāsan	*mother*
sō desu	*that's right*
musuko	*(my) son*

ℹ Bowing

Bowing is an integral part of everyday life in Japan. People bow when they meet each other; schoolchildren bow at the beginning and end of each lesson; shop assistants bow as you enter a store or elevator; roadwork signs have a picture of a workman bowing in apology for the delay; you will see mothers teaching young children to bow by pushing their heads gently forward; and you even see people bowing while on the phone!

The depth of the bow indicates the status of the person you are greeting – a shallower bow to a friend, a deep bow to someone important. Some companies now even run etiquette courses for new recruits because of concerns that young people do not know how to use respectful language and customs such as bowing correctly.

As a foreigner you may find that Japanese people will follow the western custom and shake hands with you, but it shows a positive outlook and a knowledge of Japanese customs if you bow. If you are a man, put your hands by your sides. If you are a woman, put your hands by your sides or cross your hands in front of you (see the illustrations below). Bow from the waist – not too shallow, not too deep.

Take your lead from the other person.

Explanations

1 An Jenkinsu-san desu ka *Are you Miss Anne Jenkins?*

The Japanese use **san** when they address other people. The nearest equivalent in English is the use of Mr/Mrs/Miss/Ms. However, there are some important differences. **San** is attached to the end of the name and can be used either with the surname or the first name. (In general, though, Japanese adults tend to use surnames rather than first names unless they know someone very well.)

It is very important to use **san** – it would sound impolite if you addressed a Japanese person only by their name. There are more polite and more casual forms of **san**:

- **sama** is used when addressing letters and in more formal situations;
- **kun** is used for young boys and by men who know each other well;
- **chan** may be used between children or by adults when addressing children;
- teachers and professors have **sensei** attached to their name.

2 Hajimemashite, Yamaguchi Reiko desu
How do you do? I am Reiko Yamaguchi

A second important point to know about **san** is that you only use it to address other people and never when talking about yourself (or members of your family). Look back at the dialogue – there are a number of examples of this. For example, when Jun introduces himself to Anne:

Hajimemashite. Suzuki Jun desu. *How do you do? I am Jun Suzuki.*

And when Reiko introduces her son Takeshi:

Kore wa Takeshi desu. *This is Takeshi.*

Have you noticed in the examples above that the name order is different in Japanese? The Japanese say their family name first followed by their first name:

Yamaguchi Takeshi

However, most Japanese will expect non-Japanese people to use the western convention (first name followed by surname) so you don't need to reverse the order when saying your name. This is why Anne said her name in the western order:

An Jenkinsu Anne Jenkins

In a business situation you will probably only use your surname anyway.

3 Hajimemashite, An Jenkinsu desu. Dōzo yoroshiku *How do you do? I am Anne Jenkins. I'm pleased to meet you.*

When you first meet someone you use the formal phrases, **hajimemashite** (*how do you do?*) and **dōzo yoroshiku** (*pleased to meet you or pleased to make your acquaintance*). After your name you say **desu** (*I am*). The same word (**desu**) is used for *you/we/they are* and *it/she/he is*. The important thing to remember is that **desu** comes at the end of the sentence. For example:

An Jenkinsu desu.	*I am Anne Jenkins.*
Musuko desu.	*He is my son.*

4 Yamaguchi-san desu ka *Are you Mrs Yamaguchi?*

To make a question in Japanese you say **ka** at the end of the sentence. You can think of **ka** as a spoken question mark. When **ka** is written at the end of a sentence, there is no need to write a question mark as well. For example:

Yamaguchi-san desu *ka*	*Are you Mrs Yamaguchi?*
Tōkyō desu *ka*	*Is it Tokyo?*

5 Kochira wa An Jenkinsu-san desu *This is Miss Anne Jenkins*

To introduce someone else in person you use **kochira wa** (*this is...*). For example:

Kochira wa An Jenkinsu-san desu.	*This is Miss Anne Jenkins.*
Kochira wa Yamaguchi Takeshi-san desu.	*This is Takeshi Yamaguchi.*
Kochira wa Suzuki-san desu.	*This is Mr (Mrs/Miss) Suzuki.*

However, you don't use **kochira** when introducing members of your own family. You can use **kore** (*this is* – informal) as Reiko does:

Kore wa Takeshi desu.	*This is Takeshi.*

6 Formal and informal greetings

Throughout the book you will learn a number of set phrases used by the Japanese in formal situations: meeting someone for the first time, visiting someone's home, apologizing or saying thank you.

The words you use when greeting someone depend on the time of the day to some extent. **Konnichiwa** is often translated as *hello*, but first thing in the morning you would say **ohayō gozaimasu** (*good morning*) or **ohayō** to a friend or within the family. In the evening you would use **konbanwa** (*good evening*). **Konnichiwa** is used later in the morning through to early evening.

In the same way there are different phrases for saying *goodbye*, just as there are in English.

Sayōnara is translated as *goodbye* but traditionally is used more formally with people you don't know well or with people you don't normally see every day.

Oyasumi nasai (*good night*) is a useful farewell phrase to remember when it is later in the evening, or **oyasumi** to a friend or member of your family. There is also the more casual **ja mata ne** (*see you*).

Simply using **arigatō gozaimasu** (*thank you*) is quite appropriate if you are leaving someone's house or if they have done something for you.

🛈 Learning tip

Before you begin this section, go back to the **Conversation** and listen to it or read it again. This should help to clarify all the new language you have learnt. If there is something you are still not sure about, look it up in the **Explanations** section before proceeding to the **Practice** section. Make this a habit for all the units – it will increase your confidence and improve your performance in the activities.

Practice

In this section you have the opportunity to practise what you have learnt. This will be a building-up process – later units will draw on material from earlier units so that each activity will be reinforcing what you have learnt so far as well as practising the new language items. It is therefore important to feel confident when you progress to this section that you have understood the new material. It doesn't matter if you haven't quite mastered it yet – these exercises will give you the opportunity for practice, repetition and self-testing in an enjoyable format.

▶ 1 Listen to the recording of people greeting each other at different times of the day and put the pictures **a–f** below into the order they are spoken. Alternatively, look at the pictures and say out loud the greeting you think they are saying to each other. Then check the answers at the back of the book to see if you were right.

2 Introduce the people in the pictures on the next page to each other as in the example. (The Japanese names have been written in Japanese order, with the surnames first.)

Example: Yamada Takeshi/Bill Smith
Kochira wa Yamada Takeshi-san desu.
Kochira wa Bill Smith-san desu.

▶ Now listen to the recording and practise the pronunciation of the Japanese names.

3   Using the same people as in Exercise 2, practise saying how they would introduce themselves to each other as in the example:

Example: Hajimemashite, Yamada Takeshi desu. Dōzo yoroshiku.

Hajimemashite, Bill Smith desu. Dōzo yoroshiku.

Remember that people don't use **san** when talking about themselves.

▶ 4   Now you will hear several of the characters from this book, in turn. Each time, pause the recording after a character has spoken and introduce yourself to that person, saying: **Hajimemashite,** (*your name*) desu. **Dōzo yoroshiku.**

You can still introduce yourself if you don't have the recording – speak out loud and aim to say your introduction from memory.

▶ 5   You are going to hear snippets of conversation. Note down which of the following expressions you hear and how many times. If you don't have the recording, see if you can say these words in Japanese from memory. Speak out loud.

a   Good morning
b   Good night

c   Thank you
d   Good afternoon
e   Goodbye
f   See you
g   Good evening
h   Excuse me
i   How do you do?

6   Try to decide whether **san** should be used in the sentences
     below. Write **san** in the gap if you think it should be, and X
     if not.

a   Hajimemashite, An Jenkinsu ——— desu.
b   Kochira wa Yamaguchi Reiko ——— desu.
c   Kochira wa Suzuki ——— desu ka.
d   Sumimasen, Yamaguchi ——— desu ka.

Test

1   What do you say to somebody

a   first thing in the morning?
b   when you meet them for the first time?
c   last thing at night?
d   if you want to catch their attention?

2   How would you introduce yourself to a Japanese person?
     (Make sure you say your name slowly and clearly.)

3   How would you introduce Anne Jenkins to somebody else?

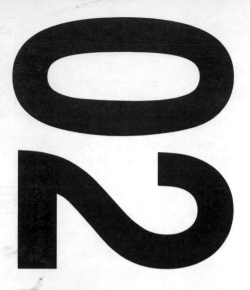

02

Igirisu-jin desu

I'm British

In this unit you will learn
- how to count from 1 to 12
- the names of countries, languages and nationalities
- the names of the months of the year
- the names of some useful objects and loan words
- how to ask for a word in Japanese

Introduction

In this unit you will be introduced to two main topics:

- Numbers and ways they are used
- Making a simple sentence – *I am, it/she/he is, they/we/you are* – using **desu**. (You have already met **desu** in Unit 1.)

There are a number of new vocabulary items but you will notice that some of them sound very similar to English, for example **tēpu** is the word for 'cassette tape'. This is because these are loanwords which the Japanese have 'borrowed' from other languages, and in particular from English. These loan words are written in their own special script – you will learn more about this in Unit 13.

▶ Let's talk

1 Read these Japanese loan words out loud and see if you can work out what they mean. You may need to read them out a few times.

a	uisukī	h	takushī
b	kēki	i	pantsu
c	aisukurīmu	j	kōto
d	tēpu rekōdā	k	beddo
e	sutereo	l	resutoran
f	kompyūta	m	pen
g	basu		

Now, if you have the recording, listen to the pronunciation and practise saying the words. This will help you to check that your answers are right. If you are still not sure about the meaning of some of the words, the answers are at the back of the book.

ℹ Loan words

Japanese language and culture have been influenced and added to over the centuries by other countries. China was the major outside influence in the pre-modern era, but from the 1850s American and European influences became predominant. The British and American influence is seen in particular in the large number of English loan words which have become a part of the Japanese language. Many of these words reflect the types of items which have been introduced from Europe and America and were not traditional to Japan.

For example, the Japanese traditionally slept on futon (a mattress laid out on the floor) but the western-style bed has become popular with young people and is called **beddo**. In the area of modern technology, the Japanese usually have adopted western words, for example **kompyūta** (*computer*) and **shī dī purēyā** (*CD player*), but the sound is changed to suit Japanese pronunciation and sometimes the word is shortened, for example, **terebi** (*television* – remember that there is no **v** sound in Japanese, it is pronounced **b** instead); **wā puro** (*word processor*). There is sometimes a Japanese word and a loan word for the same item: chicken cooked in a Japanese style is called **toriniku**, but cooked in a western style is called **chikin**.

▶ Vocabulary list

If you have the recording, listen to one item of vocabulary at a time, use the pause button the recording and say the word out loud, then move on to the next word.

If you don't have the recording, read the hints after this vocabulary list and make sure you speak out loud when practising your pronunciation of these new words.

Countries   Languages   Nationalities

Countries		Languages		Nationalities
Igirisu	(*England/UK*)	**Eigo**	(*English*)	**Igirisu-jin**
Amerika	(*America/USA*)	**Eigo**		**Amerika-jin**
Furansu	(*France*)	**Furansu-go**		**Furansu-jin**
Doitsu	(*Germany*)	**Doitsu-go**		**Doitsu-jin**
Itaria	(*Italy*)	**Itaria-go**		**Itaria-jin**
Indo	(*India*)	**Hinzū-go**	(*Hindi*)	**Indo-jin**
Nihon	(*Japan*)	**Nihon-go**		**Nihon-jin**
Chūgoku	(*China*)	**Chūgoku-go**		**Chūgoku-jin**

Useful items

tokei	*watch* or *clock*
hon	*book*
empitsu	*pencil*
pen	*pen*

Useful phrases

... wa nihon-go de nan desu ka	*what is ... in Japanese?*
nan desu ka	*what is it?*
o-namae wa?	*what's your name?*
shitsurei shimasu	*pardon me for interrupting*

ℹ️ Pronouncing loanwords

- There is no **l** sound in Japanese, and the **r** sound is somewhere between an **l** and an **r**. If you can't understand a word with an **r** sound, say it with an **l** sound instead. For example:

  Hoteru   Hotelu   = *hotel*
- Often the **u** and **i** sounds are hardly voiced, as in the example of **hotel(u)** above.
- A **b** sound is used instead of a **v** sound:

  terebi = *televi(sion)*
  bideo = *video*

The **Pronunciation guide** in the Introduction to this book explains these and other pronunciation tips.

▶ Conversation

Anne has settled into her new life with the Yamaguchi family and today is her first day at the Japanese language school. Her teacher, **Satō-sensei**, is getting the new students to introduce themselves to the whole class.

Satō-sensei	**Mina-san**, ohayō gozaimasu.
Class	Sensei, ohayō gozaimasu.
Satō-sensei	Hajimemashite, Satō desu. **Watashi wa** Nihon-jin desu. Dōzo yoroshiku. (*she points to Anne*) **Hai, dōzo**.
Anne	An desu. Watashi wa Igirisu-jin desu. Dōzo yoroshiku.
Next student	Tani desu. Furansu-jin desu. Dōzo yoroshiku.
Student 2	Ano … Haidi desu. Doitsu **kara** desu. Dōzo yoroshiku.
Student 3	Sukotto desu. **Ē to**, ē to … *America* wa nihon-go de nan desu ka.
Satō-sensei	*America* wa nihon-go de A-me-ri-ka desu.
Scott	(*amidst laughter*) Aa! so desu ka. Ja, Amerika kara desu. Dōzo yoroshiku.

A new student arrives late and Satō-sensei uses this opportunity to get the class to practise their Japanese with one another.

New student	Shitsurei shimasu. (*he bows*)
Scott	O-namae wa?

New student	Han desu. Chūgoku-jin desu.
Anne	(*looks puzzled*) Chūgoku wa eigo de nan desu ka.
Han	*China* desu.

Satō-sensei now goes on to check how many everyday objects the students know.

Satō-sensei	(*points to her watch*) **Kore wa** nihon-go de nan desu ka.
Han	Tokei desu.
Scott	(*looking at watch*) Nihon no tokei desu.
Satō-sensei	Sō desu. (*picks up Anne's coat*) Kore wa nan desu ka.
Tani	Kōto desu.
Scott	(*showing off a bit*) Igirisu no kōto desu.
Anne	Iie, **Sukottorando** no kōto desu **yo**.

mina-san	*everybody*
watashi wa	*I*
hai, dōzo	*go ahead; there you are*
kara	*from*
ē to	*another hesitation word (er, erm)*
kore wa	*this*
Sukottorando	*Scotland*
yo	*I tell you, actually*

Explanations

1 Watashi wa Nihon-jin desu *I am Japanese*

Watashi means *I* and **anata** means *you*. There are other words for *he*, *we*, etc., but the Japanese tend not to use them unless it needs to be made clear who is being talked about. **Boku** is often used by males instead of **watashi**.

When addressing other people it is more polite to use their name rather than **anata**, and unless you need to emphasize *I* you don't need to say **watashi/boku**.

Wa is used after a word to show that that word is the 'topic' (subject) of whatever is being talked about. It can sometimes be translated as as *for* in English:

Watashi wa Amerika-jin desu.	*I (subject) am American. (As for me, I am American.)*
Haidi-san wa Doitsu kara desu.	*Heidi (subject) is from Germany. (As for Heidi, she comes from Germany.)*

Don't worry too much about understanding this just yet – you will have the chance to learn and practise many more examples throughout the units, and the main thing now is to remember and use the phrases.

2 O-namae wa? *Your name?*

In point 1 above, you learnt that when addressing people it is more polite to use their name rather than **anata** (*you*). The Japanese language has other ways of avoiding the use of **anata**. One of these is the use of **o** in front of certain words to make them sound more polite or formal when you are addressing other people (you don't use it to talk about yourself or members of your family). Here are some examples:

o-namae	*your name*
namae	*(my) name*
o-shigoto	*your job*
shigoto	*(my) job*

Remember: you can only use **o** in front of certain words. You will meet more of these in future units.

3 Doitsu kara desu *I'm from Germany*

Kara means *from* and follows the word, unlike English where we say *from* first. For example:

Tōkyō *kara*	*from Tokyo*
Furansu *kara*	*from France*
(Watashi wa) Igirisu *kara* **desu.**	*I'm from England.*
Kono uisukī wa Sukottorando *kara* **desu.**	*This whisky is from Scotland.*

4 Nihon no tokei desu *It's a Japanese watch*

No inserted between two words works something like 's in English:

An-san no kōto	*Anne's coat*
sensei no tēpu	*the teacher's tape*

It also gives the meaning of *my*, *your*, etc. For example:

watashi no tokei	*my watch*
anata no hon	*your book*

It connects an item with its owner, origin or language:

Igirisu no kōto	*an English coat (a coat of/ from England)*
Doitsu-go no hon	*a German (language) book*

5 Nihon-go de nan desu ka *What is it in Japanese?*

This is a useful phrase if you want to build up your vocabulary in Japanese and you are able to speak to a willing Japanese speaker. Also, if you don't understand a Japanese word you can say:

Eigo de nan desu ka.	*What is it in English?*

If you want to specify a word, you put it at the beginning of the phrase followed by **wa** (you learnt something about **wa** in point 1 above). For example:

***Book* wa nihon-go de nan desu ka.**	*What is **book** in Japanese? (As for **book**, what is it in Japanese?)*
Tokei wa eigo de nan desu ka.	*What is **tokei** in English?*

6 Igirisu *England/Britain*

The Japanese use the word **Igirisu** to refer to Britain, although it does come from the word *England*. If you want to express Scotland, Wales or Ireland you can say **Sukottorando, Wēruzu, Airurando**.

▶ 7 Sūji *Numbers (1–12)*

If you have the recording listen to the pronunciation of the numbers 1–12. Otherwise, read them out loud.

1	ichi	7	shichi (nana)
2	ni	8	hachi
3	san	9	ku (kyū)
4	shi (yon)	10	jū
5	go	11	jū-ichi
6	roku	12	jū-ni

ℹ Remembering numbers

You can use sound association for remembering new Japanese words. Look at the suggestions below and then see if you can think of some associations.

1	ichi	sounds like 'itchy'
2	ni	sounds like 'knee'
3	san	as in **san** – *Mr/Mrs*
4	shi	in 'she' (her)
5	go	go-ing somewhere
6	roku	a large rock(-u)

You will see that there are two ways of saying 4, 7 and 9. Learn **shi**, **shichi** and **ku** first, but you will begin to see as we progress through the book that there are times when the alternative words are used.

▶ 8 The months of the year

Numbers are very useful in Japanese and are used in many ways. The first use we are going to learn is in saying the months. The Japanese call *January* 'one (first) month', *February* 'two (second) month', and so on. Study the list below and practise saying the months out loud and/or listen to them on the recording.

ichi-gatsu (*January*)
ni-gatsu (*February*)
san-gatsu (*March*)
shi-gatsu (*April*)
go-gatsu (*May*)
roku-gatsu (June)

shichi-gatsu (*July*)
hachi-gatsu (*August*)
ku-gatsu (*September*)
jū-gatsu (*October*)
jū-ichi-gatsu (*November*)
jū-ni-gatsu (*December*)

ℹ Learning tip

You may have noticed that a dash (-) is used between the number and the word for month (**gatsu**) for example **ichi-gatsu**.

In the same way, a dash was placed between country and person (**Amerika-jin**), country and language (**Furansu-go**) and in counting numbers, between 10s and units (11 = **jū-ichi**). This is to help you at first to see how the new word is made up of two words. For example, **Doitsu-go** (*German*) is made from **Doitsu** (*Germany*) and **go** (*language*).

Once this idea has been introduced to you, the dash will no longer be used, as you will see in the **Practice** section below. If later you are unsure of any words, look the word up in the index at the back. It will tell you in which unit the word was first introduced so you can refer back to it and see which two words it is derived from.

9 Denwa-bangō *Phone numbers*

Phone numbers are said using the individual digits **ichi, ni, san ... ku**. A dash between groups of numbers is usually spoken using **no**. 0 is pronounced as **zero** or **rei** (the **ze** of **zero** rhymes with the **he** of the name 'Helen'). For example:

> 020-8776-7333 = zero-ni-zero **no** hachi-nana-nana-roku **no** shichi-san-san-san

You usually use **nana** (not **shichi**) for 7, **yon** (not **shi**) for 4 and **kyū** (not **ku**) for 9, when saying phone numbers.

Note that you have learnt two words for the word *number* in this unit: **sūji** is used to describe numbers that you count – 1, 2, 3, etc. **Bangō** is used to describe items or information that you number, such as phone, bus and room numbers.

Practice

1   Practise saying out loud these Tokyo phone numbers, then check you have said them correctly against the answers in the back of the book. (Use **yon** (4), **nana** (7) and **kyū** (9).)

   a   03-3276-5453   **c**   03-7762-1234
   b   03-8893-3221   **d**   03-8283-4455

▶ 2 Satō-sensei finished off the first Japanese lesson by practising numbers. First of all, each of the students wrote down their Japanese family's phone number on the board, then Satō-sensei read them out but not always correctly. The students marked down whether they thought the numbers were read correctly or incorrectly. (She didn't say '03' because this is not needed when dialling within Tokyo.) Look at the table below, listen to the recording and see if you can do the same exercise (or simply read the numbers out loud).

	Student	Phone number	True/false
a	Anne	(03) 1353-0154	
b	Scott	(03) 9745-6622	
c	Tani	(03) 1898-1234	
d	Heidi	(03) 4222-6789	
e	Han	(03) 6969-5656	

▶ 3 Anne has been finding out the birthdays (tanjōbi) of her host family. Listen to the recording and write down in English the birthday month of each member of the family.

	Name	Month
a	Reiko Yamaguchi	
b	Mr Yamaguchi	
c	Emi	
d	Takeshi	

4 Match these two sets of months (Japanese on the left, English on the right) by drawing lines from one to the other.

a sangatsu   *January*
  shichigatsu   *September*
  kugatsu   *March*
  shigatsu   *April*
  jūichigatsu   *May*
  ichigatsu   *November*
  gogatsu   *July*

b jūnigatsu   *August*
  rokugatsu   *February*
  nigatsu   *October*
  hachigatsu   *June*
  jūgatsu   *December*

Now check your answers with the list on page 19.

▶ 5 Listen to the recording and write in English in the right
    hand column (Country/Nationality) which country each
    item/ person comes from.

	Item/Person	Country/Nationality
a	Camera	
b	Watch	
c	Whisky	
d	Coat	
e	Jean-san	
f	Maria-san	

i Listening for specific information

Many of the listening exercises contain extra vocabulary which you
haven't learnt. Do not worry about understanding every word: the
aim of the exercises is to help you develop the important skill of
scanning information and selecting the parts that you need.

Test

1 How would you say these phrases in Japanese?

  a What is 'hat' in Japanese?
  b Pardon me for interrupting (when entering a room).
  c I am English.
  d It's a Japanese (language) book.

2 How many words and phrases do you remember from the
  first two units? The clues are in English but you write the
  answers in Japanese. Try to do as many as possible from
  memory. **Gambatte!** (*good luck!*)

Yoko (*across*)

1 A greeting in the evening (8)
3 A Japanese person (8)
5 The word for *pencil* (7)
6 India (4)
9 Scott comes from this country (7)
11 The number 7 (6)
14 A farewell phrase (8)
15 Han comes from this country (7)
16 The word for *book* (3)
17 The number 12 (4)
19 A watch or clock (5)
20 See you! (2, 4, 2)

Tate (*down*)

1 September (7)
2 A casual thanks (7)
4 Britain or England (7)
7 Pleased to meet you:
   Dōzo _____ (9)
8 To catch someone's attention/
   say sorry (9)
10 *Hello* or *good afternoon* (10)
12 The Italian language (8)
13 A casual *goodnight* to
   friends/family (7)
18 No (3)

3 Write the answers to these sums in Japanese and English.

   a   ichi + san =
   b   go + ni =
   c   kyū – roku =
   d   jū – san =

03

o-shigoto wa nan desu ka

what is your occupation?

In this unit you will learn
- how to say what your job is
- how to talk about your interests
- how to say *I am not...*
- how to count from 13 to 20
- different ways to count in Japanese

Introduction

In this unit you will be introduced to a common sentence pattern – a 'person/item' is 'something'. For example:

An-san *wa* Igirisujin *desu*.   *Anne is English.*
Kore *wa* tokei *desu*.   *This is a watch.*

The pattern in Japanese is: noun **wa** noun **desu**.

Let's talk

1 Using the pattern 'noun **wa** noun **desu**', can you make statements about these people's nationalities? Say them out loud. (The first one has been done for you in the **Introduction**.)

Person	Nationality
Anne	English → An-san **wa** Igirisujin **desu**.
Scott	American
Han	Chinese
Takeshi	Japanese
Tani	French
Heidi	German

▶ Vocabulary list

If you have the recording, switch it on for practice of the new words and phrases. Try recording yourself and comparing your pronunciation with the Japanese speakers! This should help you to remember the new words too.

Next, read each word from the **Vocabulary list** out loud, remembering all you have learnt from the **Pronunciation guide** and other tips. (Have a look back at the **Pronunciation guide** every now and again to refresh your memory). If you have a Japanese friend, ask him or her to say the words for you. If you can, record them so that you can listen to them and repeat back. It's good practice to get used to different voices speaking Japanese.

Occupations

shigoto	work
sensei	teacher, professor
kaisha-in	company worker/ employee
gakusei	student
seito	pupil
shufu	housewife
isha	doctor
haisha	dentist
ten'in	shop assistant
hisho	secretary

Interests

shumi	hobby
supōtsu	sports
sakkā	football
sukī	skiing
gorufu	golf
dokusho	reading
suiei	swimming
jōba	horse riding
dansu	dancing
engei/gādeningu	gardening
ikebana	flower arranging

Kazoku *Own family*

haha	mother
chichi	father
ani	older brother
otōto	younger brother

Counting people

nan-nin	how many people?
hitori	one person, alone
futari	two people
san-nin	three people
yo-nin	four people
nan (sometimes nani)	what?

Useful phrases

Mōichido itte kudasai.	Please say it again.
Yukkuri itte kudasai.	Please say it more slowly.

▶ Conversation

Anne and her fellow classmates have brought in photos of their homestay and real families to show to the class. Anne is talking about the Yamaguchi family.

Anne   Kore wa Yamaguchi Masaki-san desu. Yamaguchi san wa kaisha-in desu. Shumi wa sukī to gorufu desu.

Tani   (*pointing to photo*) Kore wa **donata** desu ka.

Anne   Ano, Takeshi-kun desu. Takeshi-kun wa seito desu. Shumi wa suiei desu.

Heidi   **Go-kazoku** wa **zembu de** nan-nin desu ka.

Anne   Zembu de yo-nin desu.

Scott   Sumimasen, mōichido itte kudasai. Nan-nin desu ka.

Anne   Yo-nin desu.

Next Tani passes round photos of her own family and holds up one to discuss.

Tani   **Kono hito** wa haha desu. Haha wa isha desu. Shumi wa dokusho desu. Kono hito wa Henri desu. Henri wa ani desu. Shumi wa jōba desu.

Han   (*points to photo*) Kore **mo** Henri-san desu ka.

Tani   (*blushing*) Iie, Henri **ja arimasen**. Watashi no bōifurendo desu.

Scott   Nani...? Yukkuri itte kudasai.

to	*and*
donata	*who*
go-kazoku	*someone else's family*
zembu de	*altogether*
kono hito	*this person*
mo	*also, too*
ja arimasen	*is not*
bōifurendo	*boyfriend*

Now go over the dialogue once more, play the recording or read the dialogue line by line and say it out loud. Pay particular attention to how you say the words with double consonants, that is **yukkuri** (*slowly*) and **itte** (*say*). You pause slightly before the **kk** and before the **tt** (as you would when saying the English word *headdress* – see **Pronunciation guide**, page xvii).

Explanations

1 Takeshi-kun wa seito desu *Takeshi is a (school) pupil*

We have already talked about and practised the pattern 'noun **wa** noun **desu**', and in the dialogue you have come across more ways of using it when talking about jobs and hobbies. For example:

Kono hito *wa* haha *desu.*   *This (person) is my mother.*
Haha *wa* isha *desu.*   *My mother is a doctor.*
Shumi *wa* dokusho *desu.*   *(Her) hobby is reading.*

Remember that you learnt in Unit 2 (**Explanation 1**) that **wa** highlights the word that is the subject. It can sometimes be translated as *as for*. For example:

Shumi wa dokusho desu.	*As for her hobby, it is reading.*
Shigoto wa isha desu.	*As for her job, she is a doctor.*

2 Kore wa donata desu ka *Who is this?*

Donata means *who* and is a more polite version of the question word **dare** which also means *who*. **Donata** would be used on more formal occasions. In English this phrase might translate as: *Might I ask who this is?* Tani is asking about a photo but if the person is present, you use **kochira** instead of **kore** for *this*.

3 Kore mo Henri-san desu ka *Is this also Henri?* (Is this Henri as well?)

Mo means *also* and is used as follows.

- **Tani: Watashi wa gakusei desu.**   *I am a student.*
  Anne: Watashi *mo* gakusei desu.   *I am also a student. (I am a student too.)*
- **Satō-sensei wa Nihonjin desu.**   *Mrs Sato is Japanese.*
  Takeshi-kun *mo* Nihonjin desu.   *Takeshi is Japanese as well.*
- **Ani wa kaisha-in desu.**   *My older brother is a company worker.*

  Otōto *mo* kaisha-in desu.   *My younger brother is a company worker too.*

You can also use **mo** in this way:

An-san *mo* Tani-san *mo* gakusei desu.	*Both Anne and Tani are students.*
Takeshi-kun *mo* Satō-sensei *mo* Nihonjin desu.	*Both Takeshi and Mrs Sato are Japanese.*

4 Kono hito wa haha desu *This person is my mother*

Japanese people show respect for other people outside their family by using polite words and phrases. For example, you learnt in Unit 1 that **san** is attached to a name when you address someone else. And you learnt in Unit 2 that **o** is sometimes attached to certain words when talking to other people (**o-namae** – *your name*).

In contrast, Japanese people use words which are more 'humble' (or modest) to talk about themselves and their families. Therefore, Tani doesn't say **kochira wa** ... (*this person*) when talking about her mother. Instead she says **kono hito** which is a more everyday word for *this person*. She could also use **kore wa** (*this*).

▶ 5 Iie, Henri ja arimasen *No, he's not Henri*

To say *is not, am not, are not*, etc, in Japanese, you use **ja arimasen** or the more polite version, **dewa arimasen**. For example:

Tokei ja arimasen.	*It is not a watch.*
Ichigatsu ja arimasen. Nigatsu desu.	*It's not January. It's February.*

To say *was* or *were* in Japanese you change **desu** to **deshita**. For example:

Chichi wa haisha deshita.	*My father was a dentist.*
Sensei wa Furansujin deshita.	*My teacher was French.*

And to say *wasn't* or *weren't* you use **ja arimasen deshita** (or **dewa arimasen deshita**). Here is a list of these expressions which you can refer back to. You can also listen to them on the recording.

am/is/are	was/were	am not/is not/are not	was not/were not
desu	deshita	ja/dewa arimasen	ja/dewa arimasen deshita

6 Haha mo chichi mo isha desu *Both my mother and father are doctors*

There is an important difference here between Japanese and English. In English we say *one doctor* but *two doctors*, in other words we have a singular and a plural, but generally in Japanese there is no difference between one or more than one of something, and, as you saw in **Explanation 5** above, **desu** covers all the different words we use in English (*is, are, am*). This of course is good news for Japanese language learners because it means you have fewer words and changes to remember.

7 Nan-nin desu ka. Yo-nin desu *How many people are there? There are four*

Counting people

When you learnt the months of the year in Unit 2, you learnt that you simply add the numbers **ichi, ni, san** ... to the word **gatsu** (*month*). For example: **ichigatsu** ('first month' which is *January*). Japanese uses a similar method when counting people: **nin** means *person/people* (remember, there is no plural) and **san-nin** means *three people*.

However, when saying one person you use **hitori**, and for *two people* you use **futari**. Also, the word for *four* (**yon**) is shortened to **yo**.

To ask *how many people?* you say **nan-nin desu ka**. (**Nan** means *what* but translates better as *how many* in this case.)

8 Mōichido itte kudasai *Please say it again*

When you haven't understood all that is being said to you, this is a polite way of asking the speaker to repeat the information. **Yukkuri itte kudasai** is a way of getting the person to speak a little slower. You can say **sumimasen** first to be more polite. For example:

> **Sumimasen, mōichido itte kudasai.**
> *Excuse me but would you mind saying that again please?*

9 Shumi wa suiei desu *His hobby is swimming*

This is another example of the pattern you were introduced to in the **Introduction**. A word for *his, her, my*, etc. is not needed when it is understood who is being talked about. Here are some more examples:

> **Shumi wa engei desu.** *(His) hobby is gardening.*
> **Shumi wa dansu desu.** *(Her) hobby is dancing.*
> **Shumi wa ... desu.** *My hobby is ...*
> *(say your hobby)*

10 Sūji *Numbers (13–20)*

Once you have mastered the numbers 1–10, you can count to 99 using combinations of the first 10 numbers. You have already learnt that 11 is **jū-ichi**, i.e. 10 + 1, and 12 is **jū-ichi**, i.e. 10 + 2. Try to work out and say out loud how to count from 13 to 19, then look at the list below.

13	jū-san	17	jū-shichi (jū-nana)
14	jū-shi (jū-yon)	18	jū-hachi
15	jū-go	19	jū-kyū (jū-ku)
16	jū-roku	20	ni-jū

The number for 20 (**ni-jū**) is the reverse of 12 (**jū-ni**). A rule to help you to remember which is which is to think of the order like this:

10 + 2 = 12 (**jū-ni**) and 2 × 10 = 20 (**ni-jū**).

In the same way you can work out 30, 40, 50 …

3 × 10 = 30 = **san-jū**; 4 × 10 = 40 = **yon-jū** (**yon** is always used for 40, not **shi**)

Work out 50–90, say them out loud and write them down. This will prepare you for Unit 4.

Practice

▶ 1 You are going to hear some Japanese people talk about their families, their work and their interests. As you listen, write down in English the information required in the table below.

	Name	Number in family	Occupation	Interests
a				
b				
c				
d				

2   Imagine you have joined a Japanese class and have been asked to introduce all the members to each other. Look at the pictures of the class members below and read the information about them, then introduce each of them out loud. The first one has been done for you.

Example: (Steven Richards, student, likes sport)

Kochira wa Steven Richards-san desu. Steven-san wa gakusei desu. Shumi wa supōtsu desu.

Susan Bond, housewife, hobby is dancing

Example

a

b

Andrew Wall,
shop assistant,
football

c

Peter O'Connor,
doctor, golf

d

John Rogers,
company
employee

3   Tani's Japanese homework is to write out the Japanese occupations next to their English equivalent. However, she's got them confused. Imagine you are talking to her and help her to correct her work, following the example. Remember to speak out loud.

Example: *Secretary* = kaishain   **Iie, kaishain ja arimasen. Hisho desu.**

a Doctor   = gakusei   c Shop assistant = seito
b Housewife = haisha   d Student   = isha

▶ 4 Listen to the recording and write down in numbers the answers to the questions below:

   a Takeshi's age _____
   b Heidi's age _____
   c The bus number _____
   d Anne's home phone number _____
   e Mr Yamaguchi's work phone number _____
   f The number of people in Han's family _____
   g Reiko's birthday month _____

5 Make the pairs of sentences below into one sentence using **mo … mo** (*both … and*), as in the example. Speak out loud.

Example: Takeshi-kun wa seito desu. Jun-kun wa seito desu.
      = Takeshi-kun mo Jun-kun mo seito desu.

   a An-san wa gakusei desu. Haidi-san wa gakusei desu.
   b Tani-san wa Furansujin desu. Henri-san wa Furansujin desu.
   c Haha wa haisha desu. Chichi wa haisha desu.

Test

1 Read out loud the sequence of numbers below.
   7, 17, 12, 20, 14, 2, 9, 13, 16, 40, 50, 60

2 How would you ask someone:

   a to repeat something?
   b to speak more slowly?

3 **Chichi wa isha desu** means:

   a My father is a secretary.   **b** My hobby is reading.
   c My father is a doctor.

4 How would you say in Japanese: '*I am not a teacher. I am a student*'?

5 Count numbers of people backwards in sequence, beginning with **gonin**.

6 Imagine you are introducing yourself to a Japanese person. Give as much information as you can (name, occupation, interests). Speak out loud.

ℹ️ Remembering new words

You have already been introduced to a number of new words in the first three units. You may find it very useful at this stage to start organizing your own 'dictionary'. You could buy a small exercise book or even arrange vocabulary alphabetically in an address book. If you have a PC, why not set up a list of vocabulary on this?

Include in your dictionary the **Vocabulary list** and shorter word 'boxes' from Units 1–3 and the loanwords in Unit 2; then as you work through the book, continue to add new words at the end of each unit. Different people learn in different ways, but you may want to try grouping items of vocabulary by theme (family, occupations, food, etc.) or alphabetically, to help you remember them.

You will also find it useful at this stage to start your own English–Japanese glossary. Arrange the English meanings of new words alphabetically in a notebook (or on your PC) and write the Japanese next to them. This will enable you to quickly look up words for completing activities and tasks and, in general, will help you in expressing yourself in Japanese.

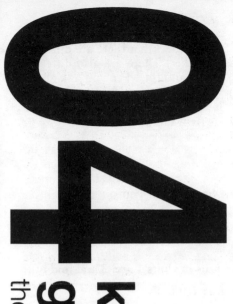

04

kazoku wa gonin desu

there are five people in my family

In this unit you will learn

- how to talk about dates and birthdays
- how to say how old you are
- how to talk about your family
- how to count from 21 to 99

Introduction

You have already met some words for family members in Units 1 and 3. You will have noticed in Unit 3 that there are different words for *older* and *younger* brother. There are also different words for *older* and *younger* sister, and for when you talk about your own family or someone else's. This may seem like a lot of extra vocabulary, but take it step by step, starting with the words that are relevant to your own family.

Let's talk

1 Using the title of this unit, how would you say *there are six people in my family*?

2 How would you say how many people there actually are in your family?

3 Look back at the conversations in Units 1 and 3 and find out:

   a how Takeshi says *mother* (Unit 1)

   b how Tani talks about her mother and older brother (Unit 3)

   c the word for *younger brother* (Unit 3)

   d how Heidi says *your family* to Anne (Unit 3).

🛈 The in-group versus the outsiders

The Japanese distinguish between the group they belong to, the 'in-group' (family, company, etc.), and the 'out-group' (other families, companies, foreigners, etc.). When referring to the in-group, they use language which expresses humility, and when referring to the out-group they use language which expresses politeness and deference.

This is illustrated well in the words used for family members. For example, when you talk to someone outside your family about your mother you use the humble word **haha**, whereas when you talk about someone else's mother you use the polite word **okāsan**. And when you talk of your own family you say **kazoku**, but for someone else's family you add the respect word go and say **go-kazoku**.

However, when Japanese people talk directly to their family they use the polite rather than the humble words. For example, Takeshi in Unit 1 calls his mother **Okāsan**.

▶ Vocabulary list

If you have the recording, use it as you did in Units 1–3 to listen to and practise saying out loud the new words, then read through the complete list.

Alternatively, say each new word out loud and read through the pronunciation tips at the end of the **Vocabulary list**.

Own family		**Someone else's family**
kazoku	*family*	**go-kazoku**
shujin	*husband*	**go-shujin**
kanai	*wife*	**okusan**
musume	*daughter*	**musume-san**
musuko	*son*	**musuko-san**
ryōshin	*parents*	**go-ryōshin**
haha	*mother*	**okāsan**
chichi	*father*	**otōsan**
ani	*older brother*	**oniisan**
ane	*older sister*	**onēsan**
imōto	*younger sister*	**imōto-san**
otōto	*younger brother*	**otōto-san**
nansai desu ka	*how old are you?*	(**sai** age)
gojussai	*50 years old*	
tanjōbi	*birthday*	

ℹ Pronunciation practice

Pay attention to the long sounds and make sure they last twice as long as single syllables. Here are some examples to help you. Each sound should smoothly run into the next; they shouldn't sound disjointed. Say them out loud.

otōto (*younger brother*)	o-to-u-to
imōto (*younger sister*)	i-mo-u-to
okāsan (*mother*)	o-ka-a-sa-n (pronounce **ka-a** like **car** with a long a)
onēsan (*older sister*)	o-ne-e-sa-n (pronounce **ne-e** like **nay**)
ane (*older sister*)	a-ne
okusan (*wife*)	o-k(u)-sa-n (**u** is almost unvoiced; sounds like **oxan**)

▶ Conversation

Anne is telling the Yamaguchis' about her family and showing them some photos.

Reiko	(*studying a photo*) Otōsan desu ka.
Anne	Ē, sō desu.
Reiko	**Wakai** desu ne.
Anne	Sō desu ka. Chichi wa gojussai desu.
Emi	Kore wa donata desu ka.
Anne	Imōto desu. Imōto wa gakusei desu.
Emi	**Kawaii** desu ne. Imōto-san wa nansai desu ka.
Anne	Jūroku-sai desu. **Are,** tanjōbi wa shichigatsu deshita. Jūnana-sai desu.
Takeshi	Kore wa okāsan desu ka.
Anne	Ē, so desu. Haha wa nijūni-sai desu.
Takeshi	Are! Okāsan wa nansai desu ka. Mōichido itte kudasai.
Anne	Nijūni-sai desu.
Takeshi	**Demo** … An-san mo nijūni-sai desu ne?
Emi	(*admist laughter*) Takeshi-kun! Jōdan desu yo.

ē	yes (softer than **hai**)
wakai	(looks) *young*
kawaii	*pretty, cute*
are	(expression of surprise)
demo	*but*
jōdan	*joke*

Explanations

1 Sūji *Numbers 21–99*

In Unit 3 you learnt how to say 20, 30, etc. by remembering this rule:

$2 \times 10 = 20 = $ ni-jū

30	sanjū	70	nanajū
40	yonjū	80	hachijū
50	gojū	90	kyūjū
60	rokujū		

To say 21, 22, etc. you simply add **ichi**, **ni**, etc. after **nijū**:

21	nijū<u>ichi</u>	22	nijū<u>ni</u>	23	nijū<u>san</u>
24	nijū<u>yon</u> (shi)	25	nijū<u>go</u>	26	nijū<u>roku</u>
27	nijū<u>nana</u> (shichi)	28	nijū<u>hachi</u>	29	nijū<u>kyū</u> (ku)

▶ Listen to the numbers 21–29 on the recording. Now you can count from 0 to 99. Practise in short spurts – try 20–30, then 30–40, etc. The main thing is to keep counting until you begin to feel more confident. There will be lots of opportunities throughout the units to keep practising and testing yourself on the numbers.

2 Imōto-san wa nansai desu ka *How old is your younger sister?*

In Unit 2 you learnt **nan desu ka** (*what is it?*). **Nan** means *what*, and if you attach **sai** to it, you form the question word **nansai** – *what age?* or *how old?* In the same way, you can ask *what month is it?* (**nangatsu desu ka**) and *how many people?* (**nannin desu ka**). You will add to these question words as you progress through the units.

To answer, you simply attach the number to **sai**: *I am 14* = **Watashi wa jūyon-sai desu**. Be careful with ages which end in 1, 8 or 10, for example, 11, 18, 30. The numbers are shortened to:

11 = **jūissai**
18 = **jūhassai**
28 = **nijū hassai**
10 = **jussai**
30 = **sanjussai**, etc.

Also, the age of 20 (when Japanese people come of age) has its own special word: **hatachi**.

Jane-san wa hatachi desu.   *Jane is 20.*

Practise saying these ages out loud. Cover up the Japanese, say the age, then check if you are right.

a	15 years old (**jūgo-sai desu**)	**c**	25 years old (**nijūgo-sai desu**)
b	44 years old (**yonjūyon-sai desu**)	**d**	18 years old (**jūhassai desu**)

▶ **3 Watashi no tanjōbi wa nigatsu jūhachi-nichi desu** *My birthday is February 18th*

You learnt how to say the months in Japanese in Unit 2. Now you are going to learn the dates. This is done by adding **nichi** (*day*) to the number. Listen to the recording and say the dates in the table below out loud to familiarize yourself with them.

11th jūichi-nichi	18th jūhachi-nichi	25th nijūgo-nichi
12th jūni-nichi	19th jūku-nichi	26th nijūroku-nichi
13th jūsan-nichi	20th **hatsuka**	27th nijūshichi-nichi
14th **jūyokka**	21st nijūichi-nichi	28th nijūhachi-nichi
15th jūgo-nichi	22nd nijūni-nichi	29th nijūku-nichi
16th jūroku-nichi	23rd nijūsan-nichi	30th sanjū-nichi
17th jūshichi-nichi	24th **nijūyokka**	31st sanjūichi-nichi

Notice that 14th, 20th and 24th differ. (In English also the rule changes when we say 1st, 2nd and 3rd rather than 1th, 2th, 3th.)

You are probably wondering where 1st–10th are. You will learn these in Unit 9 because they follow a different rule to the one above. If your own birthday is between 1st and the 10th, however, look at page 105.

When you say a date in Japanese you always say the month first and then the date. For example:

13th May = Gogatsu, jūsan-nichi

In English we have the choice between 13th May and May 13th, but there is no such choice in Japanese.

4 Go-kazoku wa nannin desu ka *How many people are in your family?*

a You've been introduced to a lot of words for family members and you're not expected to learn them all in one go! Start by learning to describe your own family using Anne's family as a model.

Anne *Kazoku wa gonin desu. Haha **to** chichi **to** (or ryōshin **to**) ane **to** imōto **to** watashi desu.*

(**to** = *and*; say yourself last. Men can use **boku**.) Now work out how to describe your own family.

If you have two brothers, three sisters …, put the people counter (see page 30) after the family word like this:

ani ga futari	(*two older brothers*)
ane ga sannin	(*three older sisters*)
musuko ga futari	(*two sons*)

Don't worry if you forget **ga**.

You can then expand this by giving information on their age:

Ane wa nijūgo-sai desu.	My older sister is 25.
Watashi wa yonjūgo-sai desu.	I am 45.

Practice

▶ 1   The odd one out. Look at the sequence of numbers overleaf as you listen to the recording and circle the number which is *not* mentioned.

a   3, 5, 9, 2, 8, 10   d   98, 89, 56, 65, 88
b   11, 17, 15, 17, 19, 14   e   1, 11, 20, 12, 21, 2
c   21, 31, 41, 51, 61, 91   f   6, 9, 66, 99, 81, 88

▶ 2 Dates. Look at the groups of dates below as you listen to
the recording and circle the one(s) you hear.

a   18th, 28th, 11th   c   14th, 24th
b   16th, 20th, 23rd   d   21st, 31st, 27th, 17th

3   Below are the birthdays of some of the characters you have
met so far. Say out loud the dates as in the example. (The
dates with * are ones which are said differently – be
careful!).

Example: Anne, February 18th = **An-san no tanjōbi wa
nigatsu jūhachi-nichi desu.**

a   Scott, May 11th   d   Han, September 25th
b   Tani, August 21st   e   Takeshi, January 14th*
c   Heidi, November 20th*   f   Emi, April 30th

Now say your own birthday out loud: **watashi no ...**

4   **Family trees**

Below are the family trees of Scott, Tani, Mr Yamaguchi
and Satō-sensei. Take the place of each of these people and
describe 'your' family tree as in the example ('you' are
underlined).

Example: Mother, father (50), older sister (25), younger
sister (17), <u>Anne</u> (22) = **Kazoku wa gonin desu.
Haha to chichi to ane to imōto to watashi desu.**

○ = male   △ = female

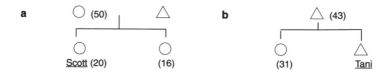

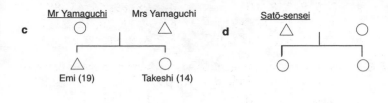

c — Mr Yamaguchi — Mrs Yamaguchi

Emi (19) — Takeshi (14)

d — Satō-sensei

5   Using the family trees in Practice 4, give the ages of each member (where you have the information), once more pretending each is your own family. Don't forget to include 'yourself'.

Example: (Anne's family) **Chichi wa gojussai desu. Ane wa nijūgo-sai desu ...**

6   Try Practice 5 again, but this time you are yourself and so you must use the words for other people's family:

Example: (Anne's family) **Otōsan wa gojussai desu ...**

▶ 7   Families. Below and overleaf are some pictures of families labelled **a–c**. You will hear four descriptions of families (1–4). As you listen, look at the pictures, decide in each case which is being described and write the appropriate number underneath. The speaker is marked **watashi**.

a   watashi

b   watashi

8 Practise saying and write out a brief introduction to your family including their ages, interests, birthdays and occupations where possible.

Test

1 Read the months and dates below out loud:

    a March 29th   **d** 13th January*

    b August 11th   **e** 31st May*

    c December 25th

(*Be careful! Remember the Japanese order.)

2 Draw lines connecting the words below to their English equivalent.

haha	*three sons*
ane	*someone else's mother*
okāsan	*someone else's father*
kazoku	*own mother*
imōto ga futari	*own older sister*
musuko ga sannin	*own family*
otōsan	*two younger sisters*

3 Say out loud this sequence of numbers.

    99, 98, 97, 96, 95, 94, 93, 92, 91 …

Can you count backwards to 1?!

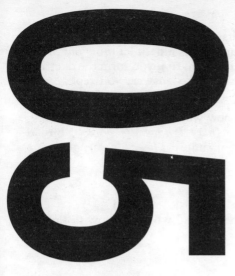

05

ima nanji desu ka

what time is it?

In this unit you will learn
- how to tell the time
- some useful shopping phrases
- saying *this* and *that*
- opening and closing times

Introduction

You learnt in the last unit that **nan** (*what*) is attached to words to make questions, for example, **nansai desu ka** (*how old (what age) are you?*). When you attach **nan** to **ji** you form the question **nanji desu ka** (*what time is it?*). To answer, you replace **nan** with a number, for example, **goji desu** means *it is 5 o'clock*.

You are also going to use a new word, **kudasai** – *may I (have)*, for example, **hon o kudasai** (*may I have the book?*), **bīru o kudasai** (*may I have a beer?* or simply *a beer please*).

Let's talk

1 Look at the clock times below and work out how to say the time for each one.

Example: Ni-ji

Example

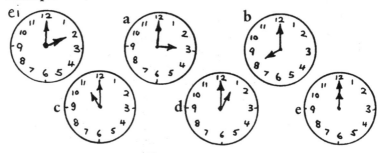

2 Ask if you may have the objects below using the phrase ... **o kudasai**. The first one is done for you.

Example: a Shimbun o kudasai.

▶ Vocabulary list

Read through the new words below, saying each one out loud. There are some pronunciation tips after the **Vocabulary list** to help you and some exercises on the recording.

Shopping phrases

... o kudasai	may I have ... (or '... please')
... o misete kudasai	please may I see ...
kore	this one/these ones
kono	this/these
sore	that one/those ones
sono	that/those
are	that one over there/those ones over there
ano	that over there/those over there
dore	which one(s)
dono	which
ōkii	big
chiisai	small
chōdo ii	just right
chotto	a little, a bit
motto	more
motto chiisai	smaller
irasshaimase	welcome! (said by shop assistants and traders)
shōshō omachi kudasai	please wait a moment (very formal)
dewa (sometimes shortened to ja)	right! (when you've made up your mind)
kara	from
made	until
depāto	department store
sūpā	supermarket
menyū	menu

ℹ Pronunciation practice

Say the sounds smoothly; each sound should run into the next:

misete (*show me*)	mi-se-te
kore (*this*)	ko-re (remember that the **r** is soft; between **l** and **r** in sound)

are (*that over there*)   a-re
irasshaimase (*welcome*)   i-ra- (slight pause) sha-i-ma-se
shōshō (*a little*)   sho-u-sho-u
made (*until*)   ma-de

▶ Conversation

Reiko has taken Anne and Emi shopping in a Tokyo department store. Anne needs a new watch.

Assistant	Irasshaimase!
Anne	(*points to display in front of assistant*) Sono tokei o misete kudasai.
Assistant	Hai, dōzo.
Anne	(tries on watch) Chotto ōkii desu. (*Points to the window display*) Ano tokei mo misete kudasai.
Assistant	Shōshō omachi kudasai. (*returns with watch*) Dōzo. (*Anne tries on watch*)
Emi	Sore wa chiisai desu ka.
Anne	Iie, chōdo ii desu.
Emi	Sono tokei wa **suteki** desu ne.
Anne	Sō desu ne. Dewa, kore o kudasai.
Assistant	Hai, arigatō gozaimasu.

Later they are having lunch in a coffee shop.

Reiko	An-san, nihongo no kurasu wa nanji kara desu ka.
Anne	Ni-ji kara desu.
Emi	Ima nanji desu ka.
Anne	(*looks proudly at watch*) Ichi-ji han desu... Are! Kurasu wa **mō sugu** desu.
Reiko	An-san! **Hayaku!**

suteki	smart, fashionable
mō sugu	soon
hayaku	quick, hurry up

ℹ️ Gift-wrapping

When you buy a gift in Japan the shop assistant will gift-wrap it for you as a free part of the service. Gift-wrapping is quite an art and the assistant with a few deft folds will produce a beautifully wrapped article, complete with a ribbon tied around it and a gift card.

Explanations

1 Irasshaimase *Welcome (May I help you?)*

Japanese shop assistants may use very formal Japanese phrases when dealing with customers. We have met two such phrases in the passage – **irasshaimase** and **shōshō omachi kudasai.** You don't have to use these phrases, but be aware that you may hear them if you go to Japan.

2 Sono tokei *That watch*

You will notice two main points about saying *this* and *that* in Japanese from the **Vocabulary list.** Firstly, there are two sets of words. For example, both **kore** and **kono** mean *this.* Think of **kore** as meaning *this one.* Anne says **Dewa, kore o kudasai** (*Right! I'll have this (one) please*). **Kono,** on the other hand, is followed directly by the item it describes: **kono tokei o kudasai** means *may I have **this watch** please.* Similarly, **sore** means *that (one)* and **sono** means *that.* Here are some examples:

Sore o misete kudasai.	*Please show me that (one).*
Sono hon o misete kudasai.	*Please show me that book.*

Also note:

Are o kudasai.	*I'll have that (one) over there.*
Ano tokei o kudasai.	*I'll have that watch over there.*

This last example takes us on to the second point. Whereas in English we have two words, *this* and *that,* in Japanese there is a third – **are** (or **ano**), meaing *that one over there.* The item in this case is at a distance from the person speaking and the person being spoken to.

The two pictures on the next page will help you to understand how this works; they also illustrate how **kore, sore** and **are** (**kono, sono** and **ano**) are used from the *speaker's* point of view. The first picture shows Anne's point of view, and the second picture shows the shopkeeper's.

1
a kore/ kono tokei
b Sore/ Sono tokei
c Are/ ano tokei

2
b Sore/ Sono tokei
a Kore/ kono tokei
c Are/ ano tokei

To ask *which one?* (*which watch?*) you say **dore** (**dono tokei?**) and this is the same for all three positions (**a, b** and **c** in the pictures).

Now read through the Conversation again with this in mind.

3 ... o kudasai/... o misete kudasai *May I have/ may I see ...*

These are two useful and easy-to-use phrases for shopping (and for other situations too). You simply put the object at the beginning of the phrase:

Kōhī o kudasai.	*May I have some coffee?*
Eigo no shimbun o kudasai.	*May I have an English newspaper?*
Shashin o misete kudasai.	*May I see the **photo** please?*

4 Ima nanji desu ka *What time is it (now)?*

In **Let's talk** in this unit you were introduced to telling the time. Let's practise now, using the clocks below as prompts. Cover up the written times, look at the clocks and say each time out loud, then check to see if you are right by uncovering the written times.

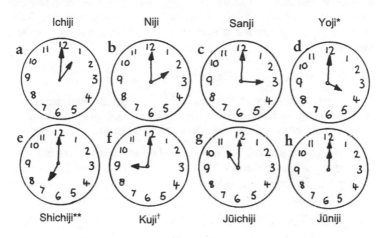

Ichiji · Niji · Sanji · Yoji*

Shichiji** · Kuji† · Jūichiji · Jūniji

*For 4 o'clock you say **yoji** (not **yon** or **shi**).
Use **shichi not **nana**.
†For 9 o'clock use **ku** (not **kyū**).

5 Ichiji han desu *It's half-past one*

Saying *half-past* is straightforward too; just add **han** (*half-past*) after **ji**.

Niji han desu. · Yoji han desu. · Kuji han desu. · Jūichiji han desu.

i Telling the time

By practising saying the time you are revising two things: the numbers 1–12 and times. Practise saying the times first in numerical order – 1 o'clock, half-past one, 2 o'clock, etc. Then make your practice real – get into the habit of saying the time in Japanese whenever you notice that the real time is on the hour or half-past. Finding opportunities to use Japanese in real situations is one of the best ways to remember it and to feel that you are making real progress.

6 Niji kara desu *(It's) from 2 o'clock*

Kara means *from* (you first met this in Unit 2, **Explanation 3** and **made** means *to/until*. They can take on the meaning of *starts/opens at* and *finishes/closes at*. For example:

Nihongo no kurasu wa niji kara goji made desu.	*The Japanese class is from 2 o'clock until 5 o'clock.*
Depāto wa kuji kara rokuji made desu.	*The department store opens at 9 and closes at 6.*

Notice that **kara** and **made** are placed *after* the time:

kuji *kara*	*from* 9
rokuji *made*	*until* 6

Kara and **made** are not just used with the time of day. For example, you can say:

nigatsu kara rokugatsu made	*From February to June* (time of year)
Igirisu kara Nihon made	*From England to Japan* (place)

7 Gozen/gogo *a.m./p.m.*

If you want to distinguish between a.m. and p.m. when saying the time, use **gozen** (*a.m.*) and **gogo** (*p.m.*). These are spoken before the time:

Ima gozen hachiji desu.	*It's now 8 a.m.*
Shigoto wa gogo goji han made desu.	*My work finishes at 5.30 p.m.*

Gogo also means *afternoon (after midday)*:

| Nihongo no kurasu wa gogo desu. | *The Japanese class is in the afternoon.* |

Practice

▶ **1 Furansu wa ima nan ji desu ka** *What time is it in France now?*

Takeshi is doing his geography homework. He has to work out the time differences between Japan and a number of other countries. Listen to the recording and write down the times next to the countries.

a	Japan	d	Germany
b	England	e	New York
c	France	f	San Francisco

▶ 2 In the left-hand column below there is a list of places/events, and in the right-hand column there is a list of times/dates. Listen to the recording and match the places and events with times/dates on the right.

a	Department store	i	11th–27th
b	Work	ii	8.30–4.30
c	Supermarket	iii	8.30–6 p.m.
d	School (**gakkō**)	iv	9 a.m.–8 p.m.
e	Holiday (**yasumi**)	v	11th–14th
f	Ski tour (**sukī tsuā**)	vi	9 a.m.–12.30

3 Below you have some information in Japanese about Japanese classes run by volunteers for non-Japanese people living in Tama City in Japan. You won't be able to read most of the information but you will be able to pick out the starting and finishing times of the three different classes. Say out loud these times using **kara** and **made**, as well as the words for a.m. and p.m. The name of the class is provided for you in Japanese in the box at the top of the next page.

a クラス：月曜クラス （10：00am～12：00am）多摩センター地区市民ホール

b 　　　金曜クラス （ 7：00pm～ 9：00pm）多摩市役所第二庁舎 (ボランティアセンター) 2F

c 　　　土曜クラス （ 2：00pm～ 4：00pm）多摩市役所第二庁舎 (ボランティアセンター) 2F

> **a** = Getsuyō kurasu (*Monday class*) = **Getsuyō kurasu wa...**
> **b** = Kinyō kurasu (*Friday class*)
> **c** = Doyō kurasu (*Saturday class*)

4 Scott is trying to increase his Japanese vocabulary by asking you the name of things around the room. Answer his questions using the information given below – make sure you use **kore**, **sore** and **are** correctly.

Example:

Scott   Kore wa nihongo de nan desu ka.

You   Sore wa (eigo no) hon desu.

a

Scott   Are wa nihongo de nan desu ka.

You   ...

b

Scott   Sore wa nihongo de nan desu ka.

You   ...

c

Scott   Kore wa nihongo de nan desu ka.

You   ...

d

Scott   Sore wa nihongo de nan desu ka.

You   ...

5 Read out loud the items on the **menyū** (menu) below and see if you can work out what they are in English (answers are at the back of the book).

Nomimono (drinks)
Kōhī
Miruku
Bīru
Aisukōhī
Jūsu

* * *

Tabemono (food)
Sandoitchi*
Supagetti
Piza
Aisukurīmu
Kēki

---

*Pronunciation tip: **sa-n-do-i** (slight pause) **chi**

Now imagine that you are at a restaurant with Anne. Can you fill in your part of the dialogue?

Waiter	Irasshaimase.
You	*Ask to see the menu.*
Anne	Kōhī to sandoitchi o kudasai.
You	*Order a food and a drink item from the menu.*

6 Underline the correct word in the sentences below.

Example: <u>Kono</u>/kore hon wa watashi no desu.

a Sore/sono o misete kudasai.
b Ja, kore/kono o kudasai.
c Are/ano shimbun wa eigo no shimbun desu ka.
d Sore/sono wa nan desu ka.
e Dore/dono hon desu ka.

7 Can you say out loud in Japanese the conversations between the shopkeeper (**ten'in**) and the customer (**o-kyakusan**) in each of these two dialogues?

a **O-kyakusan**   *Please may I see that book? (near to the **ten'in**)*
   Ten'in   *Which one?*
   O-kyakusan (*pointing*) *That one.*

b **Ten'in**   *Welcome.*
   O-kyakusan   *Could I see that watch (over there) please?*
   Ten'in   *Which watch?*
   O-kyakusan (*pointing*) *That one over there.*
   Ten'in   *Yes, there you are.*
   O-kyakusan   *Thank you.*

Test

1 Can you say these times out loud?

a 6 p.m.   d 11 o'clock
b 8 a.m.   e 7.30
c 10 a.m.   f 4.30

2 Look at the timetable below and say what time each class starts and finishes.
Example: Rekishi wa kuji kara jūji made desu.

Jikan-hyō (timetable)				
9–10	10–11	11.30–12.30	1.30–2.30	3–4
History*	Japanese	French	English	Tennis club*
(rekishi)				(tenisu kurabu)

3 How would you say in Japanese...
a May I see the menu please?
b May I have this please?
c Please show me that watch.
d May I see that watch over there?
e Which one?

06

ikura desu ka

how much is it?

In this unit you will learn
- how to count in units of 100 and 1,000
- how to ask about and say prices of things
- ways of counting objects
- how to ask for something in a shop
- shop names

Introduction

Before you begin this unit look over the numbers 1–99 (see **Appendix**). Vary the ways you practise counting – try counting in fives and tens, for example, or try counting backwards. You will increase your confidence in counting by regularly reviewing numbers, and if you vary the way that you do this, it will make the review more interesting and challenging.

In this unit you will learn to count in 100s (**hyaku**) and 1,000s (**sen**). If you go to Japan, you will find most prices are counted in these amounts – you could pay between 200 and 600 yen for a cup of coffee, for example, and around 5,000 yen for a **yukata** (*cotton kimono*).

Let's talk

1 Try saying the numbers below by adding the numbers 1–9 to the words **hyaku** (100) and **sen** (1,000). For example, 400 is **yonhyaku** and 5,000 is **gosen**. (Check your answers with the **Vocabulary list** opposite.) **Hyaku** has two 'beats': **hya-ku**.

 a 200
 b 500
 c 900
 d 2,000
 e 6,000
 f 9,000

2 Now try saying these numbers as in the example. (Answers at the back of the book.)

 Example: 250 = **nihyaku gojū**

 a 450
 b 950
 c 550
 d 2,200
 e 2,500
 f 2,250

▶ Vocabulary list

Read through and listen to the new words, saying each word out loud. When you feel familiar with them, test yourself by seeing if you can count in 100s and 1,000s starting from 100:

100	hyaku	400	yonhyaku	700	nanahyaku
200	nihyaku	500	gohyaku	800	happyaku
300	sambyaku	600	roppyaku	900	kyūhyaku
1,000	sen	4,000	yonsen	7,000	nanasen
2,000	nisen	5,000	gosen	8,000	hassen
3,000	sanzen	6,000	rokusen	9,000	kyūsen

en	yen (Japanese currency)
ikura desu ka	how much is it?
... arimasu ka	do you have ...?
hon ga arimasu ka	do you have a book?

ℹ Number tips (1): Counting in 100s

You may have noticed that the numbers 300, 600, 800, 900, 3,000 and 8,000 are said in a slightly different way from the pattern you learnt in **Let's talk**. There are some tips for remembering these in **Explanation 1**.

kyokuin	postmaster/assistant
hagaki	postcard
kitte	stamp(s)
tegami	letter
mai	counter for flat items
hon (pon/bon)	counter for cylindrical items
jū-mai	ten (stamps, tickets, etc.)
ni-hon	two (bottles, pens, etc.)
koko	here (this place)
soko	there (that place)
asoko	over there (that place over there)
kippu	ticket

▶ Conversation

Anne has gone to the local post office (**yūbinkyoku**) to post some letters home.

Anne	Sumimasen, kono tegami wa Igirisu made ikura desu ka.
Kyokuin	(*weighs the letter*) Nihyaku jū-en desu.
Anne	Ano ... hagaki wa Igirisu made ikura desu ka.
Kyokuin	Nanajū go-en desu.
Anne	Ja, nanajū go-en no kitte o jū-mai kudasai.
Kyokuin	Hai. **Ijō de yoroshii** desu ka.
Anne	Ē to, hagaki ga arimasu ka.
Kyokuin	Ē, soko desu ... Ichi-mai gojū-en desu.
Anne	Ja, kono hagaki o jū-mai kudasai.
Kyokuin	Arigatō gozaimasu. Zembu de ... (*he works it out on his abacus*) sen yonhyaku rokujū-en desu.

yūbinkyoku	*post office*
ijō de yoroshii desu ka	*is that all?*

ℹ The *soroban* or abacus

Despite the image of Japan as a technically advanced country, it is not unusual to see a **soroban** (Japanese-style abacus) instead of a calculator being used in places such as larger department stores and post offices. A **soroban** is considered to be quicker than a calculator for addition and subtraction (but not for multiplication and division). Also, the Japanese tend to be proud of their traditions and are keen to preserve them. Children can learn the **soroban** by attending special schools in the evenings. However, in recent years the numbers attending such schools have fallen.

Explanations

1 Counting above 100

You practised counting in 100s and 1,000s in the **Let's talk** section of this unit. The **Vocabulary list** section gives you the numbers between 100 and 9,000. You may have noticed that these numbers change when combined with **hyaku** (100):

300 (**sambyaku**)   600 (**roppyaku**)   800 (**happyaku**)

These numbers change when combined with **sen** (1,000).

3,000 (**san zen**)   8,000 (**hassen**)

(Also **issen** = 1,000 whereas **sen** = a 1,000 – you can use either.)

The best way to remember these changes is to keep practising them, first by themselves and then in sequence with the other 100s/1,000s. You should find that gradually the pattern will fix itself in your memory.

There is a further category of number once you reach 10,000. Whereas in English we count in 1,000s until we reach 1 million, the Japanese have another unit called **man** used for counting in 10,000s. You add the numbers **ichi, ni, san** ... to the word **man**. For example: **ichiman** = 10,000 (1 × 10,000) and **niman** = 20,000 (2 × 10,000).

You may find yourself using this unit of currency when buying long-distance train tickets or when paying for a hotel room or an expensive meal. Here are some more examples. Cover up the answers and try saying the amounts, then check to see if you are right. (The 🔳 below will help you.)

a 10,000
   (ichiman)

b 30,000
   (sanman)

c 45,000
   (yonman, gosen)

d 56,500
   (goman, rokusen, gohyaku)

e 82,450
   (hachiman, nisen,
   yonhyaku, gojū)

🔳 Number tips (2): Counting in 1,000s

Count four digits back from the end and draw a line (real or imaginary) between the fourth digit and the digits to its left. The digits on the left are the amount in **man**, the others will break down into 1,000s, 100s and 10s.

Example: 45,200 = 4 |5, 200 = yon man, go sen, ni hyaku

2 O-kane *Money*

The **yen** is the Japanese unit of currency. Here is the range of coins and notes:

coins: ichi-en (*1 yen*) go-en (*5 yen*) jū-en (*10 yen*)
gojū-en (*50 yen*) hyaku-en (*100 yen*) gohyaku-en (*500 yen*)
notes: sen-en (*1,000 yen*) nisen-en (*2,000 yen*)
gosen-en (*5,000 yen*) ichiman-en (*10,000 yen*)

If you know someone who has been to Japan or if you have a Japanese friend, have a look at some Japanese coins and notes. You will see that the amounts are written both in our Arabic numbers and in the Japanese number script.

The person pictured on the 1,000 yen note is Natsume Sōseki, a famous Japanese novelist (1867–1916). Murasaki Shikibu, the world's first female novelist (11th century) is featured on the recent 2,000 yen note. The person on the 5,000 yen note is Nitobe Inazu, a key figure in education (1862–1933). On the 10,000 yen note is Fukuzawa Yukichi, a famous scholar and founder of one of Japan's top universities (1835–1901).

3 Hagaki wa Igirisu made ikura desu ka *How much is a postcard to England?*

You ask how much something is using the phrase **... wa ikura desu ka**. For example:

Kitte wa ikura desu ka. *How much is a stamp?*
Kippu wa ikura desu ka. *How much is a ticket?*

If you want to state the destination, put **made** (*to*) (you met this in the last unit) after the name of the city or country. For example:

Kono tegami wa Amerika
  made ikura desu ka.

How much is this letter to the USA?

Kippu wa Kyōto made ikura
  desu ka.

How much is a ticket to Kyoto?

4 Hagaki ga arimasu ka *Do you have any postcards?*

If you want to enquire whether a shop or person has the thing you are looking for, use the phrase **... ga arimasu ka**. For example:

Eigo no shimbun ga
  arimasu ka.

Do you have any English newspapers?

Kitte ga arimasu ka.

Do you have any stamps?

If you want to say that you have or possess something, use **... ga arimasu**. For example:

Uchi ga arimasu. | *I own a house.*
O-kane ga arimasu. | *I have money.*
Shimbun ga arimasu. | *I've got a newspaper.*

5 More about numbers

In the following examples you will notice that two different words are used to say *one*, and also that it is not enough in Japanese simply to say **ichi** when talking about numbers of items.

Ichi-mai hyaku-en desu. | *One (postcard) is 100 yen.*
Hitotsu sambyaku-en desu. | *One (coffee, etc.) is 300 yen.*

There are actually two different ways in Japanese of counting (called system A and system B in this book).

System A

You have already learnt to count using **ichi, ni, san** .... When you talk about numbers of items you need to attach a special word – called a counter – after the number. We sometimes use counters in English, for example, *a **loaf** of bread*, *two **slices** of toast*, *three **bottles** of beer*.

The Japanese use counters to a much greater extent. In this unit you will learn two counters which are used with **ichi, ni, san** ... . Now look at these examples below.

- **Mai** is a counter for flat objects – stamps, tickets, paper, cards, etc.
  1 = ichi-mai
  2 = ni-mai
  3 = san-mai, etc.

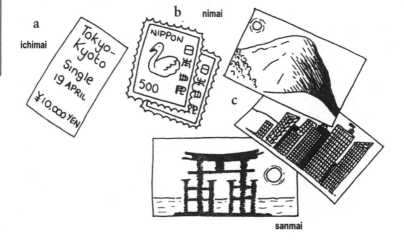

a
ichimai

b nimai

c

sanmai

- **Hon (pon, bon)** is a counter for long or cylindrical objects – bottles, pens, etc.
  1 = ippon
  2 = nihon
  3 = sambon

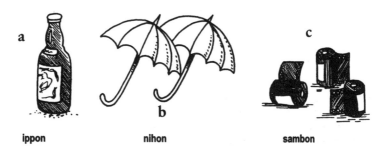

a

b

c

ippon   nihon   sambon

There are many more special counters in Japanese for counting different groups of items, for example, birds, animals, books, machines. However, the two examples on the previous page are enough for you to get by at this stage.

System B

The second set of numbers is used for the many items which don't have a special counter. You could use this system for counting any object, even those which have a special 'System A' counter (examples in **Explanation 6**). Although in some cases you might sound a little childish to a Japanese listener, you will be able to make yourself understood.

▶ This list may look daunting to begin with, but pace yourself. Learn perhaps three at a time and keep re-testing yourself. Remember 'a little, often' is the best way to learn. Use the recording to listen and repeat.

1 = hitotsu	6 = muttsu
2 = futatsu	7 = nanatsu
3 = mittsu	8 = yattsu
4 = yottsu	9 = kokonotsu
5 = itsutsu	10 = tō

a   hitotsu   b   futatsu   c   mittsu

After **tō** (10) you use **jūichi** (11), **jūni** (12), etc., just as you learnt to count in Units 3 and 4.

ℹ Tips for remembering system B

- 1–9 end in **tsu** – **hitotsu**, **futatsu**, etc.
- You learnt to count people in Unit 3. You should note that *one person* (**hitori**) and *two people* (**futari**) are similar to **hitotsu** and **futatsu**, but **tsu** is substituted for **ri** at the end of the word.
- The word *four* (**yottsu**) begins with **yo** (you already know **yon**); *seven* (**nanatsu**) is **nana** plus **tsu**.

- *Ten* (**tō**) sounds a bit like the English word *toe* – and there are ten toes on your feet!

See if you can think of some more words and sounds that will help you to remember these numbers.

6 Kitte o jūmai kudasai *May I have ten stamps, please?*

We learnt ... **o kudasai** (*may I have ...*) in the last unit. When you want to say an amount you put the number (plus counter if necessary) between **o** and **kudasai**. For example:

Kōhī o futatsu kudasai.	*May I have two coffees, please?* (system B)
Bīru o ippon kudasai.	*May I have a (bottle of) beer, please?* (system A)
Bīru o hitotsu kudasai.	*May I have a beer, please?* (system B)
Kitte o gomai kudasai.	*May I have five stamps, please?* (system A)

You could also say:

Kitte o itsutsu kudasai.	*May I have five stamps, please?* (system B)

But **gomai** sounds more sophisticated, as explained in **Explanation 5**.

7 Nanajūgo-en no kitte o jūmai kudasai *May I have 10 × 75 yen stamps, please?*

You can add information about the price, using **no**. You were introduced to **no** in Unit 2 (**Explanation 4**). It is used to show a relationship between two items/people. For example, **sensei no hon** means *the teacher's book*. In the examples below, you could think of **no** as meaning *priced*, for example:

Hyaku-en *no* kitte.	*A 100 yen **priced** stamp.*
Nihyaku-en *no* pen o nihon kudasai.	*May I have 2 × 200 yen **priced** pens, please?*
Sambyaku-en *no* aisukuriimu o mittsu kudasai.	*May I have 3 × 300 yen **priced** ice creams, please?*

8 Asoko desu *It's over there*

In Unit 5 you learnt the words **kore, sore** and **are** for *this one, that one* and *that one over there* (also **kono, sono** and **ano**). *Here/this place, there/that place* and *over there/that place over there* follow a similar pattern using the words **koko, soko** and **asoko**. For example:

Koko wa Tōkyō desu.   *This place is Tokyo.*
Hagaki wa asoko desu.   *The postcards are over there.*

The question word is **doko** (*where*) and you will meet this in Unit 7.

9 Shop names

Ya in Japanese means *shop/store*, and you add this to the end of words to make shop names. For example:

hana (*flower*) + **ya** = **hanaya** (*florist's*)

What shop names do you get when you add **ya** to the following words?

sakana (*fish*)
denki (*electric*)
pan (*bread*)
niku (*meat*)
kusuri (*medicine*)

Some words do change, however. For example:

yasai (*vegetables*) becomes **yaoya** (*greengrocer's*)
sake (*alcohol*) becomes **sakaya** (*wine shop/off-licence*)

It is worth mentioning, though, that *supermarkets* (**sūpā**) in Japan have taken over the role of the individual shop to a certain extent.

ℹ How to remember groups of vocabulary

Try drawing pictures/symbols to prompt your memory rather than writing down the English word. For example, how many shop names can you say by looking at the pictures on the next page?

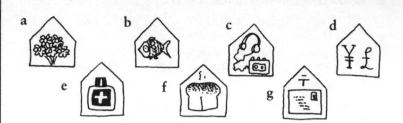

Practice

▶ 1 Below are different amounts of money. Listen to the recording and in each case circle the amount that is *not* mentioned.

a	200 yen	300 yen	400 yen
b	800 yen	600 yen	500 yen
c	450 yen	750 yen	950 yen
d	1,000 yen	2,000 yen	3,000 yen
e	1,500 yen	1,050 yen	8,050 yen
f	10,000 yen	40,000 yen	4000 yen
g	25,000 yen	20,500 yen	20,050 yen

▶ 2 You will hear people asking for amounts of the items listed below. How many do they ask for?

	Item	How many?
a	Apples (**ringo**)	
b	Stamps	
c	Tickets	
d	Bottles of beer	
e	Bottles of sake	
f	Postcards	
g	Rolls of film (**firumu**)	
h	Video tapes	

3 Below are some examples of Tokyo underground tickets with the amounts written in yen (the half-price amounts are child fares).

a Practise saying the adult fares in Japanese.

b Practise asking how much it is to the destination printed on the ticket.

Example: Shinjuku made ikura desu ka.

Example: *destination* – Shinjuku

i *destination* – Shimbashi

ii *destination* – Zushi

iii *destination* – Ōme

iv *destination* – Kōenji

4 Below are some examples of Japanese stamps.

a Practise asking for each stamp as in the example below.

Example: Nanajū-en no kitte o kudasai.

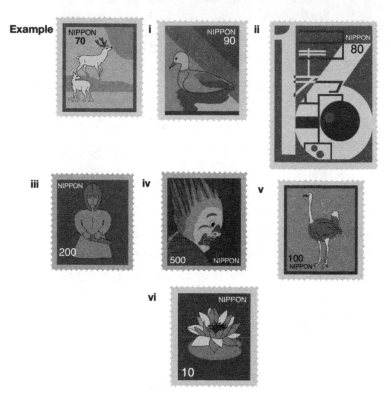

b Now practise asking for three of stamp **i**, ten of stamp **ii**, five of stamp **iii**, one of stamp **iv**, four of stamp **v** and 20 of stamp **vi**.

Example: (two stamps): Nanajū-en no kitte o nimai kudasai.

5 On the next page are some examples of the prices of journeys from Tokyo by Japan Railways (JR). Say the destination and prices out loud. Some are over 10,000 yen. The first one has been done for you.

Example: Tōkyō kara Yokohama made yonhyaku yonjū-en desu.

	Place	Fare
a	Yokohama	440
b	Narita	2,890
c	Kyoto	12,970
d	Shin-Osaka	13,480
e	Hiroshima	17,700
f	Nagasaki	23,510
g	Sapporo	21,380

6 Ask for the items below as in the example. The counter system to use is in brackets.

Example: Two cups of coffee = kōhī o futatsu kudasai

a Three postcards (**mai**)
b One bottle of beer (**hon**)
c Two glasses of milk (system B)
d Six pens (**hon**)
e Three × 200 yen cakes (system B)
f Two × 1,000 yen tickets (**mai**)

7 Practise saying these years as in the example.

Example: 1995 = sen kyūhyaku kyūjū go-**nen** (**nen** = *year*)

a 1996
b 1066
c 1963
d 1980
e 1945

Now try saying the year of your birth.

8 In which specialist shops would you buy the following items? Answer in Japanese.

a Kitte
b Ringo
c Sake
d Bīru
e Sakana
f Pan

Review

You have now completed six units of Japanese – **omedetō!** (*Congratulations!*). You have been introduced to a number of basic structures and some different ways of using numbers. You are also beginning to build up your vocabulary. Instead of a test for this unit, look back over the dialogues in the first six units. Listen to them on the recording and/or read through them and check how much you now understand. Use this opportunity to give yourself a vocabulary test on all the new words from the **Vocabulary list** section. If you have been building up your own 'dictionary' (see Unit 3, page 34), use this to test yourself.

In the next six units you will be learning new sentence structures and new vocabulary, but it is important to keep looking back and practising what you have already learnt. Go over the **Practice** exercises at the end of each unit and speak Japanese out loud – this will give you the confidence to really use it. Practise talking about yourself – there are now lots of things you can say, such as your name, age, job, nationality, birthday, interests, and you can talk about your family too. You could even record yourself and then listen to it. If you have a Japanese friend, ask him or her to listen to you and comment on your pronunciation. The main point is – keep practising what you have learnt!

07

yūbinkyoku wa doko desu ka

where is the post office?

In this unit you will learn
- how to ask for directions
- how to give directions
- how to say exactly where places are

Introduction

In Unit 5 you learnt that **kudasai** meant *please* or *may I have*. This word is also used when giving directions: *(please) go straight ahead, (please) turn left.*

In Units 4 and 5 we also talked about question words (**nan/i**, *what?*; **nanji**, *what time?*; **nansai**, *how old?* etc.).

In this unit you are going to learn a new question word **doko** (*where?*) to ask where something is (see also Unit 6, **Explanation 8**). For example, **yūbinkyoku wa doko desu ka** (*where is the post office?*). Notice the sentence order: *place* **wa doko desu ka**.

As well as asking for directions you also need to be able to understand the answer you are given. Remember that it is not important to understand every word. Learning to pick out the necessary information such as **massugu itte**, **migi ni magatte** is a very valuable skill. You may also find yourself in a situation in your own country where you need to help a Japanese person who is lost.

As a check, repeat the directions as they are given to you. You don't need to repeat **kudasai**. And don't be afraid of asking people to speak more slowly or to say something again. (See Unit 3, page 30.)

Let's talk

1 Imagine you need to stop someone to ask them for directions. How do you:

   a   catch their attention? (*excuse me*)
   b   ask where a bank (**ginkō**) is?
   c   ask them to repeat something?
   d   say thank you?

▶ Vocabulary list

To go straight on

... itte kudasai	*(please) go ...*
massugu	*straight on*
chotto	*a little way*
massugu itte kudasai	*please go straight on*
chotto itte kudasai	*please go a little way*

To turn

... magatte kudasai	*(please) turn ...*
migi	*right*
hidari	*left*
migi *ni* **magatte kudasai**	*please turn* (to the) *right*
hidari *ni* **magatte kudasai**	*please turn* (to the) *left*

Orientation points

shingō	*traffic lights*
kōsaten	*crossroads*
kado	*corner*
michi	*road*
tsugi no ...	*the next ...*
tsugi no shingō	*the next traffic lights*
nibanme no ...	*the second ...*
nibanme no kōsaten	*the second crossroads*

Giving directions

shingō o* massugu itte kudasai	*go straight at the traffic lights*
kōsaten o* migi ni magatte kudasai	*turn right at the crossroads*
tsugi no kado o* hidari ni magatte kudasai	*turn left at the next corner*

*Think of **o** in this case as meaning *at*. Note that it comes after the word: **shingō o** (*at the traffic lights*). You will learn more about **o** in Unit 8.

Some useful places

ginkō	*bank*
eki	*station*
eigakan	*cinema*

Exact location

tonari	next to
chikaku	near to
ichiban chikai	the nearest
mukaigawa	opposite (side)
mae	in front of
hidarigawa	left-hand side
migigawa	right-hand side
... no tonari	next to the ...
ginkō no tonari	next to the bank
yūbinkyoku wa ginkō no tonari desu	the post office is next to the bank

ℹ️ Itte *say/go*

You've now met two meanings for the word **itte**.

* *say* as in **mōichido itte kudasai** (*please say it again*)
* *go* as in **massugu itte kudasai** (*please go straight on*)

You will always know the meaning from the situation, so you don't need to worry about this. (There are lots of words in English with more than one meaning too, for example, bank, light, post.)

▶ Conversation

Scott is going to visit Anne's host family and he is looking for Shibuya train station. (While you listen to the recording or read the **Conversation** look at the map on the next page and see if you can follow the directions to the station.)

Scott Sumimasen, Shibuya eki wa doko desu ka.

Passer-by Ā, sumimasen, watashi wa eigo ga **dekimasen**. (*the passer-by rushes off*)

Scott Ē! (*sees another passer-by*) Sumimasen, Shibuya eki wa doko desu ka.

Passer-by Shibuya eki desu ka. Ēto, kono michi o massugu itte, tsugi no shingō o hidari ni ... Aa, sumimasen, tsugi no shingō o migi ni magatte kudasai. **Sorekara**, nibanme no kōsaten o hidari ni magatte kudasai. Shibuya eki wa Tōkyō ginkō no mukaigawa desu.

Scott Sumimasen, kono michi o massugu itte ... sorekara? Mō ichido itte kudasai.

Passer-by	Sorekara, tsugi no shingō o migi ni magatte kudasai.
Scott	**Wakarimashita. Soshite**, nibanme no kōsaten o hidari ni magatte …
Passer-by	Hai, sō desu. Nihongo ga jōzu desu ne!
Scott	**Iie, mada mada** desu. Dōmo arigato gozaimashita.

ā! ē!	(expressions of surprise)
dekimasen	*can't* (the passer-by is saying he can't speak English. Scott has spoken in Japanese but some Japanese people aren't used to this and feel they should be able to speak English)
sorokara	
soshite	and, and then
wakarimashita	*I understand* (Lit. *I've understood*)
jōzu	*good at*
iie, mada mada desu	*no, I'm no good yet**

*Japanese people are pleased if foreigners try to speak in Japanese and will praise your attempts. The way to reply to this is in a modest fashion – even if you think you are doing quite well!

Explanations

1 ... wa doko desu ka *Where is ...*

The pattern here is fairly straightforward. You put the name of the place you want to go to at the beginning of the phrase. *Place* **wa doko desu ka** means *Where is place?* To be more polite, say *excuse me* (**sumimasen**) before you ask. For example:

Sumimasen, ginkō wa doko desu ka.	*Excuse me, where is the bank?*

You might want to specify which bank, supermarket, etc. In this case, put the name first. For example:

Sumimasen, Jusco sūpā wa doko desu ka.	*Excuse me, where is Jusco supermarket?*

If you want to ask where the nearest one is, put **ichiban chikai** before the place. For example:

Sumimasen, ichiban chikai depāto wa doko desu ka.	*Excuse me, where is the nearest department store?*

▶ 2 Understanding and giving directions

In this unit you've been introduced to two important phrases for giving directions: **... itte kudasai** means *please go ...* and **... magatte kudasai** means *please turn ...*.

Once you have mastered some of the vocabulary in this unit you can gradually build up from fairly simple directions to more complex ones. Practise saying the build-up phrases on the next page. Some of these are on the recording. When you feel confident, try covering up the Japanese side and see if you can remember how to give directions using the English as a prompt.

Massugu itte kudasai.	*Please go straight ahead.*
Kōsaten o massugu itte kudasai.	*Please go straight on at the crossroads.*
Tsugi no kōsaten o massugu itte kudasai.	*Please go straight on at the next crossroads.*
Nibanme no kōsaten o massugu itte kudasai.	*Please go straight on at the second crossroads.*
Hidari ni magatte kudasai.	*Please turn left.*
Migi ni magatte kudasai.	*Please turn right.*

Shingō o hidari ni magatte kudasai.	*Please turn left at the traffic lights.*
Shingō o migi ni magatte kudasai.	*Please turn right at the traffic lights.*
Tsugi no shingō o migi ni magatte kudasai.	*Please turn right at the next traffic lights.*
Nibanme no shingō o hidari ni magatte kudasai.	*Please turn left at the second set of traffic lights.*

You can link two directions simply by leaving out the first kudasai. Thus, **massugu itte kudasai** + **shingō o migi ni magatte kudasai** becomes:

| Massugu itte, shingō o migi ni magatte kudasai. | *Go straight on and turn right at the traffic lights.* |

i Learning tips

When you are learning phrases or sentence patterns, try writing down just the first letter of each word in the phrase: so **Shingō O Hidari Ni Magatte Kudasai** (*turn left at the traffic lights*) would become: **S O H N M K**. This will help prompt your memory and also will help you to say the phrase in the correct order.

Remember that when you pronounce double consonants (**massugu, magatte, itte**) you pause slightly before you say the sound (as in the English word *headdress*). Look at the **Pronunciation guide** (page xvii) for more practice of this.

3 Giving the exact location

Ginkō no mukaigawa desu means (*it's*) *opposite the bank*. The word order is important here. In English, the word *opposite* comes before *bank*; in Japanese *opposite* comes after *bank*, with **no** in between. You could think of it as meaning *the bank's opposite*. (See Unit 2 for more information on **no**).

Yūbinkyoku no chikaku desu.	(*It's*) *near the post office.*
Eki no mae desu.	(*It's*) *in front of the station.*
Migigawa desu.	(*It's*) *on the right-hand side.*

If you want to specify the place, you put it at the beginning of the sentence followed by the particle **wa**. (Look back to Unit 3 for notes on **wa** and **desu**.)

Depāto wa ginkō no mukaigawa desu.	*The department store is opposite the bank.*
Sūpā wa eki no tonari desu.	*The supermarket is next to the station.*
Eigakan wa hidarigawa desu.	*The cinema is on the left-hand side.*

❶ Developing listening skills

As stated earlier in this unit, it is useful to develop the skill of listening for essential information, without trying to understand every word. Keep listening to the recorded dialogues to improve your understanding and build up your vocabulary.

Practice

1   a   The diagrams below represent different directions (*go straight on, turn right,* etc.). How many can you say? Speak out loud, then check your answers in the back of the book.

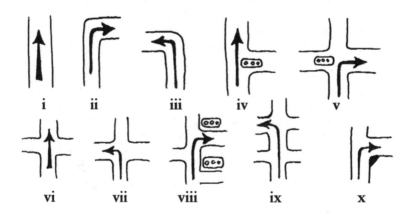

    b   Now try linking these directions together: i + ii; i + iii; iv + vii; iv + x; viii + i; vi + x.

▶ 2   As the passer-by gives you the directions to five different places, follow them on the map opposite and write the correct place name next to each of the numbers 1 to 5.

Alternatively, read the directions below and match letters a–e with the numbers on the map.

Directions

a Yūbinkyoku desu ka? Chotto itte, kado o migi ni magatte kudasai. Yūbinkyoku wa hidarigawa desu.

b Kono michi o massugu itte, tsugi no shingō o hidari ni magatte kudasai. Hanaya wa depāto no tonari desu.

c Ēto, tsugi no shingō o migi ni magatte, chotto itte kudasai. Ginkō wa eigakan no mukaigawa desu.

d Sō desu ne. Massugu itte, tsugi no shingō o migi ni magatte kudasai. Eki wa eigakan no tonari desu.

e Sūpā desu ka. Shingō o hidari ni magatte, tsugi no kōsaten o migi ni magatte kudasai. Sūpā wa kōsaten no chikaku desu.

3 How would you ask a passer-by the way to each of the places below? Try to cover up the Japanese words and use the pictures as prompts.

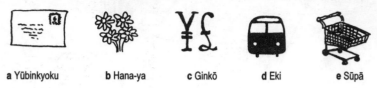

a Yūbinkyoku **b** Hana-ya **c** Ginkō **d** Eki **e** Sūpā

Next, how would you ask where the nearest of each of the above places was?

▶ **4** True or false? Listen to the directions and decide whether they correctly describe the maps **a–f** below. Mark the boxes below the maps in Japanese style: a *circle* (**maru**) if it's true or a *cross* (**batsu**) if it's false.

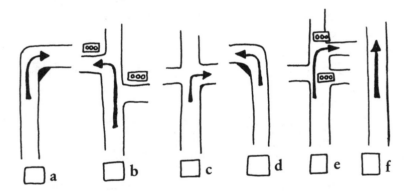

☐ **a** ☐ **b** ☐ **c** ☐ **d** ☐ **e** ☐ **f**

5 Mr Suzuki is writing a pamphlet for his local tourist information office about the facilities in his town. However, he has made some errors. Can you correct them by looking at the map and changing the underlined parts of the text if necessary? (Be careful – some are correct.)

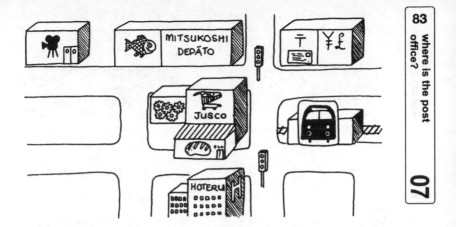

a Eigakan wa Mitsukoshi depāto no <u>chikaku</u> desu.

b Jusco sūpā wa hanaya no <u>mae</u> desu.

c Yūbinkyoku wa ginkō no <u>mukaigawa</u> desu.

d Mitsukoshi depāto wa <u>eki</u> no tonari desu.

e Ginkō wa eki no <u>mukaigawa</u> desu.

f Eki wa <u>eigakan</u> no chikaku desu.

6 Using the same map as in Practice 5, imagine you are at the *hotel* (**hoteru**) and give the directions and exact location for the places listed below. Try to link your directions and give as much information as possible. For example, in **a** you could say *Go on a little way and turn left at the next traffic lights. The bakery is in front of Jusco supermarket.*

    a The bakery   **c** The bank

    b The station   **d** The fishmonger's

7 a Hidden in the wordsearch overleaf are ten shops and services you'd expect to find in a medium-sized city in Japan. Can you find them? You can read horizontally, vertically or diagonally, and either forwards or backwards.

    b The remaining letters make up a greeting word you learnt in Unit 1. Can you work out what it is?

A	Y	A	N	A	K	A	A
O	A	Y	H	A	U	Y	O
G	O	N	O	S	S	Z	D
A	Y	A	E	I	U	M	E
A	A	P	S	K	R	P	P
N	A	K	A	G	I	E	A
D	E	N	K	I	Y	A	T
H	A	N	A	Y	A	U	O

Clues: i Where would you find the following items: sakana; tēpu rekōdā; ringo (*apple*); hana; pan; kusuri; eiga (*film/movie*); densha (*train*); yōfuku (*clothes*)?
  ii What type of shop is 'Jusco'?

Test

1 Count up in units of 100 (100, 200, etc.). Then count down in units of 1,000 from 10,000.

2 Which phrase would you choose to ask someone where the post office is?

  a Kōhī o futatsu kudasai.
  b Yūbinkyoku wa doko desu ka.
  c Yūbinkyoku no mae desu.

3 How would you say the following?

  a Good morning.
  b Go straight on and turn right at the crossroads.
  c The greengrocer's is opposite the bank.
  d May I have a coffee and some cake?
  e Where is the nearest bakery?

08

nichiyōbi ni nani o shimasu ka

what do you do on Sundays?

In this unit you will learn
- ten useful doing words for describing your day
- how to say when you do something
- how to ask about someone's future schedule
- the days of the week
- some useful question words

Introduction

In this unit you are going to learn how to talk about your daily routines and how to talk about future plans. You will find this very useful if you want to describe your day or ask somebody about their day. You will learn ten new doing or action words, (for example, *I/he/they ... eat, drink, watch* TV.) You will find that these are very simple to use once you know the new vocabulary.

Let's talk

1 Ima nanji desu ka

How well can you remember telling the time? Refresh your memory by saying the times below.

a   6 o'clock
b   4.30
c   9 p.m.
d   7.30 a.m.
e   12 o'clock
f   11.30 a.m.

2 Say the times that these places open and close (start and finish) as in the example.

Example: *Wine shop, 10–8* – Sakaya wa jūji kara hachiji made desu.

a   bank, 9–3
b   supermarket, 8–8
c   post office, 9–6
d   bakery 8–6

▶ Vocabulary list

Read and/or listen to the new words and try the exercises on the recording.

Action words

okimasu	*wake up* (get up)
nemasu	*go to bed*
tabemasu	*eat*
nomimasu	*drink*
yomimasu	*read*
shimasu	*do, make, play*
mimasu	*see, watch, look*
benkyō shimasu	*study*
gorufu o shimasu	*play golf*
kaimono o shimasu	*do the shopping*

ℹ Pronunciation tip

The final **u** of these action words is very soft and hardly spoken.

Time expressions

nanji ni	at what time
nanyōbi ni	on *what day*
asa	*morning*
hiru	*midday*
yoru	*evening*
asagohan	*breakfast*
hirugohan	*lunch*
yorugohan/bangohan	*evening meal*

Food and drink

tabemono	*food*
tōsuto	*toast*
pan	*bread*
tamago	*eggs*
niku	*meat*
yasai	*vegetables*
ringo	*apples*
gohan	*rice*
nomimono	*a drink*
ocha	*green tea*
kōcha	*black tea*
jūsu	*juice*
miruku	*milk*
kōra	*cola*
mizu	*water*

Useful objects

zasshi	*magazine*
manga	*comic book*
terebi	*television*
eiga	*movie*
soshite/sorekara/sore ni	*and (then)*
goro	*about* (used when saying times)
daitai	*more or less, generally*
tokidoki	*sometimes*

▶ Conversation

Scott has come round to the Yamaguchi home to interview Mr
Yamaguchi about his typical day, as part of a Japanese
homework project.

Scott	Asa, nanji ni okimasu ka.
Mr Yamaguchi	Daitai, rokuji han goro okimasu.
Scott	**Hayai** desu ne! Sorekara, asagohan ni nani o tabemasu ka.
Mr Yamaguchi	Sō desu ne. Tōsuto o tabemasu. Sore ni kōhī o nomimasu.
Anne	Shigoto wa nanji kara desu ka.
Mr Yamaguchi	Daitai, hachiji han kara rokuji made desu. Hirugohan wa ichi ji kara desu.
Scott	Yoru nani o shimasu ka.
Mr Yamaguchi	Bangohan o tabemasu. Soshite terebi o mimasu. Jūichiji han goro nemasu.
Scott	Nichiyōbi ni nani o shimasu ka.
Mr Yamaguchi	Sō desu ne. **Rirakkusu** shimasu ne. Zasshi o yomimasu. Tokidoki gorufu o shimasu …
Anne	(*laughing*) **Ē**? Daitai **ichinichi jū** nemasu yo.

hayai	*early*
rirakkusu	*relax*
ē?	*what?*
ichinichi jū	*all day*

ℹ The working week

The traditional image of the Japanese 'salaryman' or employee is of
someone who works six days a week and stays at work until late in
the evenings with colleagues and bosses either in the office or at
local bars. Even on Sunday he may be expected to play a round of
golf with his boss or with clients. There are increasing reports of
changes to this typical image.

Some larger companies have reduced the hours of a working week
and many have introduced a five-day week. Younger men are said to
want to spend more time with their family and are less willing to work
long hours. It remains to be seen how this will affect Japanese
working life in the future.

Explanations

1 Action words (*masu* words)

Japanese doing words are very simple to use – you will notice that they all end in **masu**. This gives the meaning *I do* or *I will do something*. For example, the question **nichiyōbi ni nani o shimasu ka** could have the meaning *what do you do on Sundays?* or *what are you going to do on Sunday?* The context will tell you which one is intended.

Also, the **masu** ending does not change whether you say *I/you/he/she/it/we/they do something*. For example:

Nichiyōbi ni Sukotto-san wa terebi o mimasu.	*Scott watches TV on Sundays.*
Nichiyōbi ni terebi o mimasu.	*I watch TV on Sundays.*

And you don't need to use the words *you/I/he*, etc. unless it's not clear who is being spoken about. It is then better to use a person's name rather than *you*. For example:

Nichiyōbi ni nani o shimasu ka.	*What do (you) do on Sundays?*
Yamaguchi-san, nichiyōbi ni nani o shimasu ka.	*Mr Yamaguchi, what do you do on Sundays?*

Tokidoki gorufu o shimasu *I sometimes play golf*

Shimasu is a useful word meaning *do, make* or *play*. Here are some examples of its use:

Tenisu o shimasu.	*I play tennis.*
Sakkā o shimasu.	*I play football.*
Kaimono o shimasu.	*I do the shopping.*
Denwa o shimasu.	*I make a phone call.*
Kuji kara jūji made eigo o benkyō shimasu.	*I study English from nine until ten.*

When you add **tokidoki** you are talking about what you do sometimes. For example:

Tokidoki denwa o shimasu.	*I sometimes make phone calls.*
Tokidoki tenisu o shimasu.	*I sometimes play tennis.*

When you add **daitai** you are saying *generally* .... For example:

Daitai rokuji ni okimasu.   *I generally get up at six.*

2 Tōsuto o tabemasu *I eat some toast*

There is no equivalent in English of the word **o**, but in Japanese you say it after the item you eat, drink, read, etc. (We call this the *object* of a sentence.) Here are some examples with the object in *italics*.

Gohan o tabemasu.	I eat *rice.*
Kōcha o nomimasu.	I drink *black tea.*
Kaimono o shimasu.	I do *the shopping.*

You should note that the **masu** word always comes at the end of the sentence.

3 Yamaguchi-san wa kōhī o nomimasu *Mr Yamaguchi drinks coffee*

When you mention the person who eats, drinks, etc., this word is followed by **wa** and is the subject of the sentence. Remember that **wa** acts like a highlighter and can be translated as *as for* .... (See Unit 2, **Explanation 1**). Here are some examples with the subject in *italics*.

An-san wa nihongo no hon o yomimasu.	*Anne* reads a Japanese book.
Watashi wa Nihongo o benkyō shimasu.	*I* study Japanese.
Sukotto-san wa kaimono o shimasu.	*Scott* is going to do the shopping.

You should note the order in which you say these sentences.

1 You say the person who does the action, followed by **wa**.
2 You say the item (or person) which has the action done to it, followed by **o**.
3 You say the action word – the **masu** word.

An-san wa	hon o	yomimasu
1 (subject)	2 (object)	3 (verb)

4 Nichi yōbi ni nani o shimasu ka *What do you do on Sundays?*

When you say the day or time that you do something, it is followed by **ni** meaning *on* or *at*. For example:

Nichiyōbi ni terebi o mimasu.	*I watch TV on Sundays.*
Hachiji ni okimasu.	*I get up at 8 o'clock.*

You can replace **ni** with **goro** (*about*) if you want to give an approximate time. For example:

Hachiji goro okimasu.	*I get up at about 8 o'clock.*

The important point to remember is that **ni** and **goro** are said *after* the time/day.

The time expression is usually said at this point in a sentence:

An-san wa *hachiji kara* terebi o mimasu.	*Anne watches TV from 8 o'clock.*
Hachiji ni asagohan o tabemasu.	*I eat breakfast at 8 o'clock.*
Rokuji ni okimasu.	*I get up at 6 o'clock.*

5 Nanji ni *At what time*

To ask when somebody does something you can use **nanji ni** (*at what time*):

Nanji ni okimasu ka.	*(At) what time do you get up?*

Or **nanyōbi ni** (*on what day*):

Nanyōbi ni gorufu o shimasu ka.	*(On) what day/s do you play golf?*

Or **nannichi ni** (*on what date/days of the month?*):

Nannichi ni sakkā o shimasu ka.	*On what date are you going to play football?*

Or the more general question **itsu** (*when*):

Itsu kaimono o shimasu ka.	*When do you do the shopping?*

You do not need to say **ni** after **itsu** because you are not saying *in*, *on* or *at*:

> **Itsu sakkā o shimasu ka.**   *When are you going to play football?* (not: on when are you going to play football?)

See **Explanation 7** for more information about this.

6 Bangohan o tabemasu *I eat dinner*

The words for the three main meals in Japanese are interesting. They are made up of the word for *rice* (**gohan**) and the words for *morning* (**asa**), *midday* (**hiru**) and *evening* (**ban** – as in **konbanwa**, *good evening*; also **yoru**). Therefore, **asagohan** (*breakfast*) literally means *morning rice*, **hirugohan** (*lunch*) is *midday rice*, and **bangohan** or **yorugohan** (*dinner/evening meal*) is *evening rice*. You've probably worked out the reason for this – traditionally in Japan every meal is accompanied by a bowl of rice. (See Unit 15 for more information on meals.)

7 Asa nanji ni okimasu ka *What time do you get up in the morning?*

In Unit 5 we learnt **gozen** (*a.m.*) and **gogo** (*p.m./afternoon*). A more informal way of saying this is to use **asa** (*morning*) and **yoru** (*evening*). For example:

> **Asa shichiji ni okimasu.**   *I get up at 8 o'clock in the morning.*
> **Yoru terebi o mimasu.**   *I watch TV in the evenings.*

You should note that you don't need **ni** after **asa** and **yoru**. **Ni** is only used with *exact* times, days and dates. (You will learn more about this in Unit 9.)

8 Asagohan ni nani o tabemasu ka *What do you eat for breakfast?*

To ask what someone eats at mealtimes, use **ni** (in this case meaning *for*) after the meal word. For example:

> **Bangohan ni nani o tabemasu ka.**   *What do you eat for dinner?*

To answer, just say the food that you eat.

Tamago o tabemasu.   *I eat eggs.*

If you want to include what you drink, use one of the *and* words (**sore ni, soshite, sorekara**). You say these at the beginning of a new sentence. For example;

Tamago o tabemasu. Sore ni   *I eat eggs. And I drink*
kōhī o nomimasu.   *coffee.*

To make a statement about what you have for breakfast (etc.), start with: **asagohan ni ....** For example:

Asagohan ni tamago   *I eat eggs for breakfast.*
o tabemasu.

9 The days of the week

Practise saying the days of the week. Speak out loud.

NB All the days of the week end in **yōbi,** meaning *day.*

Nichiyōbi	*Sunday*
Getsuyōbi	*Monday*
Kayōbi	*Tuesday*
Suiyōbi	*Wednesday*
Mokuyōbi	*Thursday*
Kinyōbi	*Friday*
Doyōbi	*Saturday*

There is more information about how to *read* the days of the week in Unit 13.

ℹ️ Learning tip

In this unit you have been introduced to whole new groups of vocabulary, for example, food and drink items, verbs and days of the week. You could make the learning process more interesting by writing out in English the days of the week, and on each of those days one or two things which you might do (it doesn't have to be true!). Then practise saying them in Japanese. For example: *Monday, eat toast for breakfast. Then study Japanese.*

Practice

▶ **1** Below are some sequences using days of the week. You have a choice of two sequences (i and ii) for each question. Listen to the recording and underline the sequence you hear.

Example: i <u>Monday</u>, <u>Wednesday</u>, <u>Friday</u>
        ii Monday, Friday, Wednesday

a   i Tuesday, Friday, Saturday
     ii Friday, Tuesday, Thursday

b   i Sunday, Monday
     ii Monday, Sunday

c   i Wednesday, Thursday, Saturday
     ii Thursday, Saturday, Wednesday

▶ **2** Takeshi has recorded his weekly schedule for Anne and she has written out the information that she has understood. Can you fill in the gaps for her as you listen to the recording?

	Day	Time/part of day	Activity
a	Wednesday	morning ?	? plays football
b	?	?	watches TV
c	Saturday	? ?	studies English watches a film
d	Sunday	? in the evening	reads comics ?
e	?	12.00	?

3 Nanyōbi desu ka

In the left column opposite are the days of the week in English; in the right column are the days in Japanese. Can you match them up by drawing lines from one to the other? There is one extra day in the Japanese list. Which one is it (in English)?

a	Monday	i	Suiyōbi
b	Thursday	ii	Nichiyōbi
c	Wednesday	iii	Kayōbi
d	Saturday	iv	Mokuyōbi
e	Sunday	v	Kinyōbi
f	Tuesday	vi	Nichiyōbi
g	Friday	vii	Getsuyōbi
h	_____	viii	Doyōbi

4 Say what each of the characters below have for their breakfast, as in the example:

Example: Yamaguchi-san wa asagohan ni tōsuto o tabemasu. Sore ni kōhī o nomimasu.

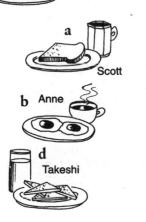

5 Describe Anne's day using the pictures and sentences overleaf. Use **sorekara, soshite** and **sore ni** as indicated. Use **daitai** (*generally/usually*) and **tokidoki** (*sometimes*).

An-san no ichinichi

Gets up at about 7.30.
Usually has eggs and black tea
(**sore ni**) for breakfast. Then
(**sorekara**) studies Japanese from 9
until 4. Generally has lunch at 12.30.

Plays tennis on Saturdays.
Sometimes watches TV in the
evening (say **yoru** before **tokidoki**).
And (**soshite**) goes to bed at about
11 p.m.

6 Anne has been writing up an interview with Emi. These are the answers to her questions. Can you write out the questions in full, in Japanese?

a What time?   Hachiji ni okimasu.
b What?   Asagohan ni tōsuto to tamago o tabemasu.
c What day?   Doyōbi ni kaimono o shimasu.
d What?   Yoru tokidoki eiga o mimasu.
e When?   Getsuyōbi kara kinyōbi made benkyō shimasu.

Test

1 Can you say these days in Japanese?

a Friday
b Tuesday
c Monday
d Thursday

2 Can you fill in the missing parts of Mr Yamaguchi's schedule? (You may wish to re-read the **Conversation** at the beginning of the unit first.)

Asa rokuji han goro _____. Sorekara _____ ni tōsuto o_____. Sore ni kōhī _____ _____. Shigoto wa hachiji han _____ roku _____ ____ desu. _____wa ichiji kara desu. Yoru _____ _____ tabemasu. Soshite terebi o _____. Jūichi ____ _____ han goro _____. Nichiyōbi_____ zasshi o _____.

3 Answer these questions to describe your own typical day.

a Nanji ni okimasu ka.
b Asagohan ni nani o tabemasu ka.
c Shigoto wa nanji kara nanji made desu ka.
d Itsu kaimono o shimasu ka.
e Nanyōbi ni nihongo o benkyō shimasu ka.
f Nanji ni hirugohan o tabemasu ka.
g Yoru nani o shimasu ka.
h Nanji goro nemasu ka.

09

pātī o shimashō

let's have a party!

In this unit you will learn
- how to say you are going to or returning from somewhere
- how to invite someone
- how to make suggestions and accept or refuse
- some useful time expressions

Introduction

In the last unit you learnt some useful action words for talking about daily activities. In this unit you are going to add three more important words to these: *go*, *come* and *return*.

You will also learn how to use the action words in a new way: to invite someone to do something or to suggest doing something as in the title of this unit: **pātī o shimashō** (*let's have a party!*).

Let's talk

To suggest doing something you change the **masu** ending of the doing word to **mashō** (*let's*). Can you change the following sentences into suggestions, as in the example?

Example Kōhī o nomi**masu**   Kōhī o nomi**mashō**.
        (*drink coffee*)   (*Let's drink some coffee.*)

1 Tenisu o shimasu (*play tennis*)
2 Kaimono o shimasu (*do some shopping*)
3 Sushi o tabemasu (*eat sushi*)
4 Ocha o nomimasu (*drink green tea*)
5 Eiga o mimasu (*watch a film*)
6 Nihongo o benkyō shimasu (*study Japanese*)

▶ Vocabulary list

Say these words out loud a few times, then test yourself by covering the Japanese words and seeing if you can say them from memory.

ikimasu	*go*
kaerimasu	*return, go back* (used to express 'going back to where you live')
kimasu	*come*

Time expressions

mainichi	*every day*
kyō	*today*
ashita	*tomorrow*
maishū	*every week*

maitsuki	*every month*
konshū	*this week*
kongetsu	*this month*
konban	*this evening*
raishū	*next week*
raigetsu	*next month*
... dō desu ka	*how about ...?*
ii desu ne	*that sounds nice*
yorokonde	*I'd love to*
yorokonde ukagaimasu	*I'd love to visit*
zannen desu	*it's a shame/pity*

▶ Conversation

Tani's stay in Japan is coming to an end.

Anne	Itsu Furansu ni kaerimasu ka.
Tani	Raishū no doyōbi ni kaerimasu.
Scott	Zannen desu ne. Ja, pātī o shimashō!
Tani	Ii desu ne.
Anne	Konshū no doyōbi wa dō desu ka.
Tani	Doyōbi wa **chotto** ... **Tomodachi** to resutoran ni ikimasu.
Scott	Ja ... Nichiyōbi wa?
Tani	Nichiyōbi wa daijōbu desu.
Satō-sensei	Mina-san, watashi no **uchi ni kimasen ka**.
Everyone	Ii desu ne!
Tani	A! Yorokonde ukagaimasu.

chotto	*a bit* (in this case '*a bit inconvenient*')
tomodachi	*friend*
uchi ni kimasen ka	*would you like to come to my house?*

Explanations

1 Ikimasu, *go*; kimasu, *come*; kaerimasu, *return*

You were introduced to **masu** words in the previous unit. These three can be learnt together as a group. For example:

Tani san wa resutoran ni ikimasu.	*Tani is going to a restaurant.*
Ashita Furansu ni kaerimasu.	*I'm going back to France tomorrow.*
An-san wa watashi no uchi ni kimasu.	*Anne is coming to my house.*

Look at the sentence order. The person doing the action is followed by **wa**. **Ni** means *to* and comes after the place you are going to. For example:

Furansi **ni**   *to France*   resutoran **ni**   *to a restaurant*

As you saw in Unit 8, the action word (or verb) always comes at the end of a Japanese sentence. (Unit 8, **Explanation 4** and **Explanation 3** in this unit practise the other meaning of **ni** that you have learnt.)

Kaerimasu is used when you return or go back to the place you come from, either your home, your town or your country. For example:

Watashi wa uchi ni kaerimasu.	*I return home/shall return home.*
Yamaguchi-san wa ashita Tōkyō ni kaerimasu.	*Mr Yamaguchi will return to Tokyo tomorrow.*

2 Ashita doko ni ikimasu ka *Where are you going tomorrow?*

In Unit 7 you learnt the question word **doko** (*where*). You can now use it with these three new verbs. For example:

Ashita doko ni ikimasu ka.	*Where are you going tomorrow?*

You answer by replacing **doko** with the place, keeping the same sentence order. For example:

Ashita Tōkyō ni ikimasu.	*I'm going to Tokyo tomorrow.*

| Yamaguchi-san wa mainichi doko ni ikimasu ka. | Where does Mr Yamaguchi go every day? |
| Yamaguchi-san wa mainichi shigoto ni ikimasu. | Mr Yamaguchi goes to work every day. |

Or more simply:

| Shigoto ni ikimasu. | He goes to work. |

3 Hachigatsu ni Igirisu ni kaerimasu *I'm returning to England in August.*

In Unit 8, **Explanation 4,** you learnt that **ni** is used after a day or time to mean *on* or *at*. In the same way, it is used when saying months or dates. For example:

| Jūichi-nichi *ni* | *on the 11th* |
| Rokugatsu *ni* | *in June* |

And you can make these question words using **nan** (*what?*):

| Nannichi ni | *On what date?* |
| Nangatsu ni | *In which month?* |

And don't forget the general question word **itsu** (*when?*).

When you use general time expressions such as **ashita** (*tomorrow*), **raishū** (*next week*) and **mainichi** (*every day*), you don't need **ni**. (In the same way, you don't say *on tomorrow* or *in next week* in English.) You have already learnt this with the words **asa** (*morning*) and **yoru** (*evening*) in Unit 8, **Explanation 7.** For example:

| Raishū Kyōto ni ikimasu. | *I'm going to Kyoto next week.* |
| Emi-san wa mainichi daigaku ni ikimasu. | *Emi goes to university every day.* |

You should note that you say the time expression before the place and the action word. (Look back at Unit 8, **Explanation 4** to remind yourself of sentence order.)

4 Raishū no doyōbi ni kaerimasu *I am going back next Saturday*

You can combine time expressions with **no** to make the following:

raishū no doyōbi	*next Saturday*
ashita no ban	*tomorrow evening*
kongetsu no hatsuka	*the 20th of this month*

ℹ Learning tip (1)

You'll meet more of these time expressions in future units, so that you can gradually build up your vocabulary. Try making sentences about your daily activities using these expressions and the new verbs you have learnt. This will help you to remember new words because you are putting them in meaningful situations (*I'm going to the cinema tonight, I'm going to the supermarket tomorrow*, etc.).

5 Pātī o shimashō *Let's have a party!*

You have already practised making suggestions in the **Let's talk** section of this unit. Here are some more examples:

Doyōbi ni eigakan ni ikimashō. *Let's go to the cinema on Saturday.*

Ashita kaimono ni ikimashō. *Let's go shopping tomorrow.*

If you want to ask somebody to do something with you, turn the phrase into a question by adding **ka**. For example:

Doyōbi ni eigakan ni ikimashō ka.	*Shall we go to the cinema on Saturday?*
Raishū no nichiyōbi ni *doraibu* ni ikimashō ka.	*Shall we go for a **drive** next Sunday?*

To answer you can say:

Ii desu ne. Sō shimashō. *That sounds nice. Let's do that!*

Or:

Yorokonde. *I'd love to.*

(To refuse, see **Explanation 7** overleaf.)

6 Watashi no uchi ni kimasen ka *Would you like to come to my house?*

This phrase literally means *won't you come to my house?* To express *I don't ...* (the negative) in Japanese you change **masu** to **masen**. For example:

Kōhī o nomi*masen*.	*I don't drink coffee.*
Asagohan o tabe*masen*.	*I don't eat breakfast.*
Ashita shigoto ni iki*masen*.	*I'm not going to work tomorrow.*

You can politely invite someone to do something by adding **ka** to the negative. For example:

Kōhī o nomimasen ka.	*Would you like to (lit. won't you) drink some coffee?*
Eigakan ni ikimasen ka.	*Would you like to go to the cinema?*
Watashi no uchi ni kimasen ka.	*Would you like to come to my house?*

(You will learn more about the negative in Unit 12.)

7 Konshū no doyōbi wa dō desu ka *How about this Saturday?*

When suggesting dates or times to do an activity, you can use the phrase **... wa dō desu ka** (*how about ...?*). For example:

Kayōbi wa dō desu ka.	*How about Tuesday?*
Rokuji wa dō desu ka.	*How about 6 o'clock?*
Ashita wa dō desu ka.	*How about tomorrow?*

To accept, use **... wa daijōbu desu** (*... is fine*). For example:

Kayōbi wa daijōbu desu.	*Tuesday is fine.*

Or simply say:

Ē, ii desu yo.	*Yes, that will be fine.*

(For other ways to accept see **Explanation 5**)

To refuse politely use **... wa chotto ...** (*It's a bit ...*). For example:

Ashita wa chotto ...	*Tomorrow's a bit ...* (implying 'inconvenient')

You can precede this with **zannen desu ga ...** (*it's a pity but ...*). For example:

Zannen desu ga ashita   *It's a shame but tomorrow*
  wa chotto ...   *is a bit ...*

When you trail your sentence off at the end like this, the listener will understand that it's inconvenient without you having to say so.

8 Tomodachi to resutoran ni ikimasu *I'm going with a friend to a restaurant*

In Unit 3 you learnt that **to** means *and* when you link two objects. For example:

Kōhī to jūsu o kudasai.   *May I have a coffee and*
    some juice?

Yamaguchi-san wa gorufu to   *Mr Yamaguchi plays golf*
  tenisu o shimasu.   *and tennis.*

To can also have the meaning *with*. For example:

tomodachi to   *with my friend*
An-san to   *with Anne*

You should note that **to** comes after the person you do something with. For example:

***An-san to* benkyō shimasu.**   *I study **with Anne**.*

You say **tomodachi to** (etc.) after time expressions and before the place/item. For example:

Ashita *tomodachi to* Rondon   *I am going to London with*
  ni ikimasu.   *a friend tomorrow.*

Sukotto-san wa *An-san to*   *Scott is going to watch a*
  eiga o mimasu.   *film with Anne.*

▶ 9 The dates 1st–10th

You learnt to say the dates from the 11th to 31st in Unit 4 by adding **nichi** to the appropriate number: 11th = **jūichi-nichi**. The exceptions to this rule were **jūyokka** (14th), **nijūyokka** (24th) and **hatsuka** (20th). The 1st–10th are also slightly different. Listen and/or read:

tsuitachi	1st	muika	6th
futsuka	2nd	nanoka	7th
mikka	3rd	yōka	8th
yokka	4th	kokonoka	9th
itsuka	5th	tōka	10th

ℹ️ Learning tip (2)

Try to find some word associations to help you remember these new numbers. You may already find these dates familiar. If you look back to Unit 6 (**Explanation 5**), you will see that the System B method of counting (**hitotsu, futatsu, mittsu** …) is similar to these dates, apart from **tsuitachi** (*1st*). The main difference is that the dates end in **ka**, whereas the numbers end in **tsu**.

Perhaps some of the same word associations will help you to remember these dates. **Tōka** (*10th*) sounds like the English word *toe*, and you have ten toes on your feet! **Nanoka** (*7th*) sounds very close to **nana** (*7*). **Itsuka** (*5th*) is like **itsu** (*when*). **Kokonoka** (*9th*) sounds like the English word *coconut*! The **yō** of **yōka** (*8th*) rhymes with *yolk*.

These are a few ideas to help you, but don't feel you have to be able to remember every item of vocabulary in one go! It takes time and practice to master vocabulary and new phrases. You will remember some words quicker than others, especially those more relevant to your life. For example, if your birthday is on the 10th you will probably remember **tōka** more easily. And of course, if you have a chance to speak with a Japanese person, these personal details will be very useful and relevant.

Practice

▶ 1 In list **a–h** below are the names of some Japanese festivals and special days. Opposite are the dates of the festivals. Listen and match each festival with its correct date by writing the letters **a–h**, as appropriate, in the brackets after the dates.

a   Girls' Day (**Hina Matsuri**)
b   Boys' Day (**Kodomo no hi**)
c   Star Festival (**Tanabata**)
d   7–5–3 Festival (**Shichi go san**)
e   Citizens' Day (**Kokumin no kyūjitsu**)
f   Culture Day (**Bunka no hi**)
g   Change of clothing day (**Koromogae**)
h   Sea Day (**Umi no hi**)

3rd November ( )
7th July ( )
15th November ( )
3rd March ( )
4th May ( )
20th July ( )
5th May ( )
1st October ( )

2 a Using the information below make sentences saying where you are going and when.

> **Example:** next week, cinema = **(Watashi wa) raishū eigakan ni ikimasu.**

i tomorrow, London
ii this evening, concert (**konsāto**)
iii today, France
iv every day, home (go back)

Remember: you don't need to say **watashi wa** (*I*) unless you need to put emphasis on it – (see Unit 2, **Explanation 1**).

b Now make sentences about Tani using the same information.

> **Example:** next week, cinema = **Tani-san wa raishū eigakan ni ikimasu.**

c Finally, can you change these sentences into questions using **doko** (*where*)?

> **Example:** next week, where? = **Raishū doko ni ikimasu ka.**

3 The sentences below have gaps, and you have to decide whether or not to write **ni** (meaning *on*, *in* or *at*). Write a **batsu** sign (✗) if **ni** is not needed.

Look back at **Explanation 3** if you need to remind yourself of the rules.

a An-san wa jūji _____ nihongo no kurasu ni ikimasu.
b Sukotto-san wa ashita _____ tenisu o shimasu.
c Tani-san wa raishū _____ Furansu ni kaerimasu.
d Mina-san wa konshū no doyōbi _____ watashi no uchi ni kimasu.
e Yamaguchi-san wa mainichi _____ kaisha ni ikimasu.
f Takeshi-san wa shichigatsu _____ Kyōto ni ikimasu.

4 Make sentences using the information in the chart below.

	Time/day	Activity	Type of suggestion
a	tomorrow	watch a film	shall we?
b	next week	go for a drive	let's!
c		read this magazine	would you like to?
d	today	have lunch	shall we?
e	this evening	come to my house	would you like to?
f	next Saturday	go shopping	let's!
g		drink some coffee	would you like to?
h	tomorrow evening	go to a restaurant	shall we?

5 Imagine you are inviting your Japanese friend out. Can you fill in your part of the dialogue using the information in English?

You *Say 'Hello'.*
Friend Konnichi wa!
You *Ask if they'd like to come to your house next week.*
Friend Ii desu ne! Yorokonde ukagaimasu.
You *Ask 'how about Wednesday?'*
Friend Suiyōbi desu ka. Suiyōbi wa chotto …
You *'How about Thursday then?'*
Friend Zannen desu ga mokuyōbi ni Rondon ni ikimasu. Doyōbi wa dō desu ka.
You *Say 'Saturday will be fine. How about 4 o'clock?'*
Friend Hai, wakarimashita. Arigatō gozaimasu.
You *Say 'See you' and 'Goodbye'.*

6 Tani is being invited out to a disco by Scott but she doesn't really want to go! Can you help her make excuses? Use **zannen desu ga …** and **chotto,** but try to think of some reasons why she can't go – playing tennis with a friend, going to a restaurant with Anne, etc.

Scott Konshū no doyōbi ni disuko ni ikimasen ka.
Tani …
Scott Ja, kinyōbi wa dō desu ka.
Tani …

Scott	Aa, sō desu ka. Mokuyōbi wa dō desu ka.
Tani	…
Scott	Ēto, raishū no getsuyōbi wa?
Tani	…
Scott	Sō desu ka. Zannen desu ne. (*sees Anne*) An-san! doyōbi ni disuko ni ikimasen ka!

Test

1 Which phrase would you choose to ask your friend where they are going tomorrow?

   a   Raishū doko ni ikimasu ka.

   b   Yūbinkyoku wa doko desu ka.

   c   Ashita doko ni ikimasu ka.

2 Change these sentences into suggestions or invitations according to the information in brackets.

   a   Ashita resutoran ni ikimasu. (*shall we?*)

   b   Raishū watashi no uchi ni kimasu. (*would you like to?*)

   c   Konban eiga o mimasu. (*let's*)

   d   Ja, sushi o tabemasu. (*shall we?*)

   e   Mokuyōbi ni doraibu ni ikimasu. (*shall we?*)

   f   Terebi o mimasu (*would you like to?*)

3 How do you say these sentences in Japanese?

   a   I'm going to London with a friend tomorrow.

   b   It's a shame but Sunday is a bit …

   c   Would you like to drink a beer?

   d   How about Thursday?

   e   Saturday is fine. I'd love to.

   f   My birthday is August 8th.

   g   Where shall we go?

10

senshū Kyōto
ni ikimashita

last week I went to Kyoto

In this unit you will learn
- **how to talk about past events (the past tense)**
- **how to say where an activity took place**
- **about types of transport**
- **more time expressions**
- **how to say you want to do something**

Introduction

In Units 8 and 9 you learnt how to talk about daily and future activities. In this unit you will learn how to talk about past events and activities. This is a simple process: you change the **masu** ending to **mashita**, as in the title of this unit:

Kyōto ni iki*mashita***.** *I went to Kyoto.*

i Pronunciation tip

The **i** sound in **mashita** is almost unspoken – **ma-sh-ta**.

Let's talk

Talk about activities that you did by changing these sentences into the past tense as in the example:

Example: Asagohan o tabe<u>masu</u>. Asagohan o tabe<u>mashita</u>. (*I ate breakfast.*)

1 Kōhī o nomi<u>masu</u>.   _____ (*I drank some coffee.*)
2 Kaimono o shi<u>masu</u>.   _____ (*I did the shopping.*)
3 Terebi o mi<u>masu</u>.   _____ (*I watched TV.*)
4 Shimbun o yomi<u>masu</u>.   _____ (*I read the newspaper.*)
5 Resutoran ni iki<u>masu</u>.   _____ (*I went to a restaurant.*)
6 Uchi ni kaeri<u>masu</u>.   _____ (*I went home.*)

▶ Vocabulary list

Transport

aruite	*on foot*
chikatetsu	*underground*
basu	*bus*
densha	*train*
fune	*boat*
jitensha	*bicycle*
shinkansen	*bullet train*
hikōki	*plane*
kuruma	*car*
takushī	*taxi*
nan de/dōyatte	*how?*

Time expressions

senshū	*last week*
kinō	*yesterday*
kesa	*this morning*
sengetsu	*last month*
yūbe	*last night*
gogo	*afternoon*
kotoshi	*this year*
kyonen	*last year*
rainen	*next year*
kakarimasu	*it takes*
jikan	*hour*
gofun	*five minutes*
juppun	*ten minutes*
gurai	*about*
ryokō shimasu	*travel*
dono gurai	*how long?*

▶ Conversation

Anne is talking to Takeshi about a recent school trip.

Takeshi Senshū Kyōto ni ikimashita. **Shūgaku ryokō** deshita.

Anne Ii desu ne! Nan de ikimashita ka.

Takeshi Tōkyō eki kara shinkansen de ikimashita. Kyōto made san jikan gurai kakarimashita.

Anne **Hē! Hayai** desu ne! Kyōto de nani o shimashita ka.

Takeshi Kayōbi ni **o-tera** o **takusan** mimashita. Sorekara **gekijō** ni ikimashita. Kyōto no **odori** o mimashita.

Anne Sō desu ka. Watashi mo odori o **mitai** desu. Suiyōbi ni nani o shimashita ka.

Takeshi **Mata** o-tera o mimashita. Soshite Tōkyō ni kaerimashita.

Anne Kyōto no **ryōri** wa dō deshita ka.

Takeshi Wakarimasen. Mainichi **kappu nūdoru** o tabemashita.

Anne Takeshi-kun! **Yokunai** desu yo!

shūgaku ryokō	school trip
hē!	hey, really!
hayai	quick, fast
o-tera	temples
takusan	many
gekijō	theatre
odori	dancing
mitai	want to see
mata	again
ryōri	cookery
kappu nūdoru	cup noodles
yokunai	no good

🅸 Kyōto

Kyoto is the old capital of Japan and today is often referred to as the religious centre of Japan. This is because there are many Buddhist temples (**o-tera**) and Shinto shrines (**jinja**) here. During the Second World War, Kyoto was one of the few cities not significantly damaged by bombing, and so many of the old buildings still stand today. Kyoto is a very popular tourist attraction both with the Japanese and with foreigners, but it is also a very peaceful place, especially if you explore places away from the main attractions.

Explanations

1 Senshū Kyōto ni ikimashita *Last week I went to Kyoto*

You have already practised talking about past activites in the **Let's talk** section of this unit. You have also been introduced to some more time expressions. Here are some more examples of sentences describing past activities. Practise them by covering the Japanese and using the English as a prompt to say the sentences:

An-san wa kinō nihongo o benkyō shimashita.
Yesterday Anne studied Japanese.

Tani-san wa senshū no doyōbi ni Furansu ni kaerimashita.
Tani went back to France last Saturday.

Scott-san wa kyonen Nihon ni kimashita.
Scott came to Japan last year.

Emi-san wa sengetsu tomodachi to ryokō o shimashita.	*Emi did some travelling last month with a friend.*

2 Kyōto de nani o shimashita ka *What did you do in Kyoto?*

To say where an activity happens or happened you use **de**, meaning *in* or *at*. You say **de** after the place. For example:

Kyōto de	*in Kyoto*
uchi de	*at home*
resutoran de	*at a restaurant*
gekijō de	*at the theatre*
Takeshi-kun wa *gekijō de* odori o mimashita.	*Takeshi watched dancing at the theatre.*
Yamaguchi-san wa *uchi de* shimbun o yomimashita.	*Mr Yamaguchi read a newspaper at home.*
Reiko-san wa mainichi *sūpā de* kaimono o shimasu.	*Reiko does the shopping every day at the supermarket.*

Notice the sentence order:

a the person who does the action (*subject*);
b the time expression;
c the place;
d the item followed by **o** (*object and object marker*)
e the action word (*verb*). (Review sentence order on pages 89–92 and 101–2.)

3 Nan de ikimashita ka *How did you get there?*

This is the other use of **de** that you will learn in this unit. When used with transport, **de** takes the meaning of *by*. For example:

densha de	*by train*
hikōki de	*by plane*
Takeshi-kun wa basu de gakkō ni ikimasu.	*Takeshi goes by bus to school.*
Reiko-san wa kuruma de sūpā ni ikimasu.	*Reiko goes to the supermarket by car.*
Shinjuki kara Shibuya made chikatetsu de ikimashita.	*I went from Shinjuku to Shibuya by underground.*

However, you don't need to use **de** when saying **aruite** (*on foot*):

Aruite tomadachi no uchi ni ikimashita.	*I went to my friend's house on foot.*

The question word is **nan de** or **dōyatte** (*how?*):

Nan de kaisha ni ikimasu ka.	*How do you get to work?*

Answer by replacing **nan** with the mode of transport:

Jitensha de ikimasu.	*I go by bicycle.*

4 Kyōto made sanjikan gurai kakarimasu *It takes about three hours to Kyoto*

To say how long a journey takes, you use **kakarimasu**. Lengths of time are expressed by adding **kan** to **ji** (*o'clock*), **nichi/ka** (*day*), **shū** (*week*), etc. For example:

ichi<u>ji</u>kan	*one <u>hour</u>*
futsuka<u>kan</u>	*two <u>days</u>*
ni<u>shū</u>kan	*two <u>weeks</u>*
go<u>fun</u> <u>(kan)</u>	*five <u>minutes</u>*

You can omit **kan** when saying minutes and days as long as the meaning is clear. For example:

yonjuppun	*40 minutes*
mikka	*three days* (or *the third day*)

One day in Japanese is **ichinichi**.

Gurai means *about*, for example, **gofun gurai** (*about five minutes*). You have already learnt **goro** meaning *about*, but this is only used when actually saying the time, not a length of time. For example:

Hachiji *goro* okimasu.	*I get up at **about** 8 o'clock.*
Hachijikan *gurai* kakarimasu.	*It takes **about** 8 hours.*

To ask *how long does it take?*, you say **dono gurai kakarimasu ka** (or **dono gurai desu ka**). For example:

Rondon kara Tōkyō made dono gurai kakarimasu ka.	*How long does it take from London to Tokyo?*
Hikōki de jūnijikan gurai kakarimasu.	*By plane it takes about 12 hours.*
Yūbinkyoku made dono gurai desu ka.	*How far is it to the post office?*

Aruite juppun gurai desu.   *On foot it's about ten
minutes.*

5 Watashi wa odori o mitai desu *I want to see some dancing*

To say that you want to do something, you replace **masu** with **tai desu**. For example:

yomi<u>masu</u>	*I read*	yomi<u>tai</u> <u>desu</u>	*I want to read*
nomi<u>masu</u>	*I drink*	nomi<u>tai</u> <u>desu</u>	*I want to drink*
tabe<u>masu</u>	*I eat*	tabe<u>tai</u> <u>desu</u>	*I want to eat*

Here are some examples:

Eigo no shimbun o yomitai
desu.

*I want to read an English
newspaper.*

Bīru o nomitai desu.   *I want to drink a beer.*

Tōkyō ni ikitai desu.   *I want to go to Tokyo.*

Uchi ni kaeritai desu.   *I want to go home.*

6 More time expressions

In the last three units you have been learning a number of time expressions. In this unit the focus has been on past time expressions as well as *year* expressions (*this/last/next year*). Below are some examples of how these phrases are used.

You may wish to practise these phrases in the following way. First familiarize yourself with the time expressions in the **Vocabulary list** section of this unit (for example, say them out loud; cover the English side, then the Japanese side; get someone to test you). Then cover up the Japanese side of the phrases below and see if you can say these time expressions:

senshū no doyōbi	*last Saturday*
kesa (no) hachi ji ni	*this morning at 8 o'clock*
kinō no gogo	*yesterday afternoon*
kyonen no hachigatsu	*last August*
rainen no sangatsu	*next March*
kotoshi no shigatsu	*this April*
sengetsu no kokonoka	*the 9th of last month*

Practice

▶ 1 The pictures **a–h** below show different forms of transport. You will hear people saying how they get to different places **i–viii**. Match up the modes of transport and the destinations.

i France
ii Shinjuku Station
iii Shibuya Station
iv Korea (**Kankoku**)

v school
vi company
vii bank

▶ 2 Anne is talking about some of the activities she did at the weekend. Listen and link each activity with where it took place. Listen carefully – the activities are not said in the order **a–e**!

a had a meal with a friend
b watched a film
c did Japanese homework (**shukudai**)
d went shopping
e bought some postcards

i in Tokyo
ii at home
iii at a restaurant
iv at a friend's house
v at a department store

3 Say out loud the approximate times from the fourth column of the chart below. The first one has been done for you.

Example: a Jūnijikan gurai kakarimasu.

	From	To	Transport	Approx. time
a	London	Tokyo	plane	12 hours
b	Tokyo	Kyoto	bullet train	5 hours
c	Derby	Sheffield	train	40 minutes
d	Anne's house	Scott's house	underground	1 hour
e	Anne's house	supermarket	on foot	5 minutes

Now, again using the chart, say out loud how long the journeys take. The first one has been done for you, but try saying it yourself first, then check that you were correct. Keep the information in the same order as it is presented in the chart.

Example: a Rondon kara Tōkyō made hikōki de jūnijikan gurai kakarimasu (*or* desu).

4 Link the time expressions in the left-hand column below with their Japanese equivalent on the right.

a	yesterday evening	i	senshū no kinyōbi
b	tomorrow night	ii	kotoshi no rokugatsu
c	next Thursday	iii	raishū no mokuyōbi
d	last February	iv	yūbe
e	this June	v	sengetsu no tōka
f	last Friday	vi	kyonen no nigatsu
g	the 10th of last month	vii	ashita no ban

5   Using the pictures and information below, make sentences about some of Reiko's past and future activities:

    a   shopping in the Ginza last Saturday
    b   at home, last Wednesday
    c   at a restaurant with a friend, tomorrow
    d   last year, in Kyoto
    e   yesterday evening
    f   last month on the 10th, at a Tokyo theatre

6   Below is a Japanese **pazuru** (*puzzle*) which has been partially completed. To fill in the spaces you need to work out how to say the English sentences below in Japanese. You then have to work out which sentence fits which line of spaces **a–g** in the **pazuru**! Put one letter in each space. **Gambatte ne!** (*Good luck!*)

    a   _ _ _ made _ _ _ _ _ _ _ _ _ _ gofun _ _ _ _ _ _ _ _ _ _
    b   _ _ _ _ _ _ _ _ _ _ _ _ _ _ shitai _ _ _ _
    c   _ _ _ _ _ _ _ _ _ _ _ _ _ _ _ kaisha _ _ _ _ _ _ _ _
    d   _ _ _ _ no _ _ _ _ _ _ _ _ _ _ tōsuto _ _ _ _ _ _ _ _ _ _ _ _
    e   Kotoshi _ _ _ _ _ _ _ _ _ _ _ _ _ _ _ _ _ _ _
    f   _ _ _ _ _ _ _ _ kugatsu _ _ _ _ _ _ _ _ ikimasu
    g   _ _ _ _ _ _ _ _ ban gekijō _ _ _ _ _ _ _ _ _ _ _ _

- Next September I am going to Japan.
- Tomorrow I want to do some shopping.
- This morning I had toast for breakfast.
- Shall we go to the theatre on Tuesday evening?
- This year I want to go to France.
- It takes five minutes to the station by bicycle.
- My father goes to work (company) by car.

Test

This test is a revision of all the units you have learnt so far. Each question refers you back to the relevant units.

1 How do you say these phrases in Japanese? (**Unit 1**)

    a Good morning
    b How do you do?
    c Good night
    d Excuse me
    e Thank you very much
    f See you!

2 A Japanese visitor is visiting your area and you have been asked by the local newspaper to interview him or her, and write a short article.

    a Think of five questions you could ask (hint: name, age, birthday, family size, nationality, job, hobbies, etc.).

    b Now imagine you are the person being interviewed and answer your questions. (**Units 2–4**)

3 Choose the correct English meaning for each of these phrases. (**Units 5–7**)

    a Sono kamera o kudasai.
        i May I have this camera please?
        ii May I see that camera please?
        iii May I have that camera please?

    b Yūbinkyoku wa kuji kara goji han made desu.
        i The supermarket is open from 9–5.30.
        ii The post office is open from 9–5.30.
        iii The supermarket is open from 9–5.

c Tsugi no shingō o hidari ni magatte kudasai.

    i Turn left at the next crossroads.

    ii Turn right at the next traffic lights.

    iii Turn left at the next traffic lights.

4 Fill in the missing parts of these sentences. (**Units 8–10**)

  a Kinō kaimono o _____ .

  b Raishū _____ doyōbi _____ pātō o _____ mashō!

  c Mainichi gakkō _____ nihongo_____ benkyō _____ .

  d Asagohan ni tamago _____ _____ .

  e Senshū Tani-san _____ Furansu ni _____ .

  f Sengetsu eiga _____ _____ .

  g Yūbe _____ jū ji _____ ne _____ .

  h Uchi _____ eki _____ basu _____ _____ masu.

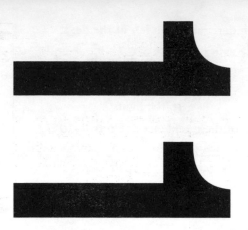

ii o-tenki desu ne

it's nice weather, isn't it?

In this unit you will learn
- how to describe people, objects and places
- two types of describing words
- how to make a comment and agree with someone
- how to talk about the weather and the seasons

Introduction

You are going to be introduced to two types of describing words (or *adjectives*) in this unit. Examples of English adjectives are: *beautiful, small, expensive*. Such words are used to describe items and people (as well as feelings, emotions, etc.).

There are of course many adjectives in Japanese (as there are in English), but this unit will select just a few of the more useful ones which you can use in everyday life. Later units will introduce you to more, but in this unit you will have the chance simply to understand how adjectives work in Japanese.

🄸 Learning tip (1)

Don't worry at this stage if there are things you don't know how to say. Concentrate on what you can say – it is this gradual building-up of vocabulary with plenty of short-term goals which will ultimately improve your confidence and grasp of Japanese.

Let's talk

You have already come across some Japanese adjectives in previous units. Look back now at the conversations of the following units and answer the questions below.

a   How does Reiko say *He looks young, doesn't he?* (Unit 4, page 38)
b   How does Emi say *She's pretty, isn't she?* (Unit 4, page 38)
c   How does Emi say *That watch is smart, isn't it?* (Unit 5, page 48)
d   How does the passer-by compliment Scott on his Japanese? (Unit 7, page 77)
e   How does Scott comment on how early Mr Yamaguchi gets up? (Unit 8, page 88)
f   How does Tani say *That will be nice?* (Unit 9, page 100)

These describing words have been included in the vocabulary list below.

▶ Vocabulary list

i adjectives

atsui (desu)	*(it is) hot*	atsukatta desu	*it was hot*
samui desu	*it is cold*	samukatta desu	*it was cold*
tanoshii desu	*it is pleasant*	tanoshikatta desu	*it was pleasant*
omoshiroi desu	*it is interesting, funny*	omoshirokatta desu	*it was interesting*
takai desu	*it is expensive*	takakatta desu	*it was expensive*
yasui desu	*it is cheap*	yasukatta desu	*it was cheap*
ōkii desu	*it is big*	ōkikatta desu	*it was big*
chiisai desu	*it is small*	chiisakatta desu	*it was small*
oishii desu	*it is delicious*	oishikatta desu	*it was delicious*
ii desu	*it is good, nice*	yokatta desu	*it was good*
warui desu	*it is bad*	warukatta desu	*it was bad*
kawaii desu	*it is cute, pretty*	kawaikatta desu	*it was pretty*
hayai desu	*it is early/quick*	hayakatta desu	*it was early*
wakai desu	*he is young*	wakakatta desu	*he was young*

Seasons

haru	*spring*
natsu	*summer*
aki	*autumn*
fuyu	*winter*

na adjectives

(o)genki	*well, healthy, lively*
benri	*convenient*
shizuka	*quiet*
shinsetsu	*kind*
suteki	*smart, fashionable*
jōzu	*good at*
(o)hisashiburi	*long time, no see*
kissaten	*coffee shop*
hontō ni	*really, in truth very*

▶ Conversation

Reiko is meeting up with a friend, Haruko, whom she hasn't seen for a while.

Haruko Ā! Reiko-san! O-genki desu ka.
Reiko Ē, **okagesama de**. Haruko-san, o-hisashiburi desu ne.
Haruko Sō desu ne. Kono kissaten de kōhī o nomimasen ka.

In the coffee shop:

Reiko Kyō wa ii o-tenki desu ne.
Haruko Sō desu ne. **Mō** haru desu.
Reiko Kyonen no natsu wa atsukatta desu ne.
Haruko Ē. Kotoshi no natsu mo atsui **ka na?**

As they are getting ready to leave:

Haruko Kono kissaten no kēki wa oishii desu ne.
Reiko Ē, chotto takai desu **ga** totemo oishii desu.
Haruko Kyō wa hontō ni tanoshikatta desu. Arigatō gozaimashita.
Reiko Dewa, mata aimashō. **O-genki de!**
Haruko Sayōnara!

okagesama de	*I'm fine, thanks* (said in reply to **o-genki desu ka**. Lit. *thanks to you*)
mō	*already*
ka na?	*I wonder* (casual speech)
ga	*but*
o-genki de	*take care*

ℹ Weather and seasons

The weather is a popular topic of conversation in Japan. When people meet up with each other they often comment on the weather – **ii o-tenki desu ne!** – rather than on a person's health (unless they haven't seen each other for a long time). Letters also often open with a comment on the weather.

Books about Japan often refer to 'four distinct seasons'. This needs some clarification. *Spring* (**haru**) is pleasantly warm and is the season of the famous cherry blossoms. The television news follows the spread of these blossoms from the south to the north of the country.

Between spring and *summer* (**natsu**) is the rainy season which lasts for about two weeks. Immediately after this, summer begins in earnest and the weather becomes very hot and increasingly humid.

Autumn (**aki**) begins in September and is sometimes preluded by another short rainy season with the occasional typhoon. The weather is fresh and fine, and the leaves on the trees change to stunning colours – this is known as the 'leaf viewing season' and it sweeps across the country from north to south, again followed avidly on the daily news.

Winter (**fuyu**) is cold and crisp with blue skies during the day, but also with plenty of snow, particularly in the northern and mountain areas.

Explanations

1 O-genki desu ka *Are you well?*

As you learnt in Unit 2 (**Explanation 2**, page 17) **o** is said in front of certain words to make them sound more polite or formal when addressing other people. It is sometimes translated as *honourable*, although this makes some words sound ridiculous in translation (for example, **o-tearai**, *the honourable toilet!*). Women in particular use **o** – it has the effect of making their speech sound more genteel. Here are some more examples of its use:

o-tenki	*the weather*
o-sushi	*sushi*
o-hisashiburi	*long time, no see*
o-hashi	*chopsticks*
o-tanjōbi	*birthday*
o-furo	*the bath*

2 Kyō wa ii o-tenki desu ne *Today is nice weather, isn't it?*

There are two types of adjectives or describing words in Japanese. These are usually referred to as **i** adjectives and **na** adjectives. This unit will mostly use **i** adjectives.

i adjectives

There are two basic ways to use adjectives in a sentence:

Oishii kēki desu ne.	*It's a delicious cake, isn't it?*
Kono kēki wa oishii desu ne.	*This cake is delicious, isn't it?*

You should note that the English and Japanese order is the same. There are some more examples below. Use these as an activity by first looking at the i adjectives in the **Vocabulary list** section. When you feel familiar with the new words, try covering the Japanese phrases below and see if you can say them from memory, using the English translations as prompts.

Kyō wa atsui desu ne.	*It's hot today, isn't it?*
Nihon no fuyu wa samui desu.	*The Japanese winters are cold.*
Kono eiga wa omoshiroi desu ne.	*This film is interesting, isn't it?*
Omoshiroi e desu ne.	*It's an interesting picture, isn't it?*
Kono pātī wa tanoshii desu ne.	*This party is enjoyable, isn't it?*
Sono sētā wa takai desu.	*That jumper is expensive.*
Yasui kōhī desu ne.	*It's cheap coffee, isn't it?*
Kono kēki wa oishii desu ne.	*These cakes are delicious, aren't they?*
Natsu wa atsui desu.	*The summer is hot.*
An-san wa kawaii desu ne.	*Anne is pretty isn't she?*

na adjectives

It will soon become clear why these adjectives are called **na** adjectives:

Kono kissaten wa shizuka desu ne.	*This coffee shop is quiet, isn't it?*
Shizukana kissaten desu ne.	*It's a quiet coffee shop, isn't it?*

When the describing word is followed immediately by the item/person it is describing, you put **na** between the two words. It may help you to think of **na** in a similar way to **no**. For example:

watashi *no* tokei	*my watch*
Reiko-san *no* tomodachi	*Reiko's friend*
benri*na* sūpā	*a useful supermarket*

Here are some more examples of phrases using **na** adjectives. (Note that **na** is not used if the adjective comes immediately before **desu**.)

O-genki desu ka.	*Are you well?*
Genki*na* hito desu ne.	*She's a lively person, isn't she?*
Kono resutoran wa shizuka desu.	*This restaurant is quiet.*
Shizuka*na* tokoro desu ne.	*It's a quiet place, isn't it?*
Satō-sensei wa shinsetsu*na* hito desu.	*Mrs Sato, the teacher, is a kind person.*
Sore wa suteki*na* tokei desu.	*That's a smart watch.*

Agreeing with someone

To agree with someone you can say **Sō desu ne** (*yes, it is*). For example:

Ii o-tenki desu ne. Sō desu ne.   *It's nice weather, isn't it? Yes, it is.*

Haruko uses this reply twice in the dialogue. Look back and see where she uses it.

ℹ Learning tip

You have been introduced to a lot of new vocabulary in this unit, in the form of adjectives or describing words. You may find it helpful to make two lists of adjectives, one called **i** adjectives and the other called **na** adjectives. You can keep adding to these lists as you learn more of these words.

It is important to keep practising these new words in phrases that you can use every day. For example, make a comment to yourself about the weather every day: **Kyō wa atsui (samui/chotto atsui/chotto samui/ii o-tenki) desu (ne)**. And try describing items and people around you. Talk to yourself or impress your friends(!) and try to keep using the new vocabulary in meaningful situations.

3 Kyonen no natsu wa atsukatta desu ne *Last summer was hot, wasn't it?*

i adjectives

In Japanese, the **i** adjectives have their own past tense. In English, we change *is* to *was*:

It is hot. → It was hot.

In Japanese, *hot* itself changes:

Atsui desu. → Atsu**katta** desu.

To make this change, you drop the last **i** of the adjective and add **katta**. Now look back at the **Vocabulary list** section for more examples, then try covering up the two right-hand columns and saying the past of the adjective from looking at the present form. (Note that **ii** (*good*) changes to **yokatta**).

na adjectives

The past tense of these adjectives is formed in the same way as English adjectives:

Shizuka desu. → Shizuka deshita.	*It is quiet.* → *It was quiet.*
Shizukana kissaten desu. →	*It is a quiet coffee shop.* →
Shizukana kissaten deshita.	*It was a quiet coffee shop.*

4 Mō haru desu *It's spring already*

To say that something has already happened, you use **mō**. For example:

Mō asagohan o tabemashita.	*I've already eaten breakfast.*
Mō aki desu.	*It's autumn now.*

To say that something hasn't happened yet, you use **mada** (*not yet*). For example:

Mō haru desu ka.	*Is is spring yet?*
Iie, mada desu.	*No, not yet.*
Mō asagohan o tabemashita ka.	*Have you eaten breakfast already?*
Iie, mada desu.	*No, not yet.*

5 Chotto takai desu ga totemo oishii desu *It's a bit expensive but very delicious*

Here **ga** means *but* and can be used between two phrases as in these examples:

Kyō wa chotto atsui desu ga ii otenki desu.	*Today is a bit hot but it's nice weather.*
Asagohan o tabemasu ga hirugohan o tabemasen.	*I eat breakfast but I don't eat lunch.*
Kono sētā wa chotto takai desu ga suteki desu.	*This jumper is a bit expensive but it's smart.*

Practice

1   Look at the pictures below and make a comment about each one using the new adjectives (describing words) you have learnt in this unit.

Example: Takai kuruma desu ne.

2   Now describe the pictures in the past tense without saying the item/person, as in the example.

Example: Takakatta desu ne.

3   Can you make the present tense from the past tense of these adjectives?

a   Atsukatta desu.
b   Shizukana gakkō deshita.
c   Tanoshikatta desu.
d   Sono eiga wa yokatta desu.
e   Kono sandoitchi wa oishikatta desu.
f   Reiko-san wa shinsetsu deshita.
g   Sutekina sētā deshita.
h   Ano hito wa kawaikatta desu.

4   Can you say these sentences in Japanese, linking them with **ga** (*but*)?

a   She was a quiet person but she was interesting.
b   This ice cream is delicious but it is a bit expensive.

c   I want to go to Japan but it's expensive.
d   Last year's spring was a little cold but this year's spring is a little hot.
e   This jumper is a bit big but that jumper is a bit small.

▶ 5 Listen to Anne and Scott chatting in Japanese and circle the correct adjective to describe what they think about various things.

Example: The film was (interesting /good/expensive)

a   The car was (big/small/fast).
b   Today's weather is (hot/cold/pleasant).
c   The supermarket is (convenient/cheap/hot).
d   The jumper is (smart/cute/nice).
e   Scott is (young/bad/kind).
f   Tokyo is (quiet/expensive/interesting).
g   The school was (convenient/quiet/nice).

▶ 6 You will hear a short weather report. Write next to each of the five cities on the map of Japan below (see next page)...

SAPPORO

HIROSHIMA   TOKYO
NAGASAKI   OSAKA

a   the temperature (this is given in centigrade);
b   a comment on the weather.

These words will help you:

ame *rain* (a-me)
hare *fine* (ha-re)
do *degrees* (**jūichido** = *11 degrees*)
nochi *later* (**hare nochi ame** = *fine later rain*)

Test

1 Underline the correct word in the brackets below.

   a   An-san no otōsan wa (wakai/wakaina) desu.
   b   Kinō no pātī wa (tanoshii/tanoshikatta) desu.
   c   (Shizukana/shizuka) tokoro desu ne.
   d   Kono sūpā wa (benri/benrina) desu ne.
   e   Ano aisukurīmu wa oishikatta (desu/deshita).

2 Link the sentences on the left with the comments on the right. There may be more than one correct answer but they should <u>all</u> make sense!

   a   Kinō resutoran ni ikimashita.   i   Ii desu ne.
   b   Mō bangohan o tabemashita ka.   ii   Atsui desu ne.
   c   Mō natsu desu ne.   iii Benri desu ne.
   d   Eiga ni ikimasen ka.   iv   Tanoshikatta desu.
   e   Eki wa uchi no chikaku desu.   v   Hai, oishikatta desu.

3 Imagine you are talking with Anne and fill in your part of the conversation.

   You   *Say you saw a Japanese language film last week.*
   Anne   Dō deshita ka.
   You   *Say that it was interesting.*
   Anne   Watashi mo nihongo no eiga o mitai desu.
   You   *Suggest that you go to the cinema together tomorrow night.*
   Anne   Kissaten ni mo ikimashō ka.
   You   *Say you'd love to and suggest going to 'Luna' coffee shop.*
   Anne   Sono kissaten wa **dō desu ka***.
   You   *Say it is a bit expensive but the ice-cream is very delicious.*

   *****dō desu ka** has the meaning *what is it like?* as well as *how about?* (see page 104).

12

supōtsu wa tenisu ga suki desu

the sport I like is tennis

In this unit you will learn
- how to talk about things that you like
- how to say that you don't like something very much
- how to say what you or another person is good at
- the negative of *masu* words
- how to describe the location of a person or an object

Introduction

This is the last unit in which you will be introduced to new language and structures. Some of the unit will already be familiar to you.

In Unit 9 (**Explanation 6**) you were introduced briefly to how to say *I/you/they do not* (etc.). In other words, the *negative* of **masu** words. To do this, you learnt to change the **masu** ending to **masen**.

In Unit 7 (**Explanation 3**) you learnt how to describe where places are. For example, **eki no mae** means *in front of the station*. You will learn more about this in this unit.

Let's talk

1   Change these verbs into the negative. The first one has been done for you. Can you remember what all these words mean?

Tabe<u>masu</u> (*I eat*)   Tabe<u>masen</u> (*I don't eat* or *I won't eat*)

Nomi<u>masu</u>
Gorufu o shi<u>masu</u>
Oki<u>masu</u>
Ne<u>masu</u>
Yomi<u>masu</u>
Iki<u>masu</u>

2   How do you say these phrases in Japanese? (Look back at Unit 7, **Explanation 3** if you need to remind yourself.)

a   The bank is next to the post office.
b   The station is near to the cinema.
c   The department store is opposite the bank.
d   The flower shop is in front of the department store.

suki	*like*
amari suki dewa/ja arimasen	*don't like very much*
jōzu, tokui	*good at, skilful*
totemo	*very (much)*
amari	*not very* (much)
zenzen	*never*

Supōtsu *Sports*

hokkē	*hockey*
yakyū	*baseball*
kuriketto	*cricket*
hyaku mētoru	*100 metres* (sprint)
kyōsō	*a race*

Ongaku *Music*

rokku	*rock music*
jazu	*jazz*
kurashikku	*classical music*
poppusu	*pop music*

Terebi bangumi *TV programmes*

eiga	*films*
komedī	*comedy*
nyūsu	*news*
dorama	*drama*
hōmu dorama	*soap opera*
manga	*cartoons/comic books*
anime	*animation/cartoons*
dokyumentarī	*documentary*
ryōri bangumi	*cookery programme*

Location

naka	*inside*
ue	*above*
ushiro	*behind, at the back*
soto	*outside*
shita	*below*
kono chikaku ni	*near here*

Dōshi *Verbs*

mottekimasu	*bring, get*
owarimasu	*end, finish*
demasu	*take part in*

Objects

tēburu	*table*
isu	*chair*
tsukue	*desk*
honbako	*bookcase*
posuto	*post-box*

▶ Conversation

Emi and Anne are watching Takeshi's school sports day and are talking to his teacher.

Sensei	An-san, supōtsu wa nani ga suki desu ka.
Anne	Sō desu ne. **Gakusei no toki**, hokkē ga suki deshita ga **saikin** amari supōtsu o shimasen.
Sensei	Tenisu wa dō desu ka.
Anne	Watashi wa amari suki dewa arimasen ga Emi-san wa tenisu ga suki desu. Totemo jōzu desu.
Emi	Iie, mada mada desu yo!
Anne	Takeshi-kun wa doko ni **imasu** ka.
Emi	**Kyōgijō** ni **imasen** ka.
Anne	A! Asoko desu. Takeshi!
Takeshi	An-san, konnichiwa. **Onēsan**, nomimono ga arimasu ka. **Nodo ga kawaiteimasu**.
Emi	Hai, jūsu o mottekimashita. Ano kaban no naka ni arimasu.
Takeshi	**Itadakimasu** … Oishii!
Emi	Takeshi, kyō nani ni demasu ka.
Takeshi	Ano … hyaku mētoru kyōsō desu. Boku wa hyaku mētoru ga tokui desu.
Anne	(*points over to sports field*) Are wa hyaku mētoru dewa arimasen ka.
Takeshi	Are! Mō owarimashita. **Hidoi** desu.

Vocabulary

gakusei no toki	*when I was at school*
saikin	*recently*
kyōgijō	*playing field*
onēsan	*older sister* (younger siblings use this)
nodo ga kawaiteimasu	*I'm thirsty*
itadakimasu	*I humbly receive* (said before eating)
hidoi	*terrible*
imasu/imasen	*is/is not* (see **Explanation 3**)

🅸 Sports day

School sports days are normally held in October when the weather is fine and not too hot. Japan has a public holiday on the second Monday of October called **Taiiku no Hi** (*Physical Education Day*) which commemorates the opening of the Tokyo Olympics in 1964. Since then it has become a tradition to hold school sports days around this date. There are even special races for parents!

Explanations

1 Supōtsu wa nani ga suki desu ka *What sports do you like?*

When you want to ask somebody what they like, you use the word **suki** (*like*) in this pattern: category **wa nani ga suki desu ka**. For example:

Supōtsu wa nani ga suki desu ka.   *What sports do you like?*

(The **u** of **suki** is hardly spoken – **s(u)-ki**.)

You can talk about other categories such as *food* (**tabemono**), *drink* (**nomimono**), *music* (**ongaku**) and *TV programmes* (**terebi bangumi**) in the same way. For example:

Tabemono wa nani ga suki desu ka.   *What food do you like?*

Nomimono wa nani ga suki desu ka. *What drink do you like?*

Ongaku wa nani ga suki desu ka. *What music do you like?*

Emi-san wa tenisu ga suki desu *Emi likes tennis*

To answer the question you replace **nani** (*what?*) with the item that you like. For example:

Watashi wa tōsuto ga suki desu. *I like toast.*

Reiko-san wa kōhī ga suki desu. *Reiko likes coffee.*

Emi-san wa kurashikku ongaku ga suki desu. *Emi likes classical music.*

You can also answer in this way (see the title of this unit):

Supōtsu wa tenisu ga suki desu. *The sport I like is tennis. (Or simply I like tennis.)*

Tabemono wa sushi ga suki desu. *The food I like is sushi. (I like sushi.)*

Ongaku wa jazu ga suki desu. *The music I like is jazz. (I like jazz music.)*

If you really like or love something, you add the word **totemo** or say **daisuki**.

Takeshi-kun wa hyaku mētoru ga totemo suki desu. *Takeshi loves the 100 metres.*

Terebi bangumi wa komedī ga totemo suki desu. *I really like TV comedies.*

Bīru ga daisuki desu. *(I) love beer.*

If you don't really like something, use **amari suki dewa/ja arimasen** (*don't like very much*):

Watashi wa niku ga amari suki ja arimasen. *I don't like meat very much.*

Sukotto-san wa kuriketto ga amari suki dewa arimasen. *Scott doesn't really like cricket.*

2 Emi-san wa tenisu ga jōzu desu *Emi is good at tennis*

Jōzu means *good at/skilful* (also **tokui**), and you use the same pattern that you learnt with **suki** to compliment other people. For example: Person **wa** skill **ga jōzu desu**. (*Someone is good at something.*)

An-san wa nihongo ga jōzu desu.	*Anne is good at Japanese.*
Reiko-san wa ryōri ga jōzu desu.	*Reiko is good at cooking.*
Takeshi-kun wa hyaku mētoru ga tokui desu.	*Takeshi is skilful at the 100 metres.*

Add **totemo** for *very*:

Emi-san wa tenisu ga totemo jōzu desu.	*Emi is very good at tennis.*

When you talk about your own skills, use **tokui** rather than **jōzu**. This word gives the idea of your strengths rather than what you are good at and so sounds less big-headed! (The Japanese tend to be very modest about themselves.) For example:

Watashi wa supōtsu ga tokui desu.	*I'm good at (my strong point is) sports.*

On the same theme of modesty, if someone compliments you, a usual reply is to deny this (just as Scott did in the **Conversation** section of Unit 7):

Nihongo ga jōzu desu ne.	*You're good at Japanese, aren't you?*
Iie, mada mada desu.	*No, I'm no good yet.*

Alternatively, to say that you're not very good at something, you can use a similar pattern to the one you learnt for *don't like very much*:

Watashi wa tenisu ga amari jōzu ja arimasen.	*I'm not very good at tennis.*

3 Takeshi-kun wa doko ni imasu ka *Where is Takeshi?*

Imasu and **arimasu** are used to talk about where an object or person is located. **Imasu** is used to talk about people and animals (i.e. animate objects), and **arimasu** is used for inanimate objects. For example:

Takeshi-kun wa kyōgijō ni imasu.	Takeshi is on the sports field.
Uchi ni imasen.	He's not in the house.
Jūsu wa kaban no naka ni arimasu.	The juice is in the bag.

(Note that you say **ni** after the location and before **imasu/arimasu**. This is a special use of **ni** with the words **arimasu** and **imasu**.)

You can often replace **arimasu/imasu** with **desu,** as you learnt in Unit 7, **Explanations 1 and 3:**

| Yūbinkyoku wa doko desu ka. | Where is the post office? |

Using **imasu/arimasu** puts more emphasis on the location:

| Yūbinkyoku wa doko ni arimasu ka. | Where is the post office located? |

But look at the difference in meaning in these two sentences:

| Uchi ni imasu. | He's at home. |
| Uchi desu. | It's a house. |

You have already learnt a different meaning of **arimasu** (page 63) – ... **ga arimasu ka** (*do you have any ...?*):

| Hagaki ga arimasu ka. | Do you have any postcards? |

4 Nomimono wa kaban no naka ni arimasu
The drinks are in the bag

In this unit you are going to add a few more 'position words' to those you learnt in Unit 7. The list below includes all the ones you have been introduced to so far:

ue	*above, on top*	shita	*below, underneath*
mae	*in front*	ushiro	*behind, at the back*
naka	*inside*	soto	*outside*
tonari	*next to*	chikaku	*near*
mukaigawa	*opposite*	kono chikaku ni	*near here*

Here are some examples of their use with **imasu/arimasu**. Try covering the Japanese words and work out how to say the phrases yourself.

Tokei wa honbako no ue ni arimasu.	*The clock is (located) on top of the bookcase.*
Inu wa beddo no shita ni imasu.	*The dog is under the bed.*
Posuto wa depāto no mae ni arimasu.	*The postbox is in front of the department store.*
An-san wa sūpā no mukaigawa ni imasu.	*Anne is opposite the supermarket.*
Furansu wa Igirisu no chikaku ni arimasu.	*France is near to England.*
Suzuki-san wa tonari no uchi ni imasu.	*Mr Suzuki is next door.*
Emi-san wa ginkō no soto ni imasu.	*Emi is outside the bank.*
Yūbinkyoku wa kono chikaku ni arimasu.	*The post office is near here.*

5 Saikin amari supōtsu o shimasen *Recently I haven't played sports very much*

You've already practised saying the negative in the **Let's talk** section of this unit. To say *I/you/he* (etc.) *didn't* (the past negative), you add **deshita** to the negative. For example:

Takeshi-kun wa kyōsō ni demasen deshita.	*Takeshi didn't take part in the race.*
Yamaguchi-san wa undōkai ni ikimasen deshita.	*Mr Yamaguchi didn't go to the sports day.*
An-san wa asagohan o tabemasen deshita.	*Anne didn't eat any breakfast.*

Amari (*not very much/not often*) and **zenzen** (*never*) are used only with the negative of the action words. For example:

Watashi wa *zenzen* kōhī o nomimasen.	*I never drink coffee.*

| Reiko-san wa *amari* terebi o mimasen. | *Reiko doesn't watch TV much.* |
| Gakusei no toki *amari* shukudai o shimasen deshita. | *When I was at school, I didn't often do homework.* |

You say **amari** and **zenzen** before the item and action word.

Practice

▶ 1 You will hear recordings of people describing the location of people/items. As you listen, decide whether the pictures (**a–f**) match the descriptions you hear. If you think the description is correct, draw a circle (**maru**) under the picture; or draw a cross (**batsu**) if you think it is not correct.

If you don't have the recordings, you can read the dialogues for this and the next exercise in the **Key to the exercises**.

▶ 2 Listen (or read in the **Key to the exercises**) as characters from this book talk about their likes and dislikes. Complete the table on the next page using one tick for *likes* (**suki**), two ticks for *loves* (**totemo/daisuki**) and × for *doesn't like* (**amari suki dewa/ja arimasen**). Leave the squares blank if no information is supplied.

	Anne	Takeshi	Emi	Mr Yamaguchi	Reiko
Tennis					
Japanese cookery					
TV news					
Soap drama					
Whisky					
Cartoons					

3 Read the three dialogues below and fill in the correct word: either **imasu** (for *people* and *animals*) or **arimasu** (for *non-living/moving objects* including *plants*).

a Q: Emi-san wa doko ni _____ ka.
   A: Ima tenisu kōto ni _____ .
   Q: Tenisu kōto wa doko desu ka.
   A: Takeshi-kun no gakkō no chikaku ni _____ .

b Q: Sumimasen, posuto wa kono chikaku ni _____ ka.
   A: Hai, _____ . Massugu itte kudasai. Posuto wa ano ginkō no mae ni _____ .

c Q: Sumimasen, Yamaguchi-san wa ima uchi ni _____ ka.
   A: Iie, _____ . Ima kaisha ni _____ .
   Q: Nan ji made imasu ka.
   A: Ano … hachi ji made _____ .

4 In response to the questions, use the pictures below to describe where the people and items are:

a Sumimasen, ginkō wa doko desu ka.

b   An-san no tokei wa doko ni arimasu ka.

c   Takeshi-kun no inu wa ima doko ni imasu ka.

d   Reiko-san wa doko ni imasu ka.

e   Watashi no hon wa doko desu ka.

5   On the next page is a family photo of the Yamaguchi family and Anne, taken on a sightseeing tour around Tokyo. Can you make sentences about where they all are? The English sentences below will help you.

Mr Yamaguchi is behind Emi.
Reiko is next to Mr Yamaguchi.
Takeshi is next to Reiko.
The dog is in front of Takeshi.
Anne is next to the dog.
Emi is in front of Mr Yamaguchi.

6 Say these sentences in Japanese.

    a   Takeshi is good at the 100 metres.
    b   Mr Yamaguchi is very good at golf.
    c   No, I'm no good at it yet.
    d   I'm good at French.
    e   Yesterday I didn't watch TV at all.
    f   I don't often read the newspaper.

7 Mr Yamaguchi is being asked how often he does certain activities. Use the prompts in the brackets to work out how he would answer. Choose between **yoku** (*often*), **tokidoki** (*sometimes*), **amari** (*not often*), **zenzen** (*never*).

Example: Yoku tenisu o shimasu ka. (*No, not often*) Iie, amari shimasen.

    a   Yoku eiga o mimasu ka. (*yes, sometimes*)
    b   Yoku gorufu o shimasu ka. (*yes, often*)
    c   Yoku hon o yomimasu ka. (*no, not often*)
    d   Tokidoki basu de kaisha ni ikimasu ka. (*no, never*)
    e   Tokidoki hōmu dorama o mimasu ka. (*no, not often*)
    f   Yoku rokku ongaku o kikimasu ka. (*no, never*)

8 **Word puzzle: Reiko-san wa _____ desu.**

The highlighted column on the grid below will give you the information you need to complete this sentence about Reiko, but first you have to work out the missing words in the sentences below and fill them in on the grid. **Gambatte!**

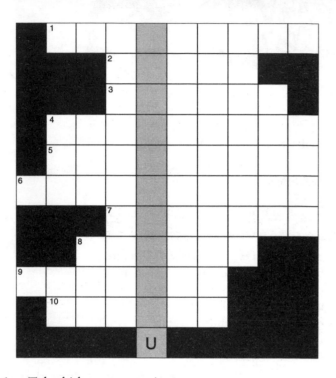

1 Takeshi-kun wa tenisu ga _____ _____ dewa arimasen. (*Takeshi doesn't like tennis very much.*)

2 Yamaguchi-san wa _____ ga daisuki desu. (*Mr Yamaguchi loves the news.*)

3 _____ ni ikitai desu. (*I want to go to Germany.*)

4 An-san no hon wa terebi no ue _____ _____. (*Anne's book is on the TV.*)

5 Zenzen manga o _____ . (*I never read comics.*)

6 Nomimono wa _____ _____ _____ desu. (*The drink I like is cola.*)

7 Supōtsu wa hokkē _____ _____ desu. (*The sport I am good at is hockey.*)

8 Emi-san wa tenisu _____ _____ desu. (*Emi is good at tennis.*)

9 Takeshi-kun wa _____ _____ demasen deshita. (*Takeshi didn't take part in the race.*)

10 An-san wa _____ jazu ongaku o kikimasen. (*Anne never listens to jazz music.*)

Revision test

This is the last test in the units with **Explanation** sections (Units 1–12), and so this revision test will be based on all these units! Each question will also indicate which unit it is based on so that you can look back at these units if you need to.

1 **Units 1–4**

Link the Japanese phrases on the left with the English meanings on the right.

a Musume wa futari desu. Jūroku sai to jūni sai desu.

b Watashi wa yonjussai desu.

c Hajimemashite. Yamaguchi Takeshi desu.

d Kanai wa haisha desu.

e Watashi wa Nihonjin desu. Ōsaka kara desu.

f Watashi wa Nissan no kaishain desu.

g Watashi no tanjōbi wa kugatsu jūsan-nichi desu.

i How do you do? My name is Takeshi Yamaguchi.

ii I am Japanese. I am from Osaka.

iii I am a company employee at Nissan.

iv I am 40 years old.

v My birthday is on 13th September.

vi I have two daughters aged 16 and 12.

vii My wife is a dentist.

Now write out your own self-introduction based on this pattern (**i–vii**) and try to learn it off by heart.

2 **Units 5–6**

How do you say these phrases in Japanese?

a May I have this one, please?

b Please show me that book (over there).

c May I have an ice cream and a coffee, please?

d Excuse me, what time is it?

e The post office is open from 9 until 5.30.

f How much is this English newspaper?

g How much is this letter to England?

h Do you have any stamps?

i May I have two bottles of beer, please?

3 **Unit 7**

Scott is in Shinjuku looking for a bank.

a How does he attract the attention of a passer-by and ask where the Japan bank is?

b How does the passer-by direct him to go a little way and turn right at the traffic lights?

c How does Scott ask him to repeat what he said?

d How does the passer-by say that the bank is opposite 'Sogo' department store?

e How does Scott say *thank you*?

4 **Units 8–10**

The pictures below show what Reiko did this morning. Describe her day using the pictures as prompts. (Remember to use **mashita** *did*.)

Got up at 6.30.

Ate egg and toast for breakfast.   Went to work by bus.

Worked from 8.30–12.   Ate lunch at a restaurant with a friend.

Next, using the information below, can you describe what she is *going to do* for the rest of the day? (Use **masu**.)

f Return home by underground.

g Prepare the evening meal from 2 p.m. to 4 p.m. (**bangohan o tsukurimasu**)

h Have chicken and rice for dinner.

i Watch TV.

j Go to bed at about 11.30.

5 **All units**

Asking questions. How do you ask:

a Excuse me, where is the post office?
b How do you say *book* in Japanese?
c What do you do on Saturdays?
d What time do you get up?
e When are you going to France?
f What did you do last night?
g What do you have for breakfast?
h How long does it take by bullet train from Tōkyō to Ōsaka?

6 **Units 9–10**

Complete the correct endings to the **masu** words from a choice of **mashō** (*let's*), **mashō ka** (*shall we?*), **masen ka** (*would you like to?*), **tai desu** (*I want to*).

a Eiga o mi _____ . (*Shall we watch a film?*)
b Kaimono ni iki _____ . (*Let's go shopping.*)
c Nihon ni iki _____ . (*I want to go to Japan.*)
d Ano resutoran de kōhī o nomi _____ . (*Shall we drink coffee at that restaurant?*)
e **Issho ni** bīru o nomi _____ . (*Would you like to have a beer with me?*)
f Omoshiroi hon o yomi _____ . (*I want to read an interesting book.*)
g Watashi no uchi de hirugohan o tabe _____ . (*Let's eat lunch at my house.*)

7 **Units 11–12**

The describing words are missing from the statements below. Choose one from the following list to make sense of the statement. Be careful! There is only one match for each sentence.

Words to choose from: **shizuka, shizukana, atsui, samukatta, jōzu, tokui**

a Kyō wa _____ desu ne.
b Kinō wa _____ desu ne.
c Koko wa _____ tokoro desu ne.
d Kono resutoran wa _____ desu ne.
e An-san wa supōtsu wa amari _____ dewa arimasen.
f Watashi wa supōtsu ga _____ desu.

13

日本語を読みましょう！

Nihongo o yomimashō

let's read Japanese!

In this unit you will learn
- about the Japanese writing system
- how to read the days of the week and numbers in Japanese characters
- how to read food and drink words and identify them on a menu

Introduction (はじめに)

It was explained in the **Introduction** that this unit is largely independent of the rest of the book, so you can miss it out or come back to it later if you choose. However, for the learner who would like to know more about Japanese script, this unit will serve as an introduction, and you will also have an opportunity to use what you have learnt in an exercise in Unit 15.

The Japanese language in this book is written in **rōmaji. Rōma** means *Roman* and **ji** means *letter* or *character*. In other words, **rōmaji** means the *Roman alphabet* (A, B, C ...). **Rōmaji** is used to write Japanese sounds in a written form that people who don't know Japanese script can read.

Although all Japanese people learn to read and write the Roman alphabet, Japanese is read and written in a different form. There are three writing forms which make up the whole Japanese writing system. Let's look at each of these in turn.

1 Kanji (漢字)

Kan is an old word for *Chinese* and **ji** means *letter* or *character*. This is because the Japanese writing system was introduced to Japan from China in the 6th century AD and was adapted to the Japanese language.

Kanji were developed originally from pictures of natural objects such as the sun, the moon, water, etc. Each kanji represents a meaning or idea. For example, the word *Japan* (**Nihon**) is written like this in kanji: 日本 .

日　means *sun* and developed from a picture of the sun:

本　means *root* and developed from a picture of the roots of a tree:

Therefore, the word *Japan* means *root/origin of the sun*, so Japan is the place where the sun rises. In other words: *land of the rising sun* (named by the Chinese because Japan lies to the east of China).

You will be introduced to more kanji later in this unit. There are several thousand kanji in the Japanese language, and you need to know about 2,000 to read a Japanese newspaper properly!

The Japanese spend their school years building up their knowledge of kanji, so don't be daunted by the amount. You will learn just a few in this unit.

2 Hiragana and katakana

The other two scripts are known collectively as **kana**. In the **Pronunciation guide** (**Introduction**) you were introduced to the Japanese sounds which make up the Japanese language. Each of these sounds is represented by a symbol or **kana**. An important difference between this system and the Roman alphabet can be shown like this:

In English, the word *house* is made up of five letters: H-O-U-S-E.

In Japanese, the word for house is **uchi** and is made up of two sounds: U-CHI.

These sounds are represented by these two **kana** symbols: うち

There are two kana scripts: hiragana and katakana. They both represent the same set of sounds but the symbols are written differently. For example, this is how the sound **a** is written in the two scripts:

Hiragana **a** = あ

Katakana **a** = ア

In a similar way, but for different reasons, the Roman alphabet also has two symbols representing one letter, known as capitals and lower case: A, a; B, b; C, c; and so on.

Below is an explanation of the different ways in which hiragana and katakana are used:

Hiragana (ひらがな)

Hiragana is used mainly to write Japanese words which don't have a kanji, and to write the grammatical parts of words and sentences. Here is an example:

I (*she, they*, etc.) *look* is written: 見 ま す
mi ma su

見 is a kanji meaning *look*, and ます are two hiragana representing **ma** and **su** and show that it is a present or future action: *I look* or *I will look*.

I looked is written: 見 ま し た
mi ma shi ta

The same kanji is used to convey the meaning of *look*. The hiragana ま ma, し shi, た ta are used to show that it is a past action (*I looked*). In other words, hiragana has a grammatical function. In this case it shows you whether the action word is **masu** or **mashita** (as you learnt in Units 8 and 10).

When Japanese children first go to school, they write all Japanese words in hiragana, and then gradually replace some of these words with kanji as they learn them.

Katakana (カタカナ)

Katakana is used mainly for writing foreign (non-Japanese) words which have been introduced into the Japanese language. In Unit 2 you were introduced to the idea of foreign words being adopted into and adapted to the Japanese language. Here are some examples of these words, written in the katakana script:

resutoran (*restaurant*) = レストラン
re su to ra n

sutereo (*stereo*) = ステレオ
su te re o

Notice that these two words have two symbols in common: ス (**su**) and レ (**re**). See if you can find them and underline them.

As well as using katakana to write all foreign words, it has also become increasingly fashionable in recent times to write Japanese words in katakana, especially in advertising, and it has the effect of making words stand out.

Now you have been introduced to the three Japanese scripts, look at the extract (on page 154) from a Japanese magazine to see how Japanese looks in the written form. The headline shows examples of all three scripts.

The article is from a school newsletter and is introducing a new teacher from England to the school. Note that the writing is printed from top to bottom. This is how Japanese is traditionally written; you begin reading from the top right-hand corner. However, Japanese can also be written 'western-style' – from left to right – and Japanese people are familiar with both styles.

英語指導をよろしく！

ロバート・ギルフーリーさん

●生年月日 一九六四年十一月二十日生（二十五才）
●国　籍　イギリス
●趣　味　クリケット・フットボール・読書・音楽鑑賞・旅行

今年町内の中学校で英語指導助手を勤めるのは、ロバート・ギルフーリーさん。九月から来年七月まで町内三中学校をローテーションして指導にあたる。

ロバートさんは、イギリス西北部の出身。ランカスター大学で英文学を学んだ。

The four kanji in the first column (top right-hand side) mean *English instruction*, and the hiragana make up the word **yoroshiku** (this word appears in Units 1 and 20). In English we might say *the school looks forward to receiving English instruction*.

The katakana in the second column make up the teacher's name (non-Japanese names are always written in katakana), and the final two hiragana make the word **san** (*Mr*).

When you have completed this unit, look back at this article and see which other words and symbols you can pick out – numbers, dates, katakana words. You won't be able to understand the whole article (and it is in small print), but it's fun and good practice to be able to identify some Japanese characters!

漢字を読みましょう！

Let's read kanji!

Practice

1 You learnt in the **Introduction** to this unit that kanji were developed from pictures of nature. Can you work out the meanings of these seven kanji from the pictures of objects that they developed from? (Cover up the answers.)

Picture	Development				Kanji

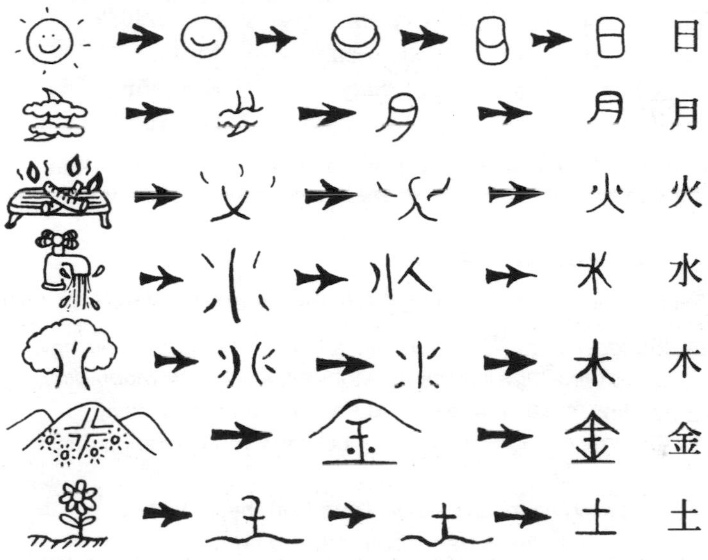

Answers

日 means *sun* and also *day* (the rising and setting of the sun defines a day).

月 means *moon* and also *month* (the cycle of the moon takes one month).

火 means *fire*.

水 means *water* (the picture shows the splashing of water).

木 means *tree* or *wood/timber*.

金 means *gold* or *money* (the picture shows a mountain with a gold mine in it).

土 means *earth* or *soil* (the picture shows plants growing from the earth).

These seven kanji are also used to represent days of the week. You learnt to say the days of the week in Unit 8. Now you are going to learn how to read them.

Kanji		English	Rōmaji
日	=	*Sunday*	Nichi (yōbi)
月	=	*Monday*	Getsu (yōbi)
火	=	*Tuesday*	Ka (yōbi)
水	=	*Wednesday*	Sui (yōbi)
木	=	*Thursday*	Moku (yōbi)
金	=	*Friday*	Kin (yōbi)
土	=	*Saturday*	Do (yōbi)

Yōbi is in brackets because it is written with two other kanji, but you can identify the days of the week from the first kanji alone.

ℹ Days of the week

To help you link the correct kanji with the correct day of the week:

日 (*Sunday*) and 月 (*Monday*) are easy because they have the same meanings in English (Monday is short for *Moon day*).

金 (*Friday*) means *money* – and Friday is often pay day!

土 (*Saturday*) means *earth day* – perhaps you do the gardening on Saturdays.

水 (*Wednesday*) means *water* – and both begin with *w*!

木 (*Thursday*) means *tree* – both begin with *t*.

2   Without looking at the kanji chart above, see if you can match the correct day with its kanji representation by writing the letters **a–f** in the brackets next to the English meaning.

a	水	Monday ( )	**d**	火	Wednesday ( )
b	木	Friday ( )	**e**	土	Sunday ( )
c	日	Saturday ( )	**f**	月	Tuesday ( )

g   金

There is one remaining kanji. Which day of the week does it represent? _____day. And which letter is it?

3 The calendar below is for the month of June. Use the information from it to answer the questions, as in the example. (You may want to look back at pages 40 and 105–6 first to remind yourself how to say the days of the month in Japanese.)

Example: Jūku-nichi wa nanyōbi desu ka. (*What day of the week is the 19th?*) = Mokuyōbi desu.

日	月	火	水	木	金	土
1	2	3	4	5	6	7
8	9	10	11	12	13	14
15	16	17	18	19	20	21
22	23	24	25	26	27	28
29	30					

a Nijūsan-nichi wa nanyōbi desu ka.
b Nijūku-nichi wa nanyōbi desu ka.
c Tōka wa nanyōbi desu ka.
d Nijūichi-nichi wa nanyōbi desu ka.
e Hatsuka wa nanyōbi desu ka.
f Yōka wa nanyōbi desu ka.
g Yokka wa nanyōbi desu ka.

Sūji *Numbers*

In Unit 2 you learnt to count from 1–12, and you have been using numbers throughout the units in different ways (months, dates, time, money, etc.). Now you are going to learn how to read them in kanji. There are some hints on the right to help you remember them.

Number	Kanji	Rōmaji	Hinto
1	一	ichi	One stroke
2	二	ni	Two strokes
3	三	san	Three strokes
4	四	shi/yon	Four sides
5	五	go	This looks like the numeral 5 – 𝟝
6	六	roku	Looks like a rocket (**roku**) taking off – 🔺

7	七	nana/shichi	looks like a French 7 upside-down 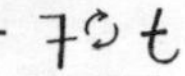 – 7〇 七
8	八	hachi	looks like a ha-t (**ha-chi**) –
9	九	kyū/ku	
10	十	jū	Like the roman numeral for 10 at an angle – x
11	十一	jūichi	10 + 1
12	十二	jūni	10 + 2 (and so on)

ℹ Learning tip

Pictures and sound association are very effective for helping you to remember new symbols (you learnt to remember some new words in the same way in earlier units). Can you think of something to help you remember 九 (9)?

4 When you feel confident that you can recognize the numbers, try the following activity.

Link the kanji number on the left with the correct rōmaji in the middle column and the correct numeral on the right, as in the example. Then check your answers with the chart above (there are no answers at the back of the book).

Kanji	Rōmaji	Numeral
一	shi	5
五	shichi	3
十二	ichi	4
七	san	1 2
三	go	1
四	jūni	7

Dates and months

You have already learnt that the kanji 日 is used to represent the day *Sunday* and that the kanji 月 is used to represent the day *Monday*. These two kanji also have another meaning:

日 means *day/date* as in 4th, 12th, etc. So 四日 = 4th; and 十二日 = 12th.

月 means *month*. You learnt to say the months in Unit 2 by adding the word **gatsu** to the numbers 1–12. For example, **Ichigatsu** = *1st month* = *January*. This is written 一月 in kanji.

5   Match the months on the left with the kanji on the right. Write the correct letter in the brackets.

a	March	六月	( )
b	November	八月	( )
c	June	十二月	( )
d	September	十一月	( )
e	December	三月	( )
f	August	九月	( )

More about numbers

You have learnt to recognize the kanji for the numbers 1–12 in this unit. The numbers 11–99 are made from a combination of 1–10. Here are some examples:

十五 = 15 = jūgo (10 + 5)
二十 = 20 = nijū (2 × 10) – you learnt this rule in Unit 3
二十三 = 23 = nijūsan (2 × 10 + 3)

6   Remember that the kanji 日 is added to a number to make a date. Below are the dates of some special events in Britain and in Japan. Can you link up the correct date with the correct event? Write the correct letter in the brackets next to the event.

	Date	Event	
a	十二月二十四日	Bonfire night	( )
b	五月五日	Girls' day (Japan: March 3rd)	( )
c	十一月十五日	Christmas Eve	( )
d	一月一日	Boys' day (Japan: May 5th)	( )
e	三月三日	Shichigosan (Japan: Nov. 15th)	( )
f	十一月五日	New Year's Day	( )

7 Match the kanji date on the left with the rōmaji in the middle by writing the correct letter in the brackets. Then write the date in English in the right-hand column. The first one has been done for you. (Look back to pages 40 and 105–6 to revise the days of the month.)

	Kanji	Rōmaji		English
a	二十三日	sanjūichi-nichi	( )	
b	一日	yōka	( )	
c	十四日	nijūsan-nichi	(a)	23rd
d	二十日	tsuitachi	( )	
e	十二日	itsuka	( )	
f	五日	jūyokka	( )	
g	八日	hatsuka	( )	
h	三十一日	jūni-nichi	( )	

8 Below is part of an advertisement for a Japanese theatre production. Can you pick out the month, date and day of the performance?

カタカナを読みましょう
Let's read katakana

You learnt in the introduction to this unit that the katakana script is used to write non-Japanese words that have been adopted into the Japanese language. You have learnt many of these words in the earlier units, and Unit 2 introduced you to the way that such words are adopted and adapted. Look back at this unit if you need to revise this before proceeding with the following section.

9 You haven't learnt to read any katakana yet, but try this recognition exercise to get you used to what katakana symbols look like. It is a simple matching exercise. Look at the katakana words **a–g**, find the same word in the right-hand column and write the correct letter **a–g** in the brackets.

a	コーヒー	ケーキ	( )
b	アイス	ミルク	( )
c	チーズ	サラダ	( )
d	ピザ	アイス	( )
e	ケーキ	チーズ	( )
f	サラダ	ピザ	( )
g	ミルク	コーヒー	( )

In the **Pronunciation guide** in the **Introduction** there is a chart of the Japanese sounds. Below is a chart of the same sounds, but written in katakana (Look back at the **Pronunciation guide** to remind yourself how to say the sounds.)

The katakana on the next page, taken from the chart, change their sound when they have the symbol ゛ added to them. Here are the rules:

Rule 1: k sounds become g sounds.

ガ (ga)　ギ (gi)　グ (gu)　ゲ (ge)　ゴ (go)

Rule 2: s sounds become z sounds.

ザ (za)　ジ (ji)　ズ (zu)　ゼ (ze)　ゾ (zo)

Rule 3: t sounds become d sounds.

ダ (da)　デ (de)　ド (do)

Katakana chart

ア	(a)	イ	(i)	ウ	(u)	エ	(e)	オ	(o)
カ	(ka)	キ	(ki)	ク	(ku)	ケ	(ke)	コ	(ko)
サ	(sa)	シ	(shi)	ス	(su)	セ	(se)	ソ	(so)
タ	(ta)	チ	(chi)	ツ	(tsu)	テ	(te)	ト	(to)
ナ	(na)	ニ	(ni)	ヌ	(nu)	ネ	(ne)	ノ	(no)
ハ	(ha)	ヒ	(hi)	フ	(fu)	ヘ	(he)	ホ	(ho)
マ	(ma)	ミ	(mi)	ム	(mu)	メ	(me)	モ	mo)
ヤ	(ya)			ユ	(yu)			ヨ	(yo)
ラ	(ra)	リ	(ri)	ル	(ru)	レ	(re)	ロ	(ro)
ワ	(wa)							ン	(n/m)

Rule 4: h sounds become **b** sounds.

バ (ba)　　ビ (bi)　　ブ (bu)　　ベ (be)　　ボ (bo)

These last five katakana change their sounds when the symbol **o** is added:

パ (pa)　　ピ (pi)　　プ (pu)　　ペ (pe)　　ポ (po)

You are not expected to learn all these katakana in order to do the exercises in this unit! The exercises will keep referring you back to the chart. However, the chart is there if you want to start memorizing the katakana. Try just a few (about five) at a time and try to link the shapes of each katakana with a picture or sound that will help you to remember it more easily. Here are a few ideas to get you started.

ア (**a**)　looks like an antelope

イ (**i**)　is a leaning **T** which rhymes with **i**

ウ (**u**)　looks like a **uisukī** (*whisky*) flask

エ (**e**)　looks like elevator doors

キ (**ki**)　looks like a door key

Katakana tips

Katakana symbols which look similar:

シ (**shi**) and ツ (**tsu**). The long stroke of **shi** slopes down more gently.

ン (**n**) and ソ (**so**). Again, the long stroke of n slopes down more gently.

Be aware of these similarities and if one sound doesn't seem to work in a word, try the other.

— This dash is used to indicate long sounds (see page xvi). In **rōmaji**, macrons are used to express long sounds as in this example:

kōhī (*coffee*) is written コーヒー in katakana. — s represented by the macrons.

10 In Practice 9 you matched pairs of katakana words. Here are those same words again, but this time you are going to find out how you say them and what they mean. Look back at the chart, match each symbol, write down the rōmaji, then work out what it means in English and select the correct word from the list on the right. The first word has been done for you.

	Katakana	**Rōmaji**	**English**	
a	コーヒー	kōhī	salad	( )
b	アイス		cake	( )
c	チーズ		milk	( )
d	ピザ		coffee	(**a**)
e	ケーキ		ice	( )
f	サラダ		cheese	( )
g	ミルク		pizza	( )

Katakana food and drink words

Below are ten common food and drink words that are found on Japanese menus, for example, in coffee shops. Try to remember them – sound and picture associations may help. Say the words out loud to yourself, then try covering the rōmaji and reading the katakana words. Finally, see how well you have remembered them by trying Practice 11. (But don't worry if you need to look back at this list!)

Katakana word	Rōmaji	English meaning
コーヒー	kōhī	coffee
アイスコーヒー	aisukōhī	iced coffee
ミルク	miruku	milk
コーラ	kōpa	cola
ケーキ	kēki	cake
カレー	karē	curry
ステーキ	sutēki	steak
ピザ	piza	pizza
サラダ	sarada	salad
ハンバーガー	hambāgā	hamburger

11 Below is a coffee shop menu written in katakana. Use the menu to answer the questions **a–d**.

メニュー　MENU

コーヒー	¥500
アイスコーヒー	¥600
コーラ	¥400
ケーキ	¥500〜700
ピザ	¥800
カレー	¥900
ハンバーガー	¥700

---

a How much is a cup of coffee?

b How much is a pizza?

c How much is a hamburger and a glass of cola?

d You and your friend each have up to 1,300 yen to spend and you both want something to eat and a drink but you don't want to order the same items. What different combinations could you order?

12 The ten food words you have learnt are hidden in this wordsearch. See how many you can find without looking back at the list on the previous page. Words are written left to right and top to bottom. Tick the words off as you find them, using the English list on the right:

ア	イ	ス	コ	ー	ヒ	ー
コ	サ	テ	｜	ミ	ル	ハ
ラ	ダ	｜	ヒ	ル	ピ	ン
ケ	ー	キ	｜	ク	シ	バ
サ	コ	ク	マ	ア	ウ	｜
キ	｜	ヒ	カ	レ	ー	ガ
サ	ラ	ダ	イ	ピ	ザ	ー

iced coffee
coffee
milk
cola
cake
curry
hamburger
salad
pizza
steak

Test テスト

1 Write the English equivalent next to the dates (month, date and day) below. The first one has been done for you.

a 八月一日（水）　　　　Wednesday 1st August

b 六月十一日（土）

c 一月三日（火）

d 九月二十五日（日）

e 四月七日 （月）

f 二月十八日 （金）

g 五月五日 (What special day is this in Japan?)

2 Select the correct katakana word from each of the choices i–iii below.

a Salad   i サンド   ii サラダ

                     iii ピザ

b Steak   i ステーキ   ii ケーキ

                     iii ステレオ

c Ice   i コーヒー   ii ケーキ

                     iii アイス

d Milk   i ホテル   ii ミルク

                     iii ミート

e Hamburger   i ハンバーガー   ii チキンバーガー

                     iii チーズバーガー

If you want to learn more about reading and writing Japanese, you could try another book in this series: *Teach Yourself Beginner's Japanese Script* by Helen Gilhooly.

14

shopping

kaimono

In this unit you will learn
- **how to find out more about shops in Japan**
- **how to practise buying clothes and other goods**
- **about typical Japanese souvenirs and presents**

As mentioned in the **Introduction,** Units 14–20 offer you the opportunity to *put into practice* the language you have learnt in the first 12 units, and to further your knowledge of Japanese in the context of situations you may find yourself in if you visit Japan or have contact with Japanese people.

Each unit is more or less independent so, for example, if you are going to eat out with Japanese friends or business colleagues, study Unit 15; or if you are meeting a Japanese person in your or their home, look at Unit 20.

Even if you do not have contact with Japanese people, these units will help you to develop your confidence in using Japanese and you will learn more about this fascinating language and culture.

Review

- Numbers (Units 2, 3)
- Saying it's a bit (small, expensive) (Unit 11, Explanation 5)
- Asking for something (Unit 5, Explanation 3)
- Asking the price (Unit 6, Explanation 3)
- Have you got/do you have? (Unit 6, Explanation 4)
- Counters for different objects (Unit 6, Explanation 5)
- Describing words (big, small, etc.) (Unit 11)

Nihon no depāto *Japanese department stores*

To find out about Japanese department stores, read the passage below. Answering the questions to Practice 1 will help you to understand it.

Nihon no depāto wa daitai kuji kara shichiji made desu. Nichiyōbi **demo aiteimasu. Iroirona** mono o **utteimasu.** **Tatoeba, nichiyōhin,** tabemono, **yōfuku** to **denki seihin** o utteimasu. Ten'in no **seifuku** wa totemo suteki desu. Ten'in no nihongo mo totemo **teinei** desu. **Kireina** depāto wa Tōkyō no Ginza ni takusan arimasu ga totemo takai desu.

demo	*even, also*	**yōfuku**	*clothes*
aiteimasu	*open*	**denki seihin**	*electrical goods*
iroirona	*various*	**seifuku**	*uniform*
utteimasu	*sell*	**teinei**	*polite*
tatoeba	*for example*	**kirei(na)**	*beautiful*
nichiyōhin	*everyday goods*		

Practice 1

a What time do Japanese department stores open and close?
b Do they open on Sundays?
c What does the passage say about the shop assistants' uniforms? What else does it say about these assistants?
d In which area of Tokyo would you find beautiful but very expensive department stores?

ℹ Learning tip

There are key **Vocabulary lists** at the beginning of each of the sections in this and future units. The best way to familiarize yourself with these words is to memorize a few words or a section at a time. Say them out loud to practise your pronunciation, then cover up the Japanese side and test yourself using the English words as prompts. Try this the other way round as well; cover the English side and see how many Japanese words you recognize. These words and phrases will recur throughout the unit and so there will be plenty of opportunity for reinforcement.

▶ Vocabulary list

Useful questions and phrases

... arimasu ka	*do you have ...?*
... uriba wa doko desu ka	*where is the ... department?*
Chotto takai (chiisai/ōkii/yasui) desu	*it's a bit expensive (small/big/cheap)*
motto yasui (ōkii/chiisai/takai) no wa arimasu ka	*do you have a cheaper (bigger/smaller/ more expensive) one?*
saizu wa?	*what size is it?*
ijō de yoroshii desu ka	*is that all?*
sore de kekkō desu	*that's all, thank you*
onegaishimasu	*please*
otsuri	*change*

Useful shop vocabulary

uriba	*department, counter*
kutsu uriba	*shoe department*
kamera uriba	*camera department*
tōki uriba	*china/pottery department*
fujinfuku uriba	*women's clothes department*

... wa nankai ni arimasu ka	*what floor is the ... located on?*
ikkai	*ground floor*
nikai	*first floor*
sankai	*second floor*
yonkai	*third floor*
chikai	*basement*
chika ikkai	*first floor of basement* (B1 – where there is more than one floor in the basement)
okujō	*rooftop*
erebētā	*elevator/lift*
esukarētā	*escalator*
kaidan	*stairs*
reji	*cash desk*
annaijo	*information desk*
sutoa gaido	*store guide*
pāsento	*per cent*
waribiki	*discount*

Phrases used by shop assistants

shōshō omachi kudasai	*please wait a moment*
arigatō gozaimashita.	*thank you. Please shop here*
Mata okoshi kudasai.	*again.*

ℹ 'First floor' and 'ground floor'

You will have noticed in the **Vocabulary list** section above that the floors in Japanese don't follow the British system: for example, **nikai** is translated as *first floor* (and not second floor as you might expect). This is because in Japan you count from the first floor, not the ground floor. The diagram below illustrates this:

yonkai _____	(3rd floor)
sankai _____	(2nd floor)
nikai _____	(first floor)
ikkai _____	(ground floor)
chika ikkai	(B1)

Practice 2

The two exercises below are designed for you to start using the new words you have learnt in the **Vocabulary list** lists above straightaway. Use them like a test to see how many words you can remember. Use the vocabulary lists to check your answers (there are no answers in the back of the book). Speak out loud.

a Can you say these phrases in Japanese? Use the example to guide you, but replace the underlined words with the alternative words given in i–iii.

> **Example:** It's a little <u>expensive</u>. Do you have a <u>cheaper</u> one? Chotto <u>takai</u> desu. Motto <u>yasui</u> no wa arimasu ka.

i   small, bigger
ii   big, smaller
iii cheap, more expensive

b Imagine you are in a Japanese department store and practise asking for the places below, as in the example.

> **Example:** Camera department: **Sumimasen, kamera uriba wa doko desu ka.**

i   china department
ii   women's clothes department
iii   shoe department
iv   elevator
v   lift
vi   stairs
vii   cash desk
viii information desk

▶ Depāto no kaimono *Department store shopping*

Items to buy

yōfuku	*clothes*
bōshi	*hat*
zubon	*trousers*
shatsu	*shirt*
wanpīsu	*dress*
burausu	*blouse*
sukāto	*skirt*
sētā	*jumper*
T. shatsu	*T-shirt*
kutsu	*shoes*
shinshi gutsu	*men's shoes*

Colour and size

akai	*red*
aoi	*blue*
shiroi	*white*
kuroi	*black*
eru (L)	*large size*
emu (M)	*medium size*
esu (S)	*small size*

Practice 3

In this exercise you are going to practise the new words for clothes and colours in the **Vocabulary list** above, so make sure you are familiar with the words.

Practise asking for the items **a–g** below using the example as your guide but replacing the underlined part with the alternative items. Then check your answers by looking back at the **vocabulary above** or listening to the recording.

Example: Do you have any <u>red jumpers</u>? <u>Akai sētā</u> ga arimasu ka.

a   red trousers
b   black shoes
c   white T-shirts
d   blue trousers

e   blue skirts
f   red dresses
g   white blouses

▶ Some of these useful phrases from Practice 2 and 3 are also recorded for you.

▶ Conversation 1

Emi is going to England during her university holidays and she has gone with Anne to a department store in Shinjuku to buy some new clothes.

Read out loud the new vocabulary for this dialogue, then listen to the recording (or read the dialogue) and, without looking back at the text, try **Practice 4**.

Annaijo de:

Emi   Sumimasen, fujinfuku uriba wa doko desu ka.

Ten'in   Hai. Nikai ni arimasu. Dōzo, sutoa gaido o **otori kudasai**.

Fujinfuku uriba de:

Ten'in	Irasshaimase.
Anne	Emi, **mite**! Kono akai sēta wa suteki desu ne.
Emi	Ē, kirei desu ne.
Ten'in	Sore wa hyaku pāsento **ūru** desu.
Emi	Sō desu ka. Ikura desu ka.
Ten'in	Nisen gohyaku-en desu.
Emi	Saizu wa?
Ten'in	Saizu wa emu desu.
Emi	Emu wa chotto ōkii desu. Motto chiisai no wa arimasu ka.
Ten'in	Hai. Shōshō omachi kudasai. Sō desu ne. Kore wa esu desu ga aoi desu.
Anne	Sore mo suteki desu yo.
Emi	Ja, chotto **kitemimasu**.

A little later:

Anne	Dō desu ka. Aa! Hontō ni niaimasu yo.
Emi	Sō desu ka. Ja kore o kaimasu.
Ten'in	Hai. Ijō de yoroshii desu ka.
Emi	Ē, sore de kekkō desu.
Ten'in	Nisen gohyaku-en de gozaimasu.
Emi	Ja, gosen-en de onegaishimasu.
Ten'in	Shōshō omachi kudasai. Nisen gohyaku-en no otsuri desu.
Emi	Domo arigatō.
Ten'in	Arigatō gozaimashita. Mata okoshi kudasai.

otori kudasai	*please take* (one)
mite	*look*
ūru	*wool*
kitemimasu	*I'll try it on*
niaimasu	*it suits you*
kaimasu	*buy*
de gozaimasu	*very polite form of* **desu** (*is*)
gosen-en de onegaishimasu	*please take it out of 5,000 yen*

Practice 4

After you've listened to the recording (you may want to listen more than once), see if you can say the Japanese for the phrases overleaf, then write them down.

a   Excuse me, where is the women's clothes department?
b   How much is it?
c   Do you have a smaller one?
d   Right, I'll just try it on.
e   Right, I'll buy this one.
f   That's all, thank you.
g   Please take it out of 5,000 yen.
h   Thank you very much for your custom.

Now read through the dialogue (remember to read out loud) and check you have understood it (check your answers in the **Key to the exercises** as well) before progressing to **Practice 5**.

Practice 5

Next imagine you are a customer in the department store and use the dialogue and the **Vocabulary list** to help you create the following scenario. Imagine the shop assistant's comments as well as your own and say the dialogue out loud.

You ask to see a pair of black trousers, you ask how much they are and are told they are 3,000 yen.

You then ask the size. When you are told the size is S, you ask if they have a larger size.

You then decide to buy them and pay out of a 10,000 yen note.

Practice 6

The larger department stores in Tokyo also stock store guides in English, as with this example of the Seibu department store on the next page. Use this store guide to answer the following questions in Japanese. You should note that there are two buildings, A and B. Indicate this with **A no** or **B no**, as in the example. Also note that the sixth floor is pronounced **rokkai**.

Example: Nekutai (*tie*) wa nankai ni arimasu ka.
        B no sankai ni arimasu.

a   Sukāto wa nankai ni arimasu ka.
b   Resutoran wa nankai ni arimasu ka.
c   Tokei wa nankai ni arimasu ka.
d   Kimono wa nankai ni arimasu ka.
e   Shatsu wa nankai ni arimasu ka.
f   Sakana wa nankai ni arimasu ka.
g   **Dansei** kutsu wa nankai ni arimasu ka.

	A		B		A		B
R GARDENINGS	M L	**R** PLAY GROUNDS & PET SHOP	T	**4** INTERNATIONAL BOUTIQUES	L T	**4** CHILDREN'S WEAR & TOYS	M L T
8 RESTAURANTS	M L T	**8** SAISON SQUARE & SPECIAL EVENT SPACE	M L T	**3** LADIES' FASHON Shoes	L T	**3** MEN'S FASHION Shoes, Neckties, Belts, Bags etc.	M T D
7 SPECIALITIES Jewelry, Watches, Boutiques	T	**7** FURNITURE & ART GALLERY	T	**2** LADIES' FASHION Skirts, Blouse, Pants, etc.	L T	**2** MEN'S FASHION	M L T
				M2 BAG ZONE			
6 KIMONO & LADIES' FASHION	L T	**6** FURNITURE & FABRICS	M L T	**1** LADIES' FASHION Accessories, Cosmetics etc.	M L T	**1** MEN'S FASHION Shoes, Bags	T
5 PRÊT-A-PORTER & INNER WEAR	M T	**5** HOUSE WARE	T	**B1** FOODS Fish Vegetables Meat	T	**B1** MEN'S FASHION	M L T

M = men's toilets   T = telephone
L = ladies' toilets   D = toilets for the disabled

---

dansei   *men's*

ℹ Discount electrical stores

These discount stores are some of the few places in Japan where you can barter. Akihabara in Tokyo is a particularly famous area, specializing in electrical and electronic goods. It's an amazing place simply to browse around, stocking all the most up-to-date equipment. You are able to buy goods tax-free if you intend to take them back to your own country and if you have a tourist visa on your passport.

Vocabulary list

denki seihin	*electrical goods*	**rajikase**	*radio cassette*
rajio	*radio*	**tēpu rekōdā**	*tape recorder*
shī dī purēyā	*CD player*	**pasokon**	*PC*
sutereo	*stereo*		

▶ Conversation 2

Familiarize yourself with the **Vocabulary list** and the new vocabulary below this dialogue, then listen to or read the dialogue.

Scott is in an electrical store in Akihabara, looking for a CD player to take back to the States.

Ten'in   Irasshaimase!

Scott   (*after a while*) Ano, kono shī dī purēyā wa Nihon-**sei** desu ka.

Ten'in   Ē, sore wa *Nashonaru* desu. Sore wa totemo ii shī dī purēyā desu yo.

Scott   A, sō desu ka. Ikura desu ka.

Ten'in   Sore wa niman-en desu.

Scott   Chotto takai desu ne. (*points to shelf*) Ano shī dī purēyā wa ikura desu ka.

Ten'in   Are wa ichiman gosen-en desu. Are wa Sanyō desu.

Scott   Ja, are o misete kudasai.

Ten'in   Hai, shōshō omachi kudasai.

A little while later:

Scott   **Disukaunto dekimasu** ka.

Ten'in   Sō desu ne. Go-pāsento no waribiki ga dekimasu.

Scott   Mmm. Juppāsento wa?

Ten'in   E! Sore wa **muri** desu. Ja, nana-pāsento **ni shimashō**! Sābisu desu yo!

Scott   Arigatō.

sei	*made in* (**Nihon-sei** = *made in Japan*)
Nashonaru	*National* (Japanese electrical company)
dekimasu	*(I) can*
disukaunto dekimasu ka	*can you do a discount?*
muri	*impossible*
... ni shimashō	*let's decide on ...*
... ni shimasu	*decide on ...*
sābisu	*service (also: on the house)*

Practice 7

Try to answer these questions without referring to the dialogue. You may need to listen or read it through several times before attempting this exercise.

a   *Nashonaru* no shī dī purēyā wa ikura desu ka.
b   *Nashonaru* no shī dī purēyā wa doko-sei desu ka.
c   Chotto _____ desu ne. (*fill in the missing Japanese word*)
d   *Sanyō* no shī dī purēyā wa ikura desu ka.
e   Diskaunto wa nan pāsento ni shimashita ka.

Now read through the dialogue (remember to read out loud) and check you have understood it (check your answers in the **Key to the exercises** as well) before progressing to **Practice 8**.

Practice 8

Imagine that you are in a store in Akihabara. You want to buy a radio-cassette (**rajikase**). Fill in the gaps in the dialogue below using the dialogue on the previous page and its related vocabulary list to help you. Say your part out loud (you could then write it down for reinforcement).

Ten'in   Irasshaimase!
You   *Ask to see that radio-cassette over there.*
Ten'in   Hai!
You   *Ask if it is made in Japan.*
Ten'in   Iie, sore wa Amerika-sei desu.
You   *Ask how much it is.*
Ten'in   Niman-en desu.
You   *Say that's a bit expensive and ask if they do a discount.*
Ten'In   Sō desu ne. Go pāsento dekimasu.
You   *Say that you will have it (use 'kore').*

Omiyage-ya de *At the souvenir shop*

Vocabulary list

omiyage	*souvenirs*
kimono	*Japanese kimono*
ningyō	*Japanese doll*
sensu	*fan*
washi	*Japanese paper*

yukata	*Japanese cotton dressing gown*
chōchin	*paper lantern*
hashi	*chopsticks*

Practice 9

To do this exercise you first need to think back to Unit 6 where you were introduced to some of the different words used for counting types of items. You learnt these in the form of two systems, A and B. You may find it useful to look back to page 63 (**Explanation 5**) and review these ways of counting before trying the exercise below.

Using the vocabulary above, ask for each of the souvenirs below, using the correct counter/number and **o kudasai** (*may I have?*). Remember that you say the counter between **o** and **kudasai**.

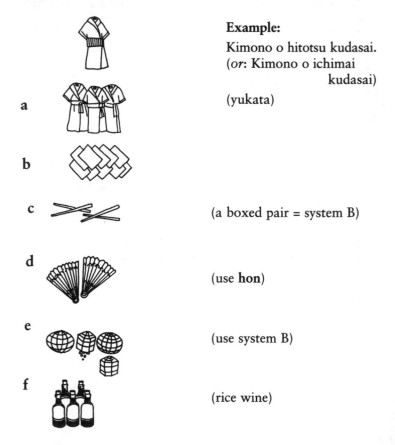

Example:
Kimono o hitotsu kudasai.
(*or*: Kimono o ichimai
 kudasai)

a   (yukata)

b

c   (a boxed pair = system B)

d   (use **hon**)

e   (use system B)

f   (rice wine)

▶ Practice 10

Emi is at a souvenir shop looking for typical Japanese gifts to take to England. Listen to the conversation and then put the dialogue below into the right order, starting with **Irasshaimase!** (You may need to listen to the recording several times.)

a   Sō desu ka. Ikura desu ka.
b   Hai. Ijō de yoroshii desu ka.
c   Hai, dōzo. Hyaku pāsento **men** desu.
d   Irasshaimase!
e   Ano ... kono o-hashi mo kudasai.
f   Sore wa kirei desu ne. Ja sore o futatsu kudasai.
g   Rokusen-en desu.
h   Hai, kore wa yonsen-en desu. Gojuppāsento men desu.
i   Ano aoi yukata o misete kudasai.
j   Chotto takai desu. Motto yasui no wa arimasu ka.

---

men   *cotton*

Test

How do you say the following in Japanese?

a   It's a bit big.
b   What size is it?
c   Do you have a cheaper one?
d   What floor is the camera department on?
e   Where is the electrical goods department?
f   Please take it out of 10,000 yen.
g   Please show me the black T-shirt over there.
h   May I have three pairs of chopsticks?

15

bīru o ippon kudasai
a bottle of beer, please

In this unit you will learn
- how to find out about eating in Japan
- how to practise ordering drinks and snacks
- how to practise ordering a meal
- how to read a coffee shop menu

Review

- Ways of counting people (Unit 3, **Explanation** 7) and items (Unit 6, **Explanation** 5)
- Saying *may I have ...* (Unit 5, **Explanation** 3)
- Asking to see something (Unit 5, **Explanation** 3)
- Asking and saying prices (Unit 6, **Explanation** 3)
- Asking *do you have any ...*? (Unit 6, **Explanation** 4)
- Food and drink items (Unit 8)
- Making suggestions and accepting (Unit 9)
- Saying what you want to do (Unit 10, **Explanation** 5)
- Expressing likes and dislikes (Unit 12, **Explanation** 1)

Famirī resutoran de *At a family restaurant*

Below is Reiko's account of eating out at a family restaurant. Before you read this account you need to understand the following phrase:

... ga taberaremasu   *you (I, they, etc.) can eat ...*

It works like the other **masu** words you have learnt except that instead of using **o** before the **masu** word, you use **ga**. For example:

Gohan ga taberaremasu.   *I can eat rice.*
Niku ga taberaremasen.   *I can't eat meat.*

Now read the passage, then check your understanding by answering the questions (in English) in **Practice 1**.

Kinō kazoku to **famirī resutoran** ni ikimashita. **Kono yōna** resutoran de wa **washoku** kara **yōshoku** made **iroirona** tabemono ga taberaremasu. Watashi wa **katsudon** o tabemashita. Shujin wa **bīfu sutēki** o tabemashita. Sorekara bīru o nihon nomimashita. Takeshi, Emi to An-san wa **mina, hambāgā** o tabemashita. **Gendai** no **wakamono** wa yōshoku ga totemo suki desu. Washoku wa amari tabemasen.

Sorekara mina kōhī o nomimashita. Kono famirī resutoran wa 'wan kappu sābisu' ga arimashita. Shujin wa takusan kōhī o nomimashita.

famirī resutoran	family restaurant (American diner-style restaurants)
kono yō (na)	this type (of)
washoku	Japanese cuisine
yōshoku	western (European and American) cuisine
iroirona	various sorts
katsudon	pork cutlets and egg on rice
bīfu sutēki	beef steak
mina	all of them, everybody
hambāgā	hamburger
gendai	these days
wakamono	young people
wan kappu sābisu	one cup service (your cup is re-filled as many times as you want at no extra charge)

Practice 1

a   Fill in the gap, in English: Yesterday I went with _____ to a family restaurant.

b   What range of food can you eat at this type of restaurant?

c   What did each person have to eat?

d   How many bottles of beer did Mr Yamaguchi drink?

e   What does Reiko say about young people these days?

🛈 About eating out (1)

The wide range of dishes, cookery styles and eating places can be quite overwhelming for the visitor to Japan. This unit will only cover a few of the dishes and types of restaurant which exist in Japan. You can divide the types of eating places into categories:

* Speciality restaurants – these offer one particular kind of cuisine, for example, a **sushi-ya** specializes in sushi, and a **soba-ya** specializes in Japanese noodles.
* **Nihon-ryōri** (*Japanese cuisine*) – these restaurants serve a variety of dishes and range from very expensive, high-class places to relatively inexpensive ones.
* Pubs and **izakaya** (*drinking places*) – these serve inexpensive food with drinks.
* 'Family' and western-style restaurants – these can be less expensive, particularly at lunchtime (this is the case with many restaurants) when they serve special **setto** (*set meals*).

- Coffee shops – these serve light snacks and coffee. You pay a higher price for coffee, so you can sit and relax for as long as you like, even if you buy only one cup.

Japanese restaurants are becoming more popular outside Japan, especially in large cities, and so you can have the opportunity to experience Japanese food without going to Japan. However, they can be expensive.

Vocabulary list

Useful expressions

chūmon shimasu	*make an order*
... ni shimasu	*I've decided on ... / I'll have ... (when ordering)*
kampai!	*cheers!*
oishisō!	*it looks delicious!*
oishikatta	*it was delicious*
mō kekkō desu	*I'm fine / I've had enough, thank you*

Vocabulary used in restaurants

nanmei-sama desu ka*	*how many people?*
kochira e, dōzo	*over here, please*
o-kimari desu ka	*have you decided?*

Yôshoku *Western food*

tabemono	*food*
chīzu sandoitchi	*cheese sandwich*
supagetti naporitan	*spaghetti neapolitan*
sarada	*salad*
piza	*pizza*
karē raisu	*curry on rice*
dezāto	*dessert*
chīzukēki	*cheesecake*
nomimono	*drink*
aisu kōhī	*iced coffee*
orenji jūsu	*orange juice*
miruku	*milk*
remon tī	*lemon tea*

*to answer, you can use the counter for people or say the number plus **mei** (**nimei** = two people).

Practice 2

Practise ordering the items below, using **... o kudasai** (*may I have ...?*) and the correct counter or number (use **hitotsu**, **futatsu**, etc. except for *bottle of beer*).

Example:  Piza o hitotsu kudasai.

a   b   c   d   e

ℹ️ About eating out (2)

Many of the restaurants and coffee shops in Japan display the types of food they serve in the form of plastic models (**shokuhin sampuru** – *food samples*). These are displayed in glass cases outside the entrance to the shop. This helps potential customers decide what food they want to eat and at which restaurant. It also can be helpful if you can't read the menu. Instead you can point to the dish you want and say **kore o kudasai**. If you are unsure what a dish is, you can point to it and say **kore wa nan desu ka**. Often the menus have pictures of all the dishes. The menus of some family restaurants and fast-food places also name the dishes in English.

▶️ Practice 3

Listen to the recording, then read the dialogue on the next page. Put the dialogue into the right order, beginning with **Irasshaimase**. Listen to the recording as many times as you need to before trying this.

If you don't have the recording, read through the sentences **a–p** and see if you can put them into the right order.

An-san to Haidi-san wa *issho ni* kissaten de hiru gohan o tabemasu.

*Heidi and Anne are going to eat lunch **together** at a coffee shop.*

a Futari desu.
b Hai! Sandoitchi hitotsu, supagetti hitotsu to kōhī o futatsu desu ne.
c E! **Dōshite?** Haidi-san wa dezāto ga totemo suki desu ne!
d (*A little later*) O-kimari desu ka.
e Hai, dōzo.
f Irasshaimase! Nanmei-sama desu ka.
g Hai, onegaishimasu.
h Hai, chīzu sandoitchi o hitotsu kudasai.
i Sō desu ne. **Demo, saikin** chotto **futorimashita**.
j Watashi wa supagetti naporitan ni shimasu.
k Watashi wa mō kekko desu.
l Kōhī o futatsu kudasai.
m Menyū o misete kudasai.
n (*After lunch*) Watashi wa dezāto o tabetai desu. Haidi-san wa?
o O-nomimono wa?

dōshite	*why?*
demo	*but*
saikin	*recently*
futorimashita	*I've put on weight*

p Hai, kochira e, dōzo.

Practice 4

How do you say the following phrases in Japanese? Use the dialogue and new vocabulary above, and speak out loud!

a How many people? Three people.
b May I see the menu, please?
c Have you decided?
d I'm going to decide on a cheese sandwich and salad.
e I love spaghetti.
f I want to eat cheesecake.
g I've had enough, thank you.

Practice 5

Use the following example of a coffee shop menu to say your side of the dialogue below it. It is written in katakana (the writing used for non-Japanese words).

If you have studied Unit 13, see if you can remember how to read this menu. Alternatively, use the katakana chart in Unit 13 to help you work out the items on the menu. There is also a rōmaji version of the menu after this activity, but try not to look at it until you've finished the activity!

```
　～　　　ルーナ　コーヒーショップ　　　～


コーヒー　　　¥４００　　　　ハンバーガー　¥６５０

アイスコーヒー　¥５００　　　　ピザ　　　　　¥７００

ミルク　　　　¥５００　　　　サラダ　　　　¥６００

ケーキ　　　　¥５００−７００　　カレー　　　¥９００
```

Waiter	Irasshaimase! Nanmei-sama desu ka.
You	*Say that you are on your own.*
Waiter	Hai, kochira e, dōzo.
You	*Ask to see the menu.*
Waiter	Hai, dōzo.
You	*Order two savoury dishes from the menu.*
Waiter	Wakarimashita. O-nomimono wa?
You	*Order something appropriate.*

A little later:

You	*Say that it was delicious.*
Waiter	Dezāto wa?
You	*Say that you're full, thank you.*

187

a bottle of beer, please

15

Rūna kōhī shoppu

Kōhī	400	Hambāgā	650
Aisu kōhī	500	Piza	700
Miruku	500	Sarada	600
Kēki	500–700	Karē	900

Fāsuto fūdo *Fast food*

Vocabulary list

Phrases used by shop assistants (*ten'in*) and waitresses (*uētoresu*)

kochira de o-meshiagari desu ka	*to eat in?*
o-mochikaeri desu ka	*to take away?*
esu, emu, eru	*small, medium, large*
kashikomarimashita	*certainly, sir/madam*
de gozaimasu	polite alternative to **desu**
gozaimasu	polite alternative to **arimasu**

Phrases used by the customer

koko de tabemasu	*I'm going to eat here*
mottekaerimasu	*I'm going to take away*
... o onegaishimasu	*please* (an alternative to **o kudasai**)
... no esu (emu/eru)	*a small (medium/large)...*
kōra no esu o onegaishimasu	*a small cola, please*

ℹ️ Pronunciation tip

Practise saying these words. Each syllable should run smoothly into the next.

O-meshiagari = o-me-shi-a-ga-ri
O-mochikaeri = o-mo-chi-ka-e-ri
Onegaishimasu = o-ne-ga-i-shi-ma-su
Mottekaerimasu – pause slightly between **mo** and **tte**

Tabemono *Food*

furaido poteto	*chips*
chīzubāgā	*cheeseburger*
teriyakibāgā	*teriyakiburger*
chikinbāgā	*chickenburger*
appuru pai	*apple pie*

Nomimono *Drink*

miruku shēku	*milk shake*
– chokorēto	*– chocolate*
– banana	*– banana*
– sutoroberī	*– strawberry*

▶ Conversation

Takeshi-kun to tomodachi no Hiroshi-kun wa 'Happībāgā' no resutoran de tabemono o kaimasu. (*Takeshi and his friend Hiroshi are going to buy some food at 'Happyburger' restaurant.*)

As you listen (or read the dialogue below) see if you can complete the table on the next page.

Uētoresu	Irasshaimase! Kochira de o-meshiagari desu ka. O-mochikaeri desu ka.
Takeshi	Mottekaerimasu.
Uētoresu	Wakarimashita. Menyū o dōzo.
Takeshi	Zembu oishisō! Hiroshi-kun, nan ni shimasu ka.
Hiroshi	Boku wa chikinbāgā to furaido poteto ni shimasu.
Uētoresu	Esu to emu to eru ga gozaimasu ga …
Hiroshi	Emu o onegaishimasu.
Uētoresu	O-nomimono wa?
Hiroshi	Sutoroberī miruku shēku no emu o onegaishimasu.

Takeshl   Boku wa chīzubāgā to furaido poteto no eru o onegaishimasu. Soshite, banana miruku shēku ni shimasu. Saizu esu o kudasai.

Uētoresu   Kashikomarimashita. Zembu de sen yonhyaku-en de gozaimasu.

Practice 6

Fill in the table below to indicate what each boy ordered and what size (where appropriate). Use 'T' for Takeshi and 'H' for Hiroshi. Then circle the correct total price that they paid.

	Item ordered?	Small?	Medium?	Large?
Hamburger				
Cheeseburger				
Chickenburger				
Potato fries				
Banana milkshake				
Strawberry milkshake				
Chocolate milkshake				

Total: **a** 1,700 yen; **b** 400 yen; **c** 1,400 yen

Practice 7

The takeaway pizza menu overleaf is written in English as well as Japanese. Use this menu and the pronunciation guide below (or try and work out how to say the words yourself by using the katakana chart in Unit 13) to say out loud your part of the dialogue. Use the dialogue below to help you (there are no answers at the back of the book).

Uētoresu   Irasshaimase! Kochira de o-meshiagari desu ka. O-mochikaori desu ka.

You   *Say you want a takeaway; ask to see the menu.*

Uētoresu   Hai, dōzo.

You   *Choose a pizza from the menu.*

Uētoresu   Ēmu to eru ga gozaimasu ga …

You   *Say the size of pizza that you want.*

Uētoresu   O-nomimono wa?

You   *Order a large coffee.*

Uētoresu   Kashikomarimashita.

Pronunciation guide:

American special	Amerikan supesharu
Fresh vegi	Furesshu bejī
Deluxe	Derakkusu
Great American	Gurēto Amerikan
Mexican DX	Mekishikan DX

PIZZA

アメリカン・スペシャル
American Special
TOPPINGS
ペパロニ、オニオン、ダブルチーズ

Ⓜ ¥1600　🄻 ¥2400

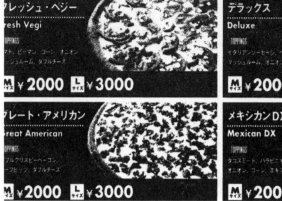

フレッシュ・ベジー
Fresh Vegi
TOPPINGS
トマト、ピーマン、コーン、オニオン、
マッシュルーム、ダブルチーズ

Ⓜ ¥2000　🄻 ¥3000

デラックス
Deluxe
TOPPINGS
イタリアンソーセージ、ペパロニ、
マッシュルーム、オニオン、ピーマン

Ⓜ ¥2000　🄻 ¥3000

グレート・アメリカン
Great American
TOPPINGS
フルクリスピーベーコン、
ビーフビッツ、ダブルチーズ

Ⓜ ¥2000　🄻 ¥3000

メキシカンDX
Mexican DX
TOPPINGS
タコスミート、ハラピニオ、トマト、
オニオン、コーン、エキストラチーズ

Ⓜ ¥2000　🄻 ¥3000

Nihon-ryōri no resutoran *Japanese-cuisine restaurants*

Vocabulary list

washoku	*Japanese food*
sushi	*vinegared rice with raw fish and other toppings*
sashimi	*raw fish*
tempura	*prawns and vegetables fried in light batter*
yakitori	*pieces of chicken and vegetables grilled on bamboo skewers*
soba	*buckwheat noodles*
udon	*thick white noodles*
miso shiru	*miso (beanpaste) soup*
tsukemono	*pickled vegetables*
teishoku	*set meal (the main dish plus rice, miso soup and pickles)*

Practice 8

To help you practise these new words, imagine that the pictures below are the plastic models outside a restaurant. Explain to a friend what each one is in answer to the question **Kore wa nan desu ka,** as in the example.

Example: Sore wa sushi desu.

Sushi

a Sashimi

b Tempura

c Soba

d Yakitori

e Miso soup

f Udon noodles

 Practice 9

Mr Yamaguchi is entertaining an American client at a Japanese restaurant. Listen to the dialogue as many times as necessary, then fill in the gaps in the dialogue below.

Uētoresu Irasshaimase! **a** ___ desu ka.

Yamaguchi **b** ___ desu.

Uētoresu Dōzo, kochira e. **c** ___ o dōzo.

Yamaguchi Ēto, bīru o **d** ___ kudasai.

Uētoresu Hai, **e** ___ ___ kudasai. (she returns with the beer)

Yamaguchi **f** ___ ___ ___ . (he pours a drink for the client)

Client **g** ___ ___ . Yamaguchi-san mo bīru o dōzo. (he pours a drink for Mr Yamaguchi)

Both men	(*raising their glasses*) h ___ !
Yamaguchi	Menyū ga i ___ .
Client	Sō desu ne. j ___ ___ wa nan desu ka.
Yamaguchi	'Sashimi teishoku' wa sashimi to k ___ ___ , ___ ___ ___ desu.
Client	Ja, sashimi teishoku ni shimasu.
Yamaguchi	Watashi wa l ___ teishoku ___ ___ .
Uētoresu	m ————— desu ka.
Yamaguchi	Ē, sashimi teishoku o n ___ to sushi teishoku o hitotsu ___. Sore ni bīru mo ___ kudasai.
Uētoresu	Kashikomarimashita.

ℹ️ About eating out (3)

You will have noticed in the previous dialogue that Mr Yamaguchi and the American client pour each other's beer. This custom is strictly adhered to in Japan. You don't pour your own drink and you don't let another person's glass become empty.

When it comes to paying the bill (**o-kanjō**), this will normally be left at your table. You take it to the cash till (**reji**) on your way out. There is no need to tip in restaurants in Japan. The service is usually included in some way.

Practice 10

Put yourself in Mr Yamaguchi's place and answer the client's questions about the following dishes. Use the dialogue above as your model and speak out loud.

a Client: 'Sushi teishoku' wa nan desu ka.
b Client: 'Yakitori teishoku' wa nan desu ka.
c Client: 'Tempura teishoku' wa nan desu ka.

Test

How do you say the following in Japanese?

a I've decided on a cheeseburger and potato fries.
b Have you decided?
c I can't eat meat. (page 181)
d That was delicious.
e I've had enough, thank you.
f Three bottles of beer, please.
g Cheers!

16

o-kane

money

In this unit you will learn

- more about Japanese money and prices
- how to change traveller's cheques at a bank
- how to send a parcel home at the post office
- how to use an international telephone

Review

- Numbers (Units 2–4, Unit 6)
- Time: **kara – made** (Unit 5, **Explanation 6**)
- Japanese money (Unit 6)
- Saying and understanding prices (Unit 6)
- Counters and buying stamps (Unit 5, **Explanations 4 & 5**)
- Giving and understanding directions (Unit 7)
- Saying you want to do something (Unit 10, **Explanation 5**)

Practice 1

1 This activity is a revision one to help you practise large numbers and prices. Look back to Practice 1 in Unit 6. This was a listening activity. This time, just practise saying each amount out loud in Japanese (answers are in the back of the book under Unit 16). If you still feel that you need more practice, try some of the other exercises in Unit 6 again (for example Practice 3, 5, 7).

Practice 2

The word for *note* in Japanese is **satsu** (for example *a five pound note* = **go-pondo satsu**) and the word for *coin* is **kōka** (for example, *a one pence coin* = **ichi-pensu kōka**).

Look back to Unit 6, **Explanation 2** at the various coins and notes in the Japanese currency. Say out loud in Japanese the amounts plus **kōka** or **satsu** as appropriate. For example, a one-yen coin is **ichi-en kōka** (there are no answers in the back of the book).

Nihon no ginkō, yūbinkyoku ni tsuite
About Japanese banks and post offices

To understand the passage below you first need to understand the key word **aiteimasu** (*is open*) and its negative form **aiteimasen** (*is not open*). For example:

Sūpā wa kuji kara rokuji   *The supermarket is open*
   made aiteimasu.   *from nine to six.*

Now read the passage below, then check your understanding by trying Practice 3.

Nihon no ginkō wa getsuyōbi kara kinyōbi made daitai kuji kara sanji made aiteimasu. **Shūmatsu** wa aiteimasen. Nihon no yūbinkyoku wa getsuyōbi kara kinyōbi made kuji kara goji made desu. Doyōbi wa kuji kara jūniji goro made desu. Nichiyōbi wa aiteimasen.

aiteimasu	*is open*
shūmatsu	*weekend*

Practice 3

Fill in the opening and closing times in the chart below using the information from the previous passage.

	Bank	Post office
Monday–Friday	–	–
Saturdays	–	–
Sundays	–	–

Vocabulary list

Ginkō de *At the bank*

ryōgae-guchi	*exchange window*
kawase rēto	*exchange rate*
genkin	*cash*
kurejitto kādo	*credit card*
toraberāzu chekku	*traveller's cheques*
pasupōto	*passport*
bank kādo	*bank card*
sain	*signature*
kyasshu mashīn	*cashpoint*
komisshon	*commission*

Useful phrases

... o kaetai desu	*I want to change ...*
... o ... ni kaetai desu	*I want to change ... into ...*
go-pondo o en ni kaetai desu	*I want to change five pounds into yen*
... en satsu de kudasai	*may I have it in ... yen notes, please?*
... en satsu de yoroshii desu ka	*is it all right in ... yen notes?*
koko ni sain shite kudasai	*please sign here*

Gaika *Foreign currency*

pondo	*pounds*
doru	*dollars*
yūro	*euro*

ℹ️ Pronunciation tips

Here are some pronunciation tips to help you master the new vocabulary. Be especially careful when saying words which derive from English. You need to make a special effort to pronounce them 'Japanese-style'. For example:

doru	do-r(u)	The last **u** is soft, almost not pronounced; the **r** is always soft – somewhere between **r** and **l**.
pondo	po-n-d(o)	The **o** is soft, almost not pronounced.
kurejitto	ku-re-ji (*pause*) to	The pause is like that in *hea**dd**ress*.
ryōgae	ryo-u-ga-e	Run the **r** and **y** together in **ryō**; **e** is pronounced as in *pen*.
kaetai	ka-e-ta-i	**E** as in *pen*; **i** as in *cheese*.

▶️ Practice 4

Before you begin this exercise, familiarize yourself with the new words. Keep saying them out loud, then use the activity as a way of testing how well you have remembered them. (There are also some useful phrases on the recording.) Say out loud in Japanese:

a   I want to change some traveller's cheques.
b   I want to change traveller's cheques into cash (or: I want to cash traveller's cheques).
c   May I have it in 5,000 yen notes, please?
d   Please sign here.
e   Excuse me, where is the exchange window?

▶️ Practice 5

Anne has gone to the bank to change some money. Listen to the recording (or read the dialogue on the next page) and work out the answers to these questions.

a   Where is Anne told the exchange window is?
b   What amount of traveller's cheques does Anne want to change?
c   What is the exchange rate on that day, and how much will Anne's cheques be in yen?
d   What is the rate of commission?
e   How does Anne want the money?

Ginkō de:

Anne   Sumimasen, ryōgae-guchi wa doko desu ka.

Ginkō-in   Asoko desu. Ano kyasshu mashīn no chikaku ni arimasu.

Anne   Dōmo arigatō.

Ryōgae-guchi de:

Anne   Sumimasen, kono toraberāzu chekku o en ni kaetai desu.

Ginkō-in   Hai. Zembu de hyaku pondo desu ne.

Anne   Ē, sō desu.

Ginkō-in   Kawase rēto wa ichi pondo hyaku nanajū-en desu. Hyaku pondo wa ichiman nanasen-en **ni narimasu**.

Anne   Komisshon wa ikura desu ka.

Ginkō-in   Komisshon wa san pāsento desu.

Anne   Hai. Ēto, gosen-en satsu to sen-en satsu de kudasai.

Ginkō-in   Hai, wakarimashita. Koko ni sain shite kudasai. Soshite pasupōto o misete kudasai.

Anne   Hai, dōzo.

---

ni narimasu   *will be*

▶ Practice 6

Listen to the recording again, but this time pause it each time the bank clerk has spoken and say out loud Anne's part using the English prompts below (**Ginkō-in** indicates when the bank clerk is speaking). You can then check your answer by continuing the recording.

Alternatively you can read the dialogue above, covering Anne's part each time. (There are no answers in the back of the book.)

> **You**   *Ask which is the exchange window.*
> **Ginkō-in**   …
> **You**   *Say thank you. Say you want to change these traveller's cheques into yen.*
> **Ginkō-in**   …
> **You**   *Agree about the amount.*
> **Ginkō-in**   …
> **You**   *Ask how much the commission is.*

Ginkō-in	...
You	*Ask for 5,000 and 1,000 yen notes.*
Ginkō-in	...
You	*Hand over your passport.*

Vocabulary list

Yūbinkyoku de *At the post office*

hagaki	*postcard*
tegami	*letter*
earoguramu	*aerogram*
kozutsumi	*parcel*
funabin de	*by seamail*
kōkūbin de	*by airmail*
kiro	*kilo*
guramu	*gramme*
... o okuritai desu	*I want to send ...*
okurimasu	*send*
tegami o kōkūbin de okuritai desu	*I want to send a letter by airmail*
naka wa nan desu ka	*what's inside?*

ℹ Pronunciation tips

kōkūbin	ko-u-ku-u-bi-n	Make sure you say the long sounds.
kozutsumi	ko-zu-tsu-mi	**Tsu** is one syllable – it may help you if you attach the **t** to **zu**.)

▶ Practice 7

Using the vocabulary above work out how to say these sentences in Japanese. Listen to the recording and practise saying some of these phrases.

- **a** I want to send a postcard.
- **b** I want to send this postcard.
- **c** I want to send a letter.
- **d** I want to send this parcel.
- **e** I want to send this parcel by seamail.
- **f** I want to send this parcel by airmail.

▶ Practice 8

Haidi-san wa kozutsumi o Doitsu ni okurimasu (*Heidi is sending a parcel to Germany*)

Listen to the recording a few times while considering these questions:

- How heavy is the parcel?
- How does she want to send it?
- What is in it?
- What else does she buy?
- How much is the total amount?

Now, without the aid of the recording, see if you can put the dialogue below into the correct order. Use the recording (or the answers at the back of the book) to check that you are right.

Follow these guidelines:

- Start by matching questions with answers
- i follows b

    a Sanzen sambyaku gojū-en desu.
    b Nihon no kimono to iroirona hon desu.
    c Funabin de onegaishimasu.
    d Kono kozutsumi o Doitsu ni okuritai desu.
    e Wakarimashita. Kono kozutsumi no naka wa nan desu ka.
    f Hai. Zembu de ikura desu ka.
    g Hai. Ichi-kiro desu ne. Sanzen-en ni narimasu.
    h Sorekara hagaki wa Doitsu made ikura desu ka.
    i Jā, koko ni sain shite kudasai.
    j Funabin desu ka. Kōkūbin desu ka.
    k Jā, nanajū-en no kitte o gomai kudasai.
    l Nanajū-en desu.
    m Gosen-en de onegaishimasu.

Practice 9

Now it's your turn. You want to send an aerogram and a parcel to England and purchase some stamps.

You	*Say you want to send this parcel to England.*
Kyoku-in	Funabin desu ka. Kōkūbin desu ka.
You	*Say by airmail.*
Kyoku-in	Gohyaku-guramu desu ne. Sen nihyaku-en ni narimasu. Kono naka wa nan desu ka.

You	*Say there are some Japanese souvenirs and a letter.*
Kyoku-in	Wakarimashita. Koko ni sain shite kudasai.
You	*Next find out how much an aerogram to England is.*
Kyoku-in	Hachijū-en desu.
You	*Now ask for ten postcard stamps.*
Kyoku-in	Hai, dōzo. Zembu de sen kyūhyaku hachijū-en ni narimasu.
You	*Hand over a 5,000 yen note.*

ℹ Public telephones

As well as public phone boxes, you can also find phones in coffee shops, bars, outside newspaper kiosks and so on. These phones (usually yellow or green) are for domestic calls only and take 10 yen or 100 yen coins. The green phones also accept **terehon kādo** (*telephone cards*).

To make an international phone call you have to use special international phones; new-style grey phones even have a monitor screen in English to help you.

Practice 10

Anne is trying to buy a phone card. Read the dialogue on the next page, then fill in the route Anne must take to find the kiosk, including any landmarks, on the following map (X is where Anne starts from).

Anne	Sumimasen, terehon kādo o kaitai desu. Doko de **utteimasu** ka.
Passer-by	Sō desu ne. **Baiten** de terehon kādo o utteimasu. Ichiban chikai baiten wa ... so desu ne. Koko kara massugu itte, tsugi no kōsaten o hidari ni magatte kudasai. Soshite, chotto itte kudasai. Baiten wa migigawa ni arimasu. Eki no mae desu.
Anne	Hai, wakarimashita. Dōmo arigatō gozaimasu.

utteimasu	*sells*
baiten	*kiosk*

Practice 11

Now imagine that Anne has stopped you in the street and give her these directions: tell her to go a little way, then turn right at the next traffic lights. Then tell her to go straight on and turn left at the crossroads. The kiosk is next to the bank.

Revision test

The following test is based on Units 14, 15 and 16.

1 Match the Japanese items on the left with the correct English description on the right.

a	Sashimi	i	Seamail
b	Baiten	ii	Set meal
c	Hashi	iii	Paper lantern
d	Teishoku	iv	Raw fish
e	Washoku	v	Western food
f	Chōchin	vi	Chopsticks
g	Funabin	vii	Kiosk
h	_____ ?	viii	Japanese food

There is one extra item on the right. When you've identified it, write it in the gap **h**, in Japanese.

2 Match the correct phrase with its English meaning.

a The exchange rate is one dollar to 70 yen.

   i Kawase rēto wa ichi yūro nanajū-en desu.

   ii Kawase rēto wa ichi doru nanajū-en desu.

   iii Toraberāzu chekku o genkin ni kaetai desu.

b How much is the commission?
  i   Komisshon wa ikura desu ka.
  ii Bank kādo wa ikura desu ka.
  iii Pasupōto wa ikura desu ka.

c What is in this parcel?
  i   Kono tegami no naka wa nan desu ka.
  ii Sono kozutsumi no naka wa nan desu ka.
  iii Kono kozutsumi no naka wa nan desu ka.

d (They) sell phone cards at kiosks.
  i   Baiten wa aiteimasu.
  ii Baiten de terehon kādo o utteimasu.
  iii Baiten de terehon kādo o kaimasu.

3 How do you say the following in Japanese?

  a It's a bit small. Do you have a larger one?
  b Please take it out of 1,000 yen.
  c A small (portion of) chips please.
  d I'll decide on a tempura set meal.
  e I want to change some traveller's cheques.
  f I want to change ten dollars into yen.
  g I want to send this letter by airmail.

17

yoyaku shitai desu

I want to make a reservation

In this unit you will learn
- about accommodation in Japan
- how to ask for information at the tourist office
- useful phrases (how many nights, type of room, etc.)
- how to make a reservation over the phone
- how to check in and out of a hotel

Review

- Giving your phone number (Unit 2, **Explanation 9**)
- Saying dates (Units 2, 4, 9)
- Counting people (Unit 3, **Explanation 7**)
- Asking *do you have ... ?* (Unit 6)
- Asking *how much?* Prices (Unit 6)
- Saying you want to do something (Unit 10, **Explanation 5**)

In the next three units you will follow Scott, Anne, Heidi and Han as they plan and carry out a trip to Hokkaido, the north island of Japan.

Familiarize yourself with the new words, then read the dialogue and try Practice 1.

▶ Vocabulary list

Shukuhaku *Accommodation*

ryokan	*Japanese inn*
hoteru	*western-style hotel*
minshuku	*family-run inn*
bijinesu hoteru	*business hotel*
penshon	*pension (family-run lodgings)*
yūsuhosuteru	*youth hostel*
washitsu	*Japanese-style room*
yōshitsu	*western-style room*
washoku	*Japanese food*
yōshoku	*western food*
tsuin	*twin*
daburu	*double*
ippaku	*one night*
nihaku	*two nights*
sampaku	*three nights*
nanpaku desu ka	*how many nights?*
heya	*room*
hitori	*per person*
(kankō) annai	*(sightseeing) information*
panfuretto/gaido	*pamphlet/guide book*

ℹ️ Remembering new words

The words for Japanese/western-style room, and Japanese/western food may seem similar and hence confusing. The first thing to remember is that **wa** refers to something Japanese, and **yō** refers to something western. (Another example is **yōfuku** – *clothes* – which you learnt in Unit 14 and actually means western-style clothes; **wafuku** is the word used for Japanese-style clothes such as **kimono**.)

The other thing to remember is that **shoku** means *food* (there are two further examples of this in the next **Vocabulary list** in this unit) and **shitsu** means *room*.

Conversation 1

Read the following dialogue, then try Practice 1.

An-san to Haidi-san wa tsūrisuto infomēshon sentā (TIC) ni imasu.
Anne and Heidi are at the TIC (tourist information centre).

Kakari-in	Irasshaimase!
Anne	Sumimasen. Raishū Hokkaidō ni ryokō shimasu. Hokkaidō no shukuhaku annai ga arimasu ka.
Kakari-in	Hai. Washitsu to yōshitsu to **dochira ga yoroshii desu ka**.
Anne	Mada **kimeteimasen**.
Kakari-in	Ja, kono Hokkaidō no gaido o dōzo. Ni-**pēji** wa ryokan no annai desu. Ryokan no heya wa daitai washitsu desu ne. Tabemono mo washoku desu. Hitori ippaku rokusen-en kara desu.
Heidi	Chotto takai desu ga ii **keiken** desu ne.
Kakari-in	Sō desu ne. Soshite san-pēji wa hoteru no annai desu. Hoteru no heya wa yōshitsu desu. Tabemono mo yōshoku desu.
Anne	Tsuin no heya wa ikura desu ka.
Kakari-in	Tsuin wa gosen-en kara desu. Soshite yūsuhosuteru wa yon-pēji desu. Hitori ippaku nisen-en kara desu. Heya wa yōshitsu de tabemono wa yōshoku desu.
Heidi	Sore wa yasui desu ne.
Anne	Sō desu ne. Watashi no uchi de kono gaido o yomimashō.
Kakarl-ln	Hokkaidō no **chizu** mo dōzo.
Anne	Dōmo arigatō.

kakari-in	attendant, person in charge
dochira ga yoroshii desu ka	which would you prefer?
kimeteimasen	(we) haven't decided
pēji	page
keiken	experience
chizu	map

Practice 1

Fill in the table below using the information in the dialogue. Write Y for *yes* and N for *no*.

	Japanese inn	Hotel	Youth hostel
Price/night Per person? Per room? Japanese room? Western room? Japanese food? Western food? Page number (in guide book)			

Practice 2

Using the previous dialogue and vocabulary, how would you say the following phrases in Japanese? Speak out loud.

a   Do you have any sightseeing information for Hokkaido?

b   Do you have a map of Tokyo?

c   Which do you prefer – Japanese or western-style rooms?

d   How much is a twin room?

e   How much is a single room (**shinguru**)?

f   Let's read this guide book at my house.

Anne, Heidi, Scott and Han are planning their trip at the Yamaguchi house. First familiarize yourself with the new words and phrases on the next page.

Vocabulary list

moshi moshi	*hello* (used on the phone)
yoyaku (shimasu)	*reservation* (make a reservation)
shokuji	*meals*
haitteimasu	*it is included*
chōshoku	*breakfast*
yūshoku	*evening meal*
... o onegaishimasu	*please* (like **... o kudasai**)

Polite language (used by receptionists, shop assistants, etc.)

de gozaimasu	(polite form of **desu** – *is*)
gozaimasu	(polite form of **arimasu** – *have*)
deshō	(polite form of **desu**)
kashikomarimashita	*certainly*
wakarimashita	*certainly* (I've understood)
nanmei-sama	*how many people?* (polite form of **nannin**)

ℹ Learning tip

You've already learnt that **asagohan** means *breakfast* and **bangohan** means *evening meal* (Unit 8, **Explanation 6**). The words **chōshoku** and **yūshoku** tend to be used in hotels and restaurants.

And remember that **shoku** means *food* (see ℹ on page 205).

▶ Practice 3

Han-san wa Sapporo yūsuhosuteru ni denwa o shimasu. *Han is phoning Sapporo youth hostel.*

Listen to the conversation (or read the dialogue) and find out the following information.

a What date is Han making the reservation for?
b How many nights is it for?
c How much is it per person per night?
d How much is breakfast? And how much is the evening meal?
e What information is requested of Han at the end?

Kakari-in	Moshi moshi. Sapporo yūsuhosuteru de gozaimasu.
Han	Sumimasen, nigatsu mikka ni yoyaku o shitai desu. Heya ga arimasu ka.
Kakari-in	Hai, shōshō omachi kudasai. Nanmei-sama desu ka.
Han	Yonin desu. **Josei** ga futari to **dansei** ga futari desu.
Kakari-in	Hai, gozaimasu. Nanpaku de gozaimasu ka.
Han	Sampaku desu. Mikka, yokka to itsuka o onegaishimasu. Ippaku ikura desu ka.
Kakari-in	Hitori nisen gohyaku-en de gozaimasu.
Han	Shokuji wa haitteimasu ka.
Kakari-in	Iie, chōshoku wa roppyaku-en de yūshoku wa sen-en de gozaimasu.
Han	Ja, chōshoku mo onegaishimasu.
Kakari-in	Hai, wakarimashita. O-namae to o-denwa bangō o onegaishimasu.

---

josei	woman/female
dansei	man/male

Now listen to the conversation again while reading the dialogue to check your understanding before moving on to Practice 4.

▶ Practice 4

Anne, Scott, Han and Heidi are also planning to go skiing in Hokkaidō; they plan to stay in another youth hostel in a place called Ōnuma, near a ski resort. You are going to make the reservation for them using the information provided in the dialogue below.

Listen to the receptionist, then pause the recording and say your part. Then switch on the recording again and check that you said it correctly (if you don't have the recording, check your answers in the **Key to the exercises**). Try not to refer back to the dialogue in Practice 3. **Gambatte!**

Kakari-in	Moshi moshi, Ōnuma yūsuhosuteru de gozaimasu.
You	*Say you want to make a reservation for February 6th.*
Kakari-in	Hai, nanmei-sama de gozaimasu ka.
You	*Say it's for four people.*
Kakari-in	Hai, gozaimasu. Nanpaku de gozaimasu ka.
You	*Say it's for two nights.*
Kakari-in	Hai, wakarimashita.

You	*Ask how much it is per night.*
Kakari-in	Hitori sanzen-en de gozaimasu.
You	*Ask if meals are included.*
Kakari-in	Iie, chōshoku wa gohyaku-en de yūshoku wa sen nihyaku-en de gozaimasu.
You	*Say you'll have breakfast and dinner then.*
Kakari-in	Kashikomarimashita. O-namae to o-denwa-bangō o onegaishimasu.
You	*Give your name and phone number.*

ℹ About Japanese inns

Heidi said that although it was expensive, it would be a good experience to stay in a **ryokan**. Staying in a Japanese inn is certainly a unique experience. Guests have the opportunity to sleep on futon, bathe in communal baths (and in spa water at hot-spring resorts), and generally to receive a very high standard of service. Meals are usually served in your room and provide you with the opportunity to try a wide range of traditional Japanese dishes.

Staying in a **ryokan** can be very expensive, but there are other Japanese inns and pensions at lower prices where you can have a similar experience.

▶ Practice 5

Here is an example of a cheaper style of Japanese inn.

25	*KOIWA*

旅館都貴 〒133 東京都江戸川区南小岩5-21-1
☞ 小岩駅南口のフラワーロード商店街を歩いて約
10分、渡辺クリニック右入る

Ryokan TOKI
TEL (03) 3657-1747
FAX (03) 3671-0655
5-21-1, Minamikoiwa,
Edogawa-ku, Tokyo 133
• city. 2F. wooden bldg

Type	Japanese Style		Western style	Meals	Japanese	Western
	without bath	with bath	with bath	Breakfast	800	700
For 1 person	5,000	5,500	5,500	Dinner	1,500	
For 2 people	8,000	8,500	8,500			
For 3 people	11,000	12,000	–			
# of rooms	3	10	4			

Japanese inn group Ryokan Toki

Listen to the phone conversation between a customer and a receptionist and fill in the gaps in the dialogue below.

If you don't have the recording, see how much you can work out using the advert and other dialogues, then fill in any gaps using the answers in the **Key to the exercises** and use the dialogue as a reading activity to check your understanding.

Vocabulary list

yokushitsu	*bathroom*
yokushitsu ga aru heya	*a room with a bathroom*
yokushitsu ga nai heya	*a room without a bathroom*

Receptionist	a	_____ _____, Ryokan Toki _____ _____ .
Customer	b	_____ _____ ni yoyaku shitai desu.
Receptionist	c	_____ _____ desu ka.
Customer	d	_____ desu. Ippaku _____ _____ _____.
Receptionist	e	_____ deshō ka. _____ deshō ka.
Customer	f	Washitsu o _____.
Receptionist	g	_____ ga aru heya wa hassen _____ de, yokushitsu ga nai heya wa _____ de gozaimasu.
Customer	h	_____ wa haitteimasu ka.
Receptionist	i	Iie, _____ wa happyaku-en de, _____ wa sen gohyaku-en de gozaimasu.
Customer	j	Ja, _____ no heya to shokuji o _____.
Receptionist	k	Kashikomarimashita. _____ to _____ o onegaishimasu.

Practice 6

Anne, Scott, Han and Heidi have decided, as part of their trip to Hokkaidō, to treat themselves to one night's stay at a reasonably priced **ryokan** in the famous hot spring resort of Noboribetsu. The information about the **ryokan** is printed on the next page.

You are the receptionist, and when Scott phones the **ryokan** you use this information to answer his questions.

Use the dialogues from Practice 4 and 5 to help you if necessary, but see how much you can understand without referring to them. (You can use the polite alternatives of **desu** – **de gozaimasu** – and **arimasu** – **gozaimasu** – if you are feeling brave, answers are given in both styles.)

3	NOBORIBETSU SPA	花鐘亭 はなや 〒059-05 登別市登別温泉町134
		☞登別駅から登別温泉行バス、花屋前バス停下車

Ryokan Hanaya
TEL (0143) 84-2521
FAX (0143) 84-2240
134, Noboribetsu-Onsenmachi,
Noboribetsu City, Hokkaido 059-05
• mountain resort. 4F. RC

Type	Japanese style		Western style
	without bath	with bath	without bath
For 1 person	5,500	–	5,500
For 3 people	10,000	12,000	10,000
For 3 people	15,000	18,000	–
# of rooms	13	5	3

Surcharge(s)			
Consumption tax 3%			
Special local consumption tax 3%		Meals	Japanese	Western
Spa tax ¥150 per person		Breakfast	1,000~	1,000~
		Dinner	2,000~	–

Noboribetsu ryokan advert

You	*Say 'hello' and the name of the inn.*
Scott	Nigatsu nanoka ni yoyaku shitai desu.
You	*Ask how many people it is for.*
Scott	Yonin desu. Ippaku ikura desu ka.
You	*Ask him if he wants Japanese or western-style rooms.*
Scott	Washitsu o onegaishimasu.
You	*Give the information for four people (use 2 × 2 people) with and without a bathroom.*
Scott	Shokuji wa haitteimasu ka.
You	*Say 'no' and give the prices of meals.*
Scott	Ja, niman-en no heya to shokuji o onegaishimasu.
You	*Now ask for his name and telephone number.*

ℹ️ About Japanese hotels

There is a wide variety of western-style hotels, ranging from the expensive and high-class type such as the New Otani Hotel in Tokyo, to the inexpensive business-style hotel aimed at business travellers in need of basic and reasonably priced rooms. A well-known type of business hotel is the capsule hotel – so-called because the rooms are about the size of the single bed within them, plus a television and light. They are usually located near to stations and are popular with city workers who have missed the last train home and need somewhere cheap to stay the night.

Conversation 2

Read the dialogue below then try Practice 7.

Mr Yamaguchi has been working late, entertaining some clients, and has missed the last train home. He tries to book into a **kapuseru hoteru** (capsule hotel).

Yamaguchi	Konban heya ga arimasu ka.
Kakari-in	Sumimasen, konban wa heya ga arimasen. Asoko no hoteru wa heya ga arimasu.
Yamaguchi	Dōmo arigatō.

At the next hotel:

Yamaguchi	Sumimasen, heya ga arimasu ka.
Kakari-in	Hai, gozaimasu.
Yamaguchi	Ippaku onegaishimasu.
Kakari-in	O-hitori-sama desu ka.
Yamaguchi	Hai, hitori desu.
Kakari-in	Koko ni o-namae to **go-jūsho** o onegaishimasu.
Yamaguchi	Hai, dōzo.
Kakari-in	Dewa, kochira e dōzo.

The next morning:

Yamaguchi	**Chekku auto** o onegaishimasu.
Kakari-in	Hai, kashikomarimashita. Zembu de kyūsen-en de gozaimasu.
Yamaguchi	Ja, ichiman-en de onegaishimasu.
Kakari-in	Arigatō gozaimasu. Sen-en no **otsuri** de gozaimasu.

go-jūsho	*address* (**go** is used when asking for someone else's address)
chekku auto	*bill/check out*
otsuri	*change*

Practice 7

Read the Japanese statements overleaf and circle **hai** if it is true, and **iie** if it is false.

saisho	*first*

a   Saisho no kapuseru hoteru ni heya ga arimashita. (hai/iie).
b   Tsugi no hoteru ni heya ga arimashita. (hai/iie)
c   Yamaguchi-san wa nihaku shimashita. (hai/iie)
d   Yamaguchi-san wa namae to denwa-bangō o kakimashita. (hai/iie)
e   Heya wa zembu de 9,000-en deshita. (hai/iie)

Practice 8

Without looking at the previous dialogue, how do you say the following phrases in Japanese?

a   Excuse me, do you have a room for tonight?
b   One night, please.
c   May I have your name and address?
d   May I have the bill, please?
e   Please take it out of 10,000 yen.
f   Here's 1,000 yen change.

Now check your answers with the dialogue. (There are no answers at the back of the book.)

Test

1   Select the correct Japanese phrase for each of these English phrases.

a   Hello, I'd like to make a reservation.
   i   Moshi moshi, heya ga arimasu ka.
   ii   Moshi moshi, washitsu o onegaishimasu.
   iii Moshi moshi, yoyaku o shitai desu.

b   Are meals included?
   i   Chōshoku wa haiteimasu ka.
   ii   Shokuji wa haitteimasu ka.
   iii Shokuji wa haitteimasen.

c   How much is it for three nights?
   i   Ippaku ikura desu ka.
   ii   Sampaku onegaishimasu.
   iii Sampaku ikura desu ka.

d   May I have your name and phone number?
   i   O-denwa bangō o onegaishimasu.
   ii   O-namae to go-jūsho o onegaishimasu.
   iii O-namae to o-denwa bangō o onegaishimasu.

    e   A room with a bathroom costs 5,000 yen.

        i   Yokushitsu ga nai heya wa gosen-en desu.

        ii   Yokushitsu ga aru heya wa yonsen-en desu.

        iii Yokushitsu ga aru heya wa gosen-en desu.

2   Match the Japanese words with their English meanings.

a	minshuku	i	a double room
b	yōshitsu	ii	a Japanese inn
c	ryokan	iii	a Japanese-style room
d	washoku	iv	a business hotel
e	daburu	v	family-run, Japanese-style inn
f	washitsu	vi	a western-style room
g	bijinesu hoteru	vii	Japanese cuisine
h	_____	viii	(per) person

There is one English phrase extra. How do you say this in Japanese? (Complete **h**.)

18

kono densha wa Sapporo-yuki desu ka

is this the train for Sapporo?

In this unit you will learn
- how to buy train and underground tickets
- how to ask where the platform is
- about food on trains
- how to catch a taxi and give directions to the driver

Review

- Saying the time (Unit 5, **Explanation 4**)
- Saying *this* and *that* (Unit 5, **Explanation 2**)
- Saying *from* and *to* (Unit 5, **Explanation 6**)
- Asking for something (Unit 5, **Explanation 3**)
- Money and prices (Unit 6)
- Counting different items (Unit 6, **Explanation 5**)
- Asking for and giving directions (Unit 7)
- The words for *go* and *return* (Unit 9, **Explanation 1**)
- Transport (Unit 10)
- Saying how long it takes (Unit 10, **Explanation 4**)
- Saying you want to (Unit 10, **Explanation 5**)
- Giving the location (Unit 7, **Explanation 3**, Unit 12, **Explanation 3**)

Familiarize yourself with these new words (test yourself by covering first the English words and then the Japanese words), then listen to or read out loud the conversation below.

Vocabulary list

jidō ken baiki	*automatic ticket machine*
... made ikura desu ka	*how much is it to ...?*
hōmu	*platform*
kippu	*ticket*
seisanjo	*fare adjustment office*
haraimasu	*pay*

▶ Conversation 1

It's the first day of the trip to Hokkaido and Anne and Heidi are at Shimbashi underground station.

Jidō ken baiki de *(at the ticket machines)*:

Anne	Ueno eki made ikura desu ka.
Heidi	Ano **chizu** o mimashō!
Anne	'Ueno' no **kanji** ga wakarimasu ka.
Heidi	Wakarimasen. *(sees a passer-by)* Sumimasen, Ueno made ikura desu ka.
Passer-by	Ueno desu ka. Hyaku rokujū-en desu.
Heidi	Arigatō gozaimashita.

Hōmu de *(on the platform)*:

Anne	A! Sukotto-san wa asoko desu. Sukotto-san!
Scott	Ohayō.
Heidi	Ohayō. **Anata no** kippu wa ikura deshita ka.
Scott	Nanajū-en deshita.
Anne	Are! Ueno made hyaku rokujū-en desu yo.
Scott	**Shimpai shinai de!** Ueno eki no seisanjo de **nokori** o haraimasu.

chizu	*map*
kanji	*Japanese writing*
anato no ...	*your ...*
shimpai shinai de!	*don't worry!*
nokori	*the rest*

Practice 1

Answer these questions in English.

- a Where do Anne and Heidi want to travel to?
- b What can't they understand?
- c How much does a ticket cost?
- d How much did Scott pay and why isn't he worried about this?

ℹ About the Japanese underground

There is an underground (or subway) system in ten of the major cities in Japan, including Tokyo, Kyoto, Osaka and Sapporo. The Tokyo system is the most complex, and often there is no English written on the ticket machines. If you don't know how much to pay, you can buy the cheapest ticket, as Scott did, and pay the difference at the **seisanjo** *(fare adjustment office)* at your destination. There are no penalties for doing this. Alternatively, you can do as Anne and Heidi did – ask someone!

Unlike on the ticket machines, all the station names are written in **rōmaji** (Japanese written in English) as well as Japanese (see the example below). Not only are the station names supplied, but the previous and the next station are also shown so that you can check when your station is coming up.

Practice 2

Without looking back at the dialogue, can you work out how Anne, Heidi and Scott said these phrases in Japanese?

- **a** Excuse me, how much is it to Ueno station?
- **b** Let's look at that map over there!
- **c** Do you understand the Japanese writing (kanji) for 'Ueno'?
- **d** It's 160 yen to Ueno.
- **e** I will pay the rest at the fare adjustment office.

Practice 3

Now it's your turn! You are at Shinjuku station and you want to go to Ginza (exclusive and expensive shopping area). Stop a passer-by and say:

You	*Excuse me, how much is it to Ginza?*
Passer-by	160-en desu.
You	*Excuse me, could you repeat that please?*
Passer-by	160-en desu.
You	*Repeat the price and say thank you.*

Vocabulary list

sen	*line*
(example) **Hibiya-sen**	*the Hibiya line*
nani sen	*which line?*
eki-in	*rail employee*
norikaemasu	*change, transfer*
norikaete kudasai	*please change*
... sen ni norikaete kudasai	*please change to the ... line*
doko de norikaemasu ka	*where do I change at?*

ℹ️ Pronunciation tip

Norikaemasu   No-ri-ka-e-ma-su (**e** is spoken as the *e* in *met*; the final **su** is soft – the **u** is hardly spoken)

▶ Conversation 2

Han has a more complicated journey to make to Ueno from Kiba. He is asking how to get there at the information office. Look at the map below as you listen to the recording (or read the dialogue).

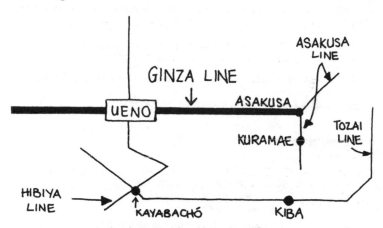

Han	Sumimasen, Ueno ni ikitai desu. Doko de norikaemasu ka.
Eki-in	Hai, koko kara Kayabachō ni itte kudasai. Soshite, Hibiya-sen ni norikaete kudasai.
Han	Kayabachō de norikaemasu ne?
Eki-in	Hai, sō desu. Hibiya-sen ni norikaemasu.
Han	Wakarimashita. Arigatō gozaimashita.

Practice 4

Can you match the Japanese questions with the correct answers without looking at the dialogue above? (You may need to listen to the recording several times first.)

a   Han-san wa doko ni   i   Kayabachō de norikaemasu.
    ikimasu ka.   ii   Hibiya-sen ni norikaemasu.
b   Doko de norikaemasu ka iii Ueno ni ikimasu.
c   Nani sen ni norikaemasu
    ka.

Notice **doko** *de* (*at which station?*); **nani sen** *ni* (*to which line?*)

Practice 5

Look again at the map and this time imagine that Han is making the journey to Ueno from Kuramae. Say out loud the conversation between Han and the station employee using the English prompts below (? indicates information you must find from the map).

Han	a	*Says 'excuse me' and that he wants to go to Ueno.*
Eki-in	b	*Tells him to go from here (Kuramae) to ? station. Then to change to the ? line.*
Han	c	*Checks that he changes at ? station.*
Eki-in	d	*Says 'that's right' and repeats which line he should change to.*
Han	e	*Says he's understood and 'thank you'.*

Ueno eki de *At Ueno station*

Vocabulary list

midori no mado-guchi	*green window*
kaimasu	*buy*
kaisatsu-guchi	*ticket gate*
kippu uriba	*ticket office*
katamichi	*single*
ōfuku	*return*
shitei seki	*reserved seat*
jiyū seki	*unreserved seat*
... yuki	*destined for ...*
Sapporo-yuki	*destined for Sapporo*
waribiki kippu	*discount ticket*

Familiarize yourself with the new words above, then listen to or read **Conversation 3**. Try Practice 6 when you have listened to or read it at least once.

▶ Conversation 3

Ueno eki de Han-san wa An to Haidi to Sukotto ni aimasu. At
Ueno station Han meets up with Anne, Heidi and Scott.

Anne	Han-san, ohayō!
Han	A! Yokatta. Ja, shinkansen no kippu o kaimashō.
Heidi	Doko de kippu o kaimasu ka.
Anne	Asoko desu. Ano midori no mado-guchi de.
Scott	Boku ga kippu o kaitai desu.
Anne	Dōzo!
Scott	Sumimasen, Sapporo-yuki no kippu o yonmai kudasai.
Eki-in	Katamichi desu ka, ōfuku desu ka.
Scott	Chotto …
Anne	(*whispers*) Ōfuku desu.
Scott	E? Hai, ōfuku o onegaishimasu.
Eki-in	Shitei seki desu ka, jiyū seki desu ka.
Scott	Ēto …
Heidi	Jiyū seki wa **motto yasui** desu ne.
Scott	Ja, jiyū seki o onegaishimasu.
Eki-in	Hai, zembu de …
Han	(*whispers*) Sukotto-san, waribiki kippu desu yo!
Scott	A! Sumimasen, **watashitachi** wa gakusei desu. Waribiki kippu ga arimasu ka.
Eki-in	Arimasu yo. **Pasupōto** o misete kudasai … Arigatō gozaimasu. Ja, zembu de rokuman nisen-en desu.
Scott	Hai, nanaman-en de onegaishimasu.
Anne, Han, Heidi	Sukotto-san, **omedetō**!

motto yasui	*cheaper*
watashitachi	*we*
pasupōto	*passport*
omedetō	*congratulations*

Practice 6

Try this exercise without referring back to the dialogue. Some of
the Japanese sentences below are true and some are false. Write
a circle (**maru**) in the brackets next to the ones you think are
true and a cross (**batsu**) next to the ones you think are false.

a Sukotto-san wa Sapporo-yuki no kippu o kaimashita. ( )
b Kaisatsuguchi de kippu o kaimashita. ( )
c Kippu o go-mai kaimashita. ( )
d Katamichi no kippu o kaimashita. ( )
e Gakusei no waribiki kippu ga arimasen deshita. ( )
f Jiyū seki no kippu o kaimashita. ( )
g Kippu wa zembu de 6200-en deshita. ( )

Practice 7

Use the dialogue and new words as necessary to work out how to say the following.

a Where do we buy the tickets for the Shinkansen?
b I'd like four tickets for Kyōto, please.
c Return or single?
d I'd like a reserved seat, please.
e Do you have any discount tickets?
f Please show me your passports.

Practice 8

Now it's your turn. You're going to Hiroshima by bullet train: you want two single tickets for unreserved seats and you want a discounted ticket for the person travelling with you who is a child (**kodomo**). Use this information to complete the conversation below. Speak out loud.

You *Say 'excuse me', then state your destination and how many tickets you want.*
Eki-in Katamichi desu ka, ōfuku desu ka.
You *Give the information required.*
Eki-in Shitei seki desu ka, jiyū seki desu ka.
You *Give the information required, then ask about the child discount ticket.*
Eki-in Hai arimasu yo.

ℹ️ About discount tickets

Visitors to Japan can purchase a Japan rail pass which can be used during a trip to Japan on JR (Japan Railways) trains, buses and ferries. As Japan Rail travel is very expensive, the rail pass can mean huge savings. You must purchase the voucher for the pass outside Japan (travel agents will have details) and exchange it for a pass when you arrive in Japan. You have to enter Japan under the status of 'temporary visitor' to be eligible to use the pass. Anne, Scott, Heidi and Han do not have passes because they have a study visa; however, other discounts are available, for example for group travel or for long-distance round-trips.

Vocabulary list

nanban-sen	*what platform numbers? (Lit. what track number?)*
tsugi no ...	*the next*
chotto matte kudasai	*Please wait a while*

Practice 9

Han is asking for some information at the travel centre (**ryokō sentā**) on the station. Look at the new words, then put the dialogue below into the correct order. Begin with **Sumimasen ...**

a Rokuban-sen desu.
b Jūichiji desu.
c Sumimasen, Sapporo-yuki no densha wa nanban-sen desu ka.
d Tsugi no densha wa nanji desu ka.
e Arigatō gozaimashita.

Practice 10

Now it's your turn to find out about the Hiroshima train. Try to say your part out loud from memory.

You *Say 'excuse me' and ask what platform your train goes from.*
Eki-in Yonban-sen desu.
You *Ask what time the next train is.*
Eki-in 4-ji desu.
You *Repeat the time and say thank you.*

Practice 11

Read the following conversation.

Anne Sumimasen, kono densha wa Sapporo-yuki desu ka.
Passer-by Iie, sono densha wa Yamagata-yuki desu. Tsugi no densha wa Sapporo-yuki desu. Chotto matte kudasai.

Now try to re-write the dialogue so that Anne asks if this is the train for Hiroshima; the answer is 'no, it's the Ōsaka train; it's the next train that is for Hiroshima'.

🅘 Inside the bullet train

O-bentō or *packed lunches*, usually comprising rice with meat or fish and various pickles, are beautifully presented in a box with a small pair of wooden chopsticks and can be bought at railway stations or on board bullet trains and express trains from as little as 600 yen. These **o-bentō** are known as **ekiben** (**eki** means *station* and **ben** is a shortened form of **o-bentō**). Many railway stations have their own speciality **ekiben** – the two mentioned in the dialogue on the next page can actually be bought at stations along the train line between Hakodate and Sapporo, in South Hokkaido.

Railway food vendors (**uriko**) walk up and down the length of the bullet train selling a wide assortment of **o-bentō** and **omiyage** (*souvenirs*). They use very polite Japanese language, bowing and apologizing for the interruption as they enter and leave each carriage.

Vocabulary list

tōi	*far*
ikura	*salmon roe*
(o)-bentō	*packed lunches*
ekiben	*packed train lunches*
kani-meshi	*crab and rice*
tōchaku shimasu	*arrive*

Polite language (used by railway food vendors)

shitsurei itashimasu	*excuse me* (said when entering the train carriage)
... ikaga desu ka	*how about ...?* (polite version of **... dō desu ka** – Unit 9)
gozaimasu	*have* (polite version of **arimasu**)
de gozaimasu } **deshō** }	*is* (polite version of **desu**)

▶ Practice 12

Listen to the conversation taking place on the bullet train and fill in the gaps in the dialogue below. Listen several times before you try to fill in the gaps.

Scott	a	An-san! Sapporo made ___ ___ kakarimasu ka.
Anne	b	___ ___ gurai desu yo.
Scott	c	___ desu ne! Nani o shimashō ka.
Uriko		(*enters carriage pushing food trolley*) Shitsurei itashimasu.
Scott	d	A! O-bentō o ___ .
Uriko		(*walking down carriage*)
	e	___ o-bentō wa ___ deshō ka.
Scott		Sumimasen.
Uriko		Hai!
Scott	f	Ekiben wa ___ ___ ___ ___.
Uriko	g	Ikura-bentō to kani-meshi ga ___ .
Scott	h	E? An-san, 'kani' wa ___ ___ nan desu ka.
Anne	i	'Crab' desu. ___ desu yo.
Scott	j	Sō desu ka. Ja, kani-meshi o ___ to ocha ___ ___ .
Uriko	k	Kashikomarimashita. Zembu de ___ de gozaimasu.
Scott		Sen-en de onegaishimasu.
Uriko	l	Arigatō gozaimasu. Hyaku-en no ___ de gozaimasu.

A little later:

Scott	m	Aa! Oishikatta desu. An-san, nanji ni ___ ___ ka.
Anne	n	___ ___ desu.
Scott		Ima nanji desu ka.
Anne	o	Ima ___ desu.
Scott	p	E! Mada desu ne. Hontō ni tōi desu. ___ ___ ___ ___ .

Anne, Heidi and Han   Sukotto-san, **Shizuka ni!**

---

shizuka ni   *be quiet*

Sapporo eki de *At Sapporo station*

Vocabulary list

takushī noriba	*taxi rank*
untenshu	*driver*
yoku dekimashita	*well done*
nan demo nai desu	*it's nothing*

▶ Practice 13

Listen to the dialogue and, as Scott gives the directions to the taxi driver from Sapporo station, follow them on the map and decide whether the youth hostel is at the place marked **a**, **b** or **c**. (The arrows and points (**i**), (**ii**), (**iii**) refer to Practice 15; you don't need them for this exercise.)

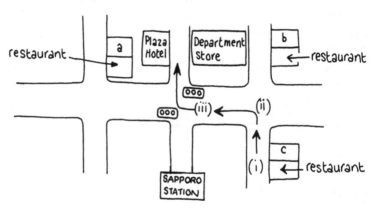

▶ Practice 14

Listen to the taxi dialogue again, then see if you can say these phrases in Japanese. Or try without the recording and check the answers in the **Key to the exercises**.

    a   Let's go by taxi.
    b   Where is the taxi rank?
    c   I want to go to Sapporo youth hostel.
    d   Do you have a youth hostel map?

e   The youth hostel is over there. It's next to that restaurant.

Practice 15

Now it's your turn. Use the map in Practice 13 to give the following directions. You are setting out from the restaurant next to **c** on the map and are taking a taxi to the Plaza Hotel.

You	*Say where you want to go.*
Untenshu	Sore wa doko deshō ka.
You	*Give the first direction (i). And then the next direction (ii)*
Untenshu	Koko desu ka.
You	*Say 'that's right'. Now give the third direction (iii).*
Untenshu	Hai, wakarimashita.
You	*Say that the hotel is over there, then give its exact location.*
Untenshu	Koko desu ne. Roppyaku-en desu.
You	*Say 'thanks' and hand over a 1,000 yen note.*
Untenshu	Yonhyaku-en no otsuri desu. Arigatō gozaimashita.

ℹ️ About taxis

Taxi ranks are found in main public places such as stations and large hotels. If a taxi is vacant, there will be a red light in the windscreen; a green light shows that it is occupied. The doors of taxis are opened and closed automatically by the driver. In large cities it is a good idea to have a map or address of where you want to go, to show the driver. There is no custom of tipping – the exact fare will be shown on the meter.

Test

1   Say the following sentences in Japanese.

   a   Ask a passer-by how much it is to Shinjuku station.
   b   Say that you want to go to Shibuya station.
   c   Ask where you change.
   d   Ask where you buy tickets for the bullet train.
   e   Ask for one ticket to Kyōto.
   f   Tell a taxi driver to turn left at the next traffic lights.
   g   Ask which platform the train for Maebashi goes from.

2   Choose the correct English equivalent for each of the following Japanese phrases.

a   Tōzai-sen ni norikaete kudasai.
    i   Change to the Tozai line.
    ii   Change at Tozai.
    iii Take the Tozai train.

b   Katamichi desu ka. Ōfuku desu ka.
    i   Do you want a single ticket?
    ii   Do you want a single or a return?
    iii Do you want a packed lunch?

c   Jiyūseki desu ka. Shitei seki desu ka.
    i   I'll have a reserved seat, please.
    ii   I'll have an unreserved seat, please.
    iii Do you want a reserved or unreserved seat?

d   Hachi-ji ni tōchaku shimasu.
    i   We arrive at 7 o'clock.
    ii   We arrive at 8 o'clock.
    iii We leave at 8 o'clock.

e   O-cha, o-bentō wa ikaga deshō ka.
    i   Does anyone want green tea or packed lunches?
    ii   May I have green tea and a packed lunch?
    iii We have green tea and packed lunches.

19

sukī ni ikimashō

let's go skiing!

In this unit you will learn
- how to ask for information about sightseeing
- how to find out about places and leisure activities
- how to hire sports equipment
- how to book a theatre ticket by phone
- about traditional Japanese theatre

Review

- Dates (Units 2, 4, 9)
- Time (Unit 5)
- Prices (Unit 6)
- Counters (Unit 6)
- Understanding and saying directions (Unit 7)
- Making suggestions and invitations (Unit 9)
- Time expressions (Units 9, 10)
- Saying what you want to do (Unit 10)
- Saying likes and dislikes (Unit 12)
- Saying what you are good at (Unit 12)
- Floors (Unit 14)

Kankō *Sightseeing*

Vocabulary list

ryokō annai-jo	*tourist information office*
gaido bukku	*guide book*
chizu	*map*
hakubutsukan	*museum*
daigaku	*university*
Ainu kinenkan	*Ainu memorial museum*
kōen	*park*
Yuki-Matsuri	*Snow Festival*
matsuri	*festival*
basu noriba	*bus stop*
bīru-en	*beer garden*
... wa, doko desu ka/doko ni arimasu ka	*where is the ...?*
kankō	*sightseeing*
kankō basu	*sightseeing bus*

▶ Conversation 1

On their first morning in Sapporo, Heidi, Anne, Scott and Han have gone to the tourist information office. Once you have learnt the new words on the previous page, listen to the recording (or read the dialogue below) as you look at the map of Sapporo in Practice 1. See if you can fill in the information required.

Ryokō annai-jo de (*At the tourist information office*):

Heidi	Sumimasen, Sapporo no chizu ga arimasu ka.
Kakari-in	Hai, dōzo.
Anne	Yuki-matsuri wa doko desu ka.
Kakari-in	Koko desu. Ōdōri-kōen no naka desu.
Han	Sapporo ni omoshiroi hakubutsukan ga arimasu ka.
Kakari-in	Ē. Hokkaidō daigaku no chikaku ni Ainu kinenkan ga arimasu.
Heidi	Sore ni, Sapporo no kankō o shitai desu. Kankō basu ga arimasu ka.
Kakari-in	Arimasu yo. Kankō basu noriba wa koko ni arimasu. Eki no mae desu. Tsugi no basu wa jūichiji desu.
Scott	Ano ... **yūmeina** bīru-en wa doko ni arimasu ka.
Kakari-in	Sapporo bīru-en desu ne. Koko desu. Sōgō depāto no chikaku ni arimasu. Gozen jūichi-ji kara gogo kuji made aiteimasu.
Han	Soshite, konban disuko ni ikitai desu.
Kakari-in	Ja, **Susukino no hen** ni disuko ya **bā** ga takusan arimasu. Koko kara chikatetsu de Susukino eki made itte kudasai.
Han	Arigatō gozaimashita.

yūmei (na)	*famous*
Susukino no hen	*the Susukino area*
bā	*bar(s)*

Practice 1

Below is a street map of Sapporo. Use the information in the dialogue to match the points 1–5 on the map with the places **a–e** below. Write 1–5 in the brackets after the places.

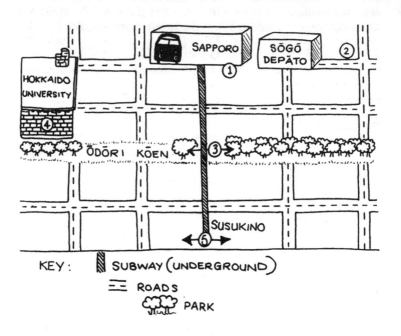

a Sapporo beer garden ( )
b Sightseeing bus stop ( )
c Disco area ( )
d Ainu memorial museum ( )
e Snow Festival ( )

Now fill in these times:

f Beer garden (opening time):
(closing time):
g Next sightseeing bus:

ℹ About Sapporo

Hokkaido, the north island of Japan, has only been fully inhabited by the Japanese since the late 19th century. Before that it was almost exclusively inhabited by the Ainu, a group of people believed to be the original inhabitants of the Japanese islands. The climate is generally cooler than the rest of Japan, and winters are long and severe. Sapporo, the capital of Hokkaido, is a modern city, laid out in a checker-board pattern. The Odori park slices east to west through the middle of the city, and it is here that the famous **Yuki-matsuri** or *Snow Festival* is held in February. Vast numbers of tourists descend on the city at this time to see the amazing snow and ice sculptures.

Practice 2

Try to work out, without referring back to the dialogue, how the speakers said:

- a   Do you have a map of Sapporo?
- b   Where is the Snow Festival?
- c   Are there any interesting museums in Sapporo?
- d   I want to do a sightseeing tour of Sapporo.
- e   Where is the famous beer garden?
- f   We want to go to a disco this evening.

Practice 3

Now it's your turn to find out some information at the tourist office. This time you are in Tokyo, planning your day. Say out loud your part of the conversation, then fill in the table on the next page with the information you are given. Here is the vocabulary that you will need:

bijutsukan	*art gallery*
kokuritsu	*national*
toku ni	*in particular*
meiji jingū	*meiji shrine*
omiyage	*souvenirs*
utteimasu	*sell*
Sunshine 60 biru	*Sunshine 60 building* (one of Japan's highest buildings – 60 floors)
kabuki-za	*kabuki theatre*

Areas of Tokyo mentioned in the dialogue: **Ueno, Yoyogi park, Asakusa, Ikebukuro, Ginza.**

Ryokō annai-jo de:

You	*Ask if they have a map of Tokyo.*
Kakari-in	Hai, dōzo.
You	*Ask if there are any interesting museums in Tokyo.*
Kakari-in	Ē. Ueno no hen ni takusan arimasu. Toku ni, Tōkyō bijutsukan to kokuritsu hakubutsukan wa omoshiroi desu. Kuji kara yoji han made aiteimasu.
You	*Ask where the Meiji shrine is.*
Kakari-in	Koko desu. Yoyogi kōen no naka ni arimasu. Kuji kara yoji han made aiteimasu.
You	*Say you want to buy some Japanese souvenirs.*
Kakari-in	Sō desu ka. Asakusa de ii omiyage o utteimasu.
You	*Ask where Asakusa is.*
Kakari-in	Koko desu. Ueno kōen no chikaku desu.
You	*Ask where the famous Sunshine 60 building is.*
Kakari-in	Ikebukuro no hen ni arimasu.
You	*Say you want to see kabuki this evening. Ask where the kabuki theatre is.*
Kakari-in	Koko desu. Higashi-Ginza no chikaku ni arimasu. Kabuki wa shichiji han kara desu.
You	*Say thank you.*

Place	Location	Opening times (where relevant)
National Museum		
Tokyo Art Gallery		
Meiji shrine		
Japanese souvenirs		
Sunshine 60 building		
Kabuki theatre		

Vocabulary list

sukī-jō	*ski ground*
nyūjōken	*admission ticket*
sukī yōgu	*ski equipment*
... o karitai	*I want to rent ...*
hitori	*(per) person*
rifuto	*lift*
muzukashisō	*it looks difficult*
sukī surōpu	*ski slopes*

▶ Conversation 2

Anne, Heidi, Scott and Han have moved on from Sapporo to a youth hostel near a ski resort. Listen to the recording (or read the dialogue below), then answer the questions in Practice 4.

Scott Kyō wa nani o shimashō ka.
Han Sukī ni ikimashō!
Heidi Sō shimashō. Watashi wa sukī ga totemo suki desu.
Scott Boku wa amari ...
Anne Watashi mo chotto ...
Han An-san, Sukotto-san, hayaku! Sukī-jō ni ikimashō.

Sukii-jō de:

Han Sumimasen, nyūjōken wa ikura desu ka.
Kakari-in Ichi-jikan wa sen-en desu. Ichinichi wa gosen-en desu.
Han Ja, ichinichi no nyūjōken o yonmai kudasai. Sore ni, sukī yōgu o karitai desu. Ikura desu ka.
Kakari-in Hitori sen-en desu.
Han Hai, sukī yōgu mo onegaishimasu.
Kakari-in Zembu de niman yonsen-en desu.

A little later:

Heidi Ja, rifuto de sukī surōpu ni ikimashō ne.
Scott Chotto ... muzukashisō desu ne.
Han E! Sukotto-san, Amerika de yoku sukī ni ikimashita ka.
Scott Iie, amari shimasen deshita. Amari jōzu dewa arimasen.

Anne	Watashi mo amari jōzu dewa arimasen.
Han	Hontō desu ka. Dō shimashō ka.
Anne	Ja, Sukotto-san, issho ni sukī no renshū o shimashō.
Scott	Ii desu ne. Sō shimashō.

Practice 4

Answer the questions below in Japanese.

a Haidi-san wa sukī ga suki desu ka.
b Yūsuhosuteru kara doko ni ikimashita ka.
c Ichinichi no nyūjōken wa ikura desu ka.
d Han-san wa nani o karitai desu ka.
e Nan de sukī surōpu ni ikimashita ka.
f Sukotto-san wa Amerika de yoku sukī o shimashita ka.
g An-san wa sukī ga jōzu desu ka.
h Dare ga sukī no renshū o shimashita ka.

Practice 5

Using the dialogue on the previous page, say these phrases out loud in Japanese:

a What shall we do today?
b Excuse me, how much is an admission ticket?
c May I have four one-day admission tickets, please?
d Also, I want to hire ski equipment.
e I'm not very good at skiing.

Practice 6

Anne and Scott have finished their skiing lesson and have decided to try ice-skating at a nearby outdoor ice rink. Imagine that you are the ice rink attendant; answer their questions using the following information.

Admission ticket cost: One hour = 500 yen   One day = 2,000 yen
Skate hire: 300 yen per person
Skating lessons: 1,000 yen per hour

sukēto gutsu	*ice skates*
sukēto no ressun	*skating lessons*
soku	*a pair* (shoes, socks, etc.)
ni-soku	*two pairs*

Sukēto-jō de:

Scott Sumimasen, nyūjōken wa ikura desu ka.
You *Give both costs.*
Scott Sore ni sukēto gutsu o karitai desu. Ikura desu ka.
You *Give the information required.*
Scott Sukēto no ressun wa ikura desu ka.
You *Give the information required.*
Scott Chotto takai desu ne. Ja, ichijikan no nyūjōken o nimai to sukēto gutsu o ni-soku karitai desu.
You *Say how much it is altogether.*
Scott Nisen-en de onegaishimasu.
You *Say how much change you are giving.*
Scott Dōmo arigatō.

▶ Practice 7

Reiko is booking tickets by phone for the kabuki theatre as a surprise for Anne when she comes back from Hokkaido. Read through the new words, then listen to the conversation a few times. Then switch off the recording and see if you can fill in the gaps in the dialogue below. Check your answers by re-playing the dialogue (or look at the answers at the back of the book.)

If you don't have the recording, fill in the gaps from the answers at the back, then use the dialogue as a reading activity to test your understanding before going on to Practice 8.

kabuki-za	*the kabuki theatre in Tokyo*
man-in	*full house* (sold out)
seki	*seats*
kodomo	*children*
hangaku	*half the price*
otona	*adults*
kyūkei	*interval, break*
sankai	*three times*
Eigo no gaido	*English guide*
iyahōn	*earphones*

Kakari-in	a	___ ___ Kabuki-za de gozaimasu.
Reiko	b	Sumimasen, ___ ___ ___ ni mada seki ga arimasu ka.
Kakari-in	c	Sō desu ne. Doyōbi no ban wa ___ desu ga doyōbi no ___ wa dō desu ka. Mada ___ ga arimasu.
Reiko	d	Seki wa ___ desu ka.
Kakari-in	e	___ ___ seki wa gosen-en to ___ de, ni-kai no seki wa ___ en to ___ en de gozaimasu. ___ ___ ___ wa hangaku de gozaimasu.
Reiko	f	Ja, ___ en no seki o ___ mai kudasai. Sore ni kodomo no seki o ___ mai kudasai.
Kakari-in	g	Kashikomarimashita, Zembu de ___ ___ ___ en de gozaimasu.
Reiko	h	Kabuki wa ___ ___ desu ka.
Kakari-in	i	___ ji kara ___ ji made desu. Kyūkei ga ___ kai arimasu.
Reiko	j	Eigo no ___ ga arimasu ka.
Kakari-in	k	Ē, eigo no ___ to ___ o utteimasu.
Reiko		Ā, yokatta!
Kakari-in	l	Sore dewa ___ to ___ o onegaishimasu.
Reiko	m	Yamaguchi Reiko desu. Denwa-bangō wa Tōkyō ___ desu.
Kakari-in		Arigatō gozaimashita.

Practice 8

Match the Japanese phrases on the left with the correct English phrases on the right.

a Seki ga arimasu ka.

b Doyōbi no ban wa man-in desu.

c Seki wa ikura desu ka.

d Rokusen-en no seki o yonmai kudasai.

e Kabuki wa nanji kara desu ka.

f Eigo no gaido ga arimasu ka.

g O-namae to o-denwa-bangō o onegaishimasu.

i What time does the kabuki performance start?

ii Your name and phone number, please.

iii Do you have any guides in English?

iv Do you have any seats?

v How much is a seat?

vi May I have 4 × 6,000-yen seats, please?

vii Saturday night is sold out.

ℹ About the theatre

The three main traditional forms of Japanese theatre are **kabuki**, **bunraku** and **noh**. Kabuki theatre offers its audience exciting and intriguing drama accompanied by a colourful and varied display of music, costume, stage sets and dance. All parts, including those of women, are played by men, and the actors usually have a long family tradition of involvement in the kabuki theatre.

Bunraku is similar in style to kabuki theatre, but its actors are puppets. The puppets are about four feet tall and are very life-like, with many moving parts including eyes, eyebrows and fingers. They are each operated by three puppeteers who are visible on stage. It takes many years to train as a puppeteer. A narrator tells the story and provides the voices of the puppets. Musical accompaniment is provided by a shamisen player.

Noh theatre is a more controlled style of drama. It uses a minimum of props, actors and sets, and its stories are performed through the medium of controlled dance, movement, poetry and song. A Greek-style chorus tells the story, and musicians accompany the action with flutes and drums. Some of the actors wear intricate masks, and the costumes are very sumptuous.

Although these forms of theatre go back several centuries, some of the forms have been transferred to modern or western theatre such as the kabuki-style Macbeth which toured Europe and the States to high acclaim.

Practice 8

The Bunraku theatre occasionally tours abroad. Imagine that you are working at your local theatre and a Japanese person phones to inquire about tickets. Use the schedule below to answer these questions.

Performances:	Saturday 12 and Sunday 13 September at 7.30 p.m.
Tickets:	Stalls (ground floor) £8/£10; balcony (1st floor) £6/£9
Children:	Half the above prices.

Customer Moshi, moshi. Konshū no doyōbi ni seki ga arimasu ka.

You *Saturday is sold out; there are still seats for Sunday.*

Customer Ikura desu ka.

You *Give the information asked for.*

Customer Ja, hachi-pondo no seki o nimai to kodomo no seki o nimai kudasai.

You *Say how much that will be altogether.*

Customer	Bunraku wa nanji kara desu ka.
You	*Give the information required.*
Customer	Dōmo arigatō.
You	*Ask for his/her name and phone number.*

Revision test

1 Units 17–19

Find 12 words which you have learnt in Units 17–19. There are some English clues to help you. Words can be found left to right, right to left, top to bottom, and bottom to top.

Clues: *Japanese cuisine, Japanese-style room, reservation, two nights, reserved seat, return (ticket), train lunch, discount* (use **waribiki**), *museum, entrance ticket, art gallery, tour bus.*

H	A	K	U	B	U	T	S	U	K	A	N
A	I	E	R	I	J	O	H	R	I	N	U
U	N	Y	U	J	O	K	E	N	R	E	S
K	I	S	Y	U	K	O	H	S	A	W	A
A	S	H	I	T	E	I	S	E	K	I	B
Y	O	W	A	S	H	I	T	S	U	K	O
O	F	U	K	U	N	Y	U	H	R	A	K
Y	U	S	H	K	A	U	H	A	H	I	N
A	R	U	W	A	R	I	B	I	K	I	A
J	O	H	N	N	E	B	I	K	E	S	K

2 Units 17–19

Select one word from the box on the next page to complete the Japanese phrases. Use each word once.

a Kyōto no chizu ga ————— ka.

b Nigatsu futsuka ni yoyaku o ————— desu.

c Shokuji wa ————— ka.

d Ōsaka-yuki no kippu o ———— kudasai.
e Hiroshima-yuki no densha wa ———— desu ka.
f Sapporo made dono gurai ———— ka.
g Nichiyōbi no ban ———— ga arimasu ka.
h Nyūjōken wa ———— desu ka.
i O-namae to o-denwa-bangō o ————.

---

gomai   onegaishimasu   ikura   arimasu   kakarimasu
    haitteimasu   seki   shitai   nanban-sen

---

3 **Units 17–19**

Can you ask for the following?

a a Tokyo sightseeing guide
b the price of a double room
c if there are any rooms for tonight
d a single ticket
e whether there are discount tickets for students
f if there are any art galleries in *this area* (**kono hen**)
g where to change trains

4 **Units 17–19**

Complete the following sentences by choosing the endings **i**, **ii** or **iii**.

a Tsugi no shingō o migi ni
   i   itte kudasai.
   ii   norikaete kudasai.
   iii magatte kudasai.

b Hakubutsukan wa kuji kara yoji han made
   i   aiteimasu.
   ii   haitteimasu.
   iii utteimasu.

c Sukēto gutsu o
   i   shitai desu.
   ii   karitai desu.
   iii ikitai desu.

d Watashi wa sukī ga amari
   i   suki desu.
   ii   jōzu desu.
   iii jōzu dewa arimasen.

20

asobi ni kite kudasai

please come and visit

In this unit you will learn
- about visiting a Japanese home
- about Japanese houses
- how to invite a Japanese person to your home
- how to introduce yourself in a business or formal situation
- about the exchange of business cards
- how to make a phone call to a Japanese home and office

This unit will look at a few formal Japanese phrases you may come across in the Japanese home and in working life. It is particularly useful if you are planning to go to Japan or if you have Japanese friends in your own country.

Review

- Greetings (Unit 1)
- Days of the week (Unit 8, **Explanation 9**)
- Inviting someone (Unit 9, **Explanation 6**)
- Asking if someone is well (Unit 11, **Explanation 1**)
- Describing words (Unit 11)
- Useful expressions (Unit 15, page 183)

Satō-sensei no ie de *At Sato-sensei's house*

The new phrases below are recorded for you to practise your pronunciation. Listen to one phrase at a time, then pause the recording and repeat it. When you have listened and repeated all the phrases once, go back to the beginning and see if you can say each phrase first, then play the recording to check your pronunciation. Try recording yourself and compare this with the recording. This will help you to correct and improve your pronunciation – and it will help you to remember the words too!

▶ Vocabulary list

gomen kudasai	*may I come in?* (Lit. *excuse me* – said when entering the entrance of a home)
genkan	*the entrance porch*
ima	*living room*
yoku irasshaimashita	*welcome* (to my home)
o-genki desu ka	*are you well?* (used if someone has been ill or if you haven't see them for some time)
o-kagesama de	*I'm fine, thank you* (in reply to **o-genki desu ka**)

o-hairi kudasai	please come in
hairimasu	enter
shitsurei shimasu	pardon me for interrupting (said when entering a home or room)
surippa	slippers
o-kake kudasai	please sit down
tsumaranai mono	it's nothing much (said when handing over a gift) (Lit. a boring thing)
ikaga desu ka	how about…? would you like? (formal version of **dō desu ka**)
dochira ga ii desu ka	which would you prefer?
itadakimasu	(said before a meal – like 'Bon appétit')
gochisōsama deshita	(said after a meal – Lit. 'That was a feast!')
oishisō desu	it looks delicious
… no okawari	another helping of …
mō kekkō desu	I'm full, thank you
o-ki o tsukete!	take care

▶ Conversation 1

Listen to the conversation or read it below. Focus particularly on Anne's part.

An-san wa Satō-sensei no ie e asobi ni ikimashita. *Anne has gone to visit Satō-sensei's home.*

Anne	(*sliding open the front door*) Gomen kudasai!
Satō-sensei	Ā, An-san! Yoku irasshaimashita. O-genki desu ka.
Anne	Ē, o-kagesama de.
Satō-sensei	Dōzo, o-hairi kudasai.
Anne	Shitsurei shimasu. (*Anne enters the **genkan***)
Satō-sensei	Surippa o dōzo. (*Anne takes off her shoes and steps into the slippers*)
Satō-sensei	Kochira e dōzo.

Ima ni hairimasu. *They enter the living room.*

Satō-sensei	O-kake kudasai.
Anne	Shitsurei shimasu.
Satō-sensei	Hokkaidō wa dō deshita ka.
Anne	Totemo tanoshikatta desu. Kireina tokoro desu ne.
Satō-sensei	Sō desu ne. Samukatta desu ka.
Anne	Ē, chotto samukatta desu. Ano, tsumaranai mono desu ga, dōzo.
Satō-sensei	**Ara! Nan deshō?**
Anne	Hokkaidō no omiyage desu.
Satō-sensei	Dōmo arigatō gozaimasu. An-san, o-cha to kōhī to dochira ga ii desu ka.
Anne	Ocha o onegaishimasu.
Satō-sensei	Kēki wa ikaga desu ka.
Anne	Oishisō desu ne. Itadakimasu.

Later:

Satō-sensei	An-san, itsu Igirisu ni kaerimasu ka.
Anne	Mō sugu desu ne. Raigetsu desu.
Satō-sensei	Nihongo ga jōzu **ni narimashita** ne.
Anne	Iie, mada mada desu.
Satō-sensei	Jōzu desu yo. Ocha no okawari wa ikaga desu ka.
Anne	Mō kekō desu.

As Anne is leaving:

Anne	Gochisōsama deshita. Kēki wa oishikatta desu.
Satō-sensei	Mata asobi ni kite kudasai.
Anne	Arigatō gozaimashita.
Satō-sensei	O-ki o tsukete!
Anne	Oyasumi nasai.

---

ara! nan deshō?	*hey, what's this?*
... ni narimashita	*you have become ...*

Practice 1

Can you link the Japanese phrases on the left with their English meanings on the right? See if you can do this exercise without referring back to the dialogue.

a	Ocha o onegaishimasu.	i	May I come in?
b	Shitsurei shimasu.	ii	I'm fine, thank you.
c	Tsumaranai mono desu ga, dōzo.	iii	Pardon me for interrupting.
d	Gochisōsama deshita.	iv	It's nothing, but please accept this.
e	Hokkaidō no omiyage desu.	v	It's a souvenir from Hokkaido.
f	Gomen kudasai.	vi	May I have green tea, please?
g	Kēki wa oishikatta desu.	vii	They look delicious.
h	O-kagesama de.	viii	That was delicious (a feast), thank you.
i	_____	ix	The cakes were delicious.

There is one English phrase remaining. Can you supply the Japanese for it (i)?

Practice 2

Now that you have familiarized yourself with the new words and the dialogue above, try taking Anne's part in the conversation. If you have the recording, pause it after each of Satō-sensei's lines and say Anne's part out loud. Try to do this from memory, but don't worry if you need to look back at the dialogue to prompt you. When you've said the line, play the recording to check how you did. Continue like this through the dialogue.

If you don't have the recording, use a piece of paper to cover each part of Anne's dialogue until you have said it, then uncover it and check.

Practice 3

What can you say in Japanese:

a   As you slide open the front door of a Japanese home?
b   As you enter the house?
c   After your host(ess) asks you to sit down?
d   When you hand over a gift?
e   Before you start to eat or drink?
f   If you are offered a choice of drinks and you want coffee?

g If you are offered more and you are full?
h When you want to say something was delicious?
i At the end of a meal?

i About Japanese homes

The Japanese live in a variety of accommodation ranging from apartment blocks and 'mansions' (blocks of flats) in the cities through single-storey wooden or pre-fabricated houses in the suburbs and smaller cities, to larger houses for those who can afford them, and farmhouses in the country areas.

Standard to all Japanese homes is the **genkan** or *porch* which separates the outside from the interior of the home. There is often a step up from the genkan to the main body of the house, and it is in the genkan that you must remove your shoes and step up into the slippers that are set out for you. This reinforces the idea of a separation between the outside and the interior, and of course, in practical terms, it keeps the home freer from dirt.

Many, but not all, Japanese homes have rooms with **tatami** floors. Tatami mats are made from rice straw and rushes woven around a frame. When you enter a tatami room you always take off the slippers and leave them in the hallway. Many homes (and restaurants too) also have a pair of plastic slippers or wooden clogs for use only in the toilet.

Owing to the lack of land space Japanese houses tend to be smaller than their western counterparts. They also tend to be much less cluttered with furniture, and rooms, particularly the main living room, are often multi-functional. It is not unusual, for example, for the living room to be turned into the parents' bedroom at night simply by laying out the futon bedding. The next day the futon is aired outside and then put away again in the cupboard.

▶ Practice 4

Look at the dialogue on page 244 again and this time take the role of Satō-sensei. Listen to the recording (or read the dialogue) and repeat Satō-sensei's lines after her. Then, as you did in Practice 2, try pausing the recording after Anne's lines and saying Satō-sensei's lines out loud.

Practice 5

Link the English phrases on the left with their Japanese equivalents on the right.

a Welcome (to my home).
b Are you well?
c Please come in.
d Come this way.
e Please sit down.
f Thank you very much.
g Would you prefer beer or wine?
h Would you like some coffee?
i Would you like some more coffee?
j Please visit again.
k Take care.

i Bīru to wain to dochira ga ii desu ka.
ii Dōmo arigatō gozaimasu.
iii Mata asobi ni kite kudasai.
iv O-ki o tsukete.
v Yoku irasshaimashita.
vi Kōhī wa ikaga desu ka.
vii O-genki desu ka.
viii Dōzo o-hairi kudasai.
ix Kochira e, dōzo.
x O-kake kudasai.
xi _____

There is one extra English phrase. Can you say the Japanese equivalent (**xi**)?

Practice 6

Emi is in England and is planning to visit Anne's mother. Anne's mother has been studying Japanese by herself so that she can welcome Emi in Japanese. Take the part of Anne's mother and say out loud your part in the dialogue below.

Emi	Gomen kudasai!
Mrs Jenkins	*Welcome Emi to your house and invite her in.*
Emi	Shitsurei shimasu.
Mrs Jenkins	*Guide her to the living room, then ask her to sit down.*
Emi	Shitsurei shimasu.
Mrs Jenkins	*Ask her how London was.*
Emi	Omoshirokatta desu.
Mrs Jenkins	*Ask her where she went.*
Emi	'Madame Tussauds' to **Daiei hakubutsukan** ni ikimashita. Ano, tsumaranai mono desu ga, dōzo.
Mrs Jenkins	*Thank her very much for the gift.*
Emi	Nihon no **ningyō** desu.
Mrs Jenkins	*Ask her if she'd prefer tea or coffee.*
Emi	Kōcha o onegaishimasu.

Mrs Jenkins	*Then offer her some sandwiches.*
Emi	Hai, itadakimasu.
Mrs Jenkins	*Ask her if Anne is well.*
Emi	Hai, totemo genki desu. Nihongo ga jōzu ni narimashita.
Mrs Jenkins	*Ask her if she'd like some more tea.*
Emi	Iie, mō kekkō desu. Gochisōsama deshita. **Sorosoro shitsurei shimasu.**
Mrs Jenkins	*Ask her to visit again.*
Emi	Arigatō gozaimasu. Totemo tanoshikatta desu.
Mrs Jenkins	*Tell her to take care and say goodbye.*
Emi	Sayōnara.

daiei hakubutsukan	*British Museum*
ningyō	*doll*
sorosoro	*soon*
sorosoro shitsurei shimasu	*I shall be leaving (excusing myself) soon*

ℹ Gift-giving

When you visit a Japanese home for the first time, take a small gift to show your appreciation. If you are planning a trip to Japan, 'typical' gifts from your country such as small items of china, tea-towels or drink coasters would be adequate. For a more important person, such as a company head or someone who has or is going to do you a great favour, a good quality bottle of whisky would be greatly appreciated. The Japanese usually have gifts specially wrapped when they buy them. If you don't have this custom in your country, you can either wrap the gift yourself or simply present it in the shop bag.

You may find that when you offer your gift, your host(ess) will put it to one side and not open it in front of you. This is a Japanese custom and certainly doesn't mean that the person is not pleased to receive it. On the other hand, if a Japanese person visits you, it is fine to follow the western tradition and open the present in front of him or her so that you can show your appreciation and maybe ask some questions about it.

Watashi wa Yamaguchi to mōshimasu
I am called Mr Yamaguchi

In this section you will learn some useful phrases for more formal and business situations. First of all, familiarize yourself with the new words below and then look at Unit 1 again – how to introduce yourself.

Vocabulary list

Eikoku	*England* (also **Igirisu**)
... to mōshimasu	*I am called ...*
yoroshiku onegaishimasu	*pleased to meet you*
	(also **dōzo yoroshiku**)
meishi	*business card*
watashi no desu	*This is/it's mine*

▶ Conversation 2

Listen to the conversation (or read the dialogue), then fill in the table in Practice 7 with the information required.

Mr Yamaguchi is meeting a British business client at a reception in Tokyo.

Business client Hajimemashite, **Eikoku** Ginkō no Maiku Robinson **to mōshimasu**. Dōzo yoroshiku. (*they both bow*)

Yamaguchi Hajimemashite, Nihon Ginkō no Yamaguchi to mōshimasu. **Yoroshiku onegaishimasu.**

Business client Watashi no **meishi** o dōzo.

Yamaguchi **Watashi no desu**. Dōzo. (*they both exchange business cards*)

Practice 7

	Business client	Mr Yamaguchi
Name		—
Place of work		

ℹ️ About business cards

The information on a **meishi** or *business card* helps the Japanese business person to quickly establish the rank of the other person, and thus how formally they should greet someone or how deeply they should bow (a deeper bow to a more senior person). In meetings with non-Japanese people, however, this information is less necessary, as non-Japanese people do not have a place within this ranking. Nevertheless, a business card, especially if it is in Japanese as well as English, helps a Japanese person in pronouncing your name and understanding your position and status.

There is a certain etiquette involved in the exchanging of **meishi**. You offer the card to the other person with the writing facing them, and usually with both hands. When you receive a business card, you should read it carefully and treat it with respect, putting it away carefully once you have studied it. If things become a little confused, you can use **sumimasen** or **shitsurei shimasu** (*excuse me*) to show that the situation is unfamiliar to you.

Practice 8

When a Japanese person introduces him or herself within a work situation, he or she invariably says the name of the company they belong to before their own name. This demonstrates the importance which is attached in Japan to identifying yourself with your place of work. Mr Yamaguchi introduced himself like this: **Nihon Ginkō no Yamaguchi to mōshimasu**. The English equivalent of this is: *I am Mr Yamaguchi of the Bank of Japan.*

Below is a list of work places. Imagine you work at these places and practise introducing yourself (use your own name). Speak out loud and practise bowing too. (But remember that the Japanese are well aware of the western custom of shaking hands and may do this with a foreign client.)

   a   Eikoku Ginkō (*The Bank of England*)
   b   Amerika Taishikan (*The American Embassy*)
   c   Higashi Denki (*East Electric*)
   d   Eikoku Gasu (*British Gas*)
   e   Mainichi Shinbun (*The 'Mainichi' newspaper*)
   f   Rondon Daigaku (*London University*)
   g   Nihon Shōji (*Japan Trading*)
   h   Daiei Hakubutsukan (*The British Museum*)

Denwa o suru koto *Making phone calls*

Say these new words out loud. There are also some phrases on the recording for you to practise. Play one at a time, pause the recording and repeat it. Listen carefully to the pronunciation.

▶ Vocabulary list

moshi moshi	*hello* (when telephoning)
irasshaimasu ka	*is he in?* (polite version of **imasu**)
rusu desu	*he's not in* (the house)
kaigi-chū	*in a meeting*
denwa-chū	*on the phone*
shutchō-chū	*on a business trip*
gaishutsu-chū	*out (of the office)*
dengon	*a message*
dengon o onegai dekimasu ka	*may I leave a message?*
watashi ni denwa o onegaishimasu	*please phone me*
yoroshiku onegaishimasu	*I'm indebted to you* (used when meeting someone for the first time and when someone is going to do you a favour)
mata denwa o shimasu	*I'll phone again*
o-taku	*home* (someone else's)
shitsurei shimasu	*sorry for interrupting* (said by the caller at the end of a call)

Practice 9

Yamaguchi-san wa Robinson-san ni denwa o shimasu. *Mr Yamaguchi telephones Mr Robinson.*

Read this dialogue, then indicate whether the statements below it are correct or not by placing a circle (**maru**) by the correct ones and a cross (**batsu**) by the incorrect ones.

Yamaguchi	Moshi moshi, Tōkyō Ginkō no Yamaguchi desu ga Robinson-san wa irasshaimasu ka.
Hisho	Sumimasen, ima kaigi-chū desu. Go-dengon ga arimasu ka.
Yamaguchi	Hai, watashi ni denwa o onegaishimasu. Kaisha no denwa-bangō wa zero san no hachi san kyū

no go ichi ichi go desu. Shichiji made koko ni imasu. Soshite uchi e kaerimasu. Uchi no denwa-bangō wa zero san ichi no hachi san roku no nana kyū ichi nana desu.

Hisho   Hai, wakarimashita.

Yamaguchi   Yoroshiku onegaishimasu.

a Robinson-san wa Yamaguchi-san ni denwa
   o shimashita.   ( )
b Robinson-san wa denwa-chū deshita.   ( )
c Yamaguchi-san wa dengon o shimashita.   ( )
d Yamaguchi-san no kaisha no denwa-bangō
   wa 03-836-7917 desu.   ( )
e 7-ji made kaisha ni imasu.   ( )
f Soshite resutoran e ikimasu.   ( )

Practice 10

Can you say the conversation below between the receptionist and Ms Gates in Japanese? Speak out loud.

Ms Gates a *Hello, this is Ms Gates of **London Insurance**. Is Mr Suzuki in?*

Hisho   b *I'm sorry, he's out at the moment. Do you have a message?*

Ms Gates c *Yes, please could he phone me? My work (company) number is 020-7663-2198. I will be here until 5.30.*

Hisho   d *Yes, certainly.*

Ms Gates e *Thanks for your help (I'm indebted to you).*

Rondon Hoken   *London insurance*

▶ Practice 11

Robinson-san wa Yamaguchi-san no uchi ni denwa o shimasu.
Mr Robinson telephones Mr Yamaguchi's house.

Listen to the recording, then fill in Mr Robinson's weekly diary.

---

hima   *free, not busy*
tanoshimi ni shitemasu   *look forward to something*

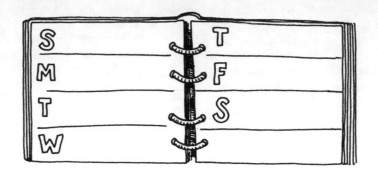

Test

1   Fill in the gaps in the dialogue below:

Visitor	**a**	*(Slides open door)* _____ _____!
Host	**b**	Aa! Tanaka-san, _____ _____.
Visitor	**c**	*(Says 'Hello')* _____.
Host	**d**	*(Asks her to come in)* _____ _____ _____.
Visitor	**e**	*(As enters house)* S_____ s_____.
Host	**f**	*(Offers slippers)* _____ _____ _____.

2   Making phone calls. What do you say in Japanese:

   a   When you ask if it's the Yamaguchi residence?
   b   If you want to leave a message?
   c   If you're going to phone again?
   d   If you want the person to phone you?
   e   When you ask someone if they want to leave a message?
   f   If someone calls and the person they want to speak to is on the phone?
   g   At the end of a call (two choices)?

Omedetō gozaimasu! *Congratulations!*

We hope you have enjoyed working your way through the course. We are always keen to receive feedback from people who have used our course, so why not contact us and let us know your reactions? We'll be particularly pleased to receive your positive comments, but we should also like to know if you think things could be improved. We always welcome comments and suggestions and we do our best to incorporate constructive suggestions into later editions.

You can contact us through the publishers at: Teach Yourself Books, Hodder Headline Ltd, 338 Euston Road, London NW1 3BH.

You have completed *Teach Yourself Beginner's Japanese* and are now a competent speaker of basic Japanese. You should be able to carry out conversations in Japanese in a variety of different situations, whether in Japan or with a Japanese person in your own country. Japanese is an exciting language and is becoming more and more popular to learn. So why not try to increase your knowledge and ability by taking your study further with the full *Teach Yourself Japanese* course?

Gambatte! *Good luck!*
Sayōnara! *Goodbye!*

taking it further

There is a wealth of workbooks and internet sites that can help you to take your study of Japanese further. The suggestions below are taken from my own teaching experience and feedback from students and other teachers. It is by no means an exhaustive list and the internet in particular is continuously producing new and often improved possibilities. However, the list does include some of the real 'backbones' and classics for learning Japanese.

Books

- *Teach Yourself Beginner's Japanese Script*, Helen Gilhooly, 2003
- *Teach Yourself World Cultures: Japan*, Helen Gilhooly, Hodder and Stoughton, 2003. For a general introduction to all aspects of Japanese life and society.
- *Kodansha Bilingual Encyclopedia of Japan*, 1998. An easy-to-read, comprehensive encyclopedia with entries and index in English and Japanese.
- *Kodansha Encyclopedia of Japan*, 1999. A detailed and comprehensive English language reference book on all aspects of Japan. Also available on CD-ROM with various extras such as dictionary and links to worldwide web.
- *Japan Made Easy – All You Need to Know to Enjoy Japan*, Boye Lafayette De Mente, Passport Books, 1995. Practical advice and information for visiting Japan including lots of dos and don'ts.
- *Japan*, Chris Taylor, Lonely Planet, 1997. Traveller's guidebook includes lots of interesting facts and advice about Japan.

Magazines

These are available from Japanese bookshops.

- *Hiragana Times* (monthly). Written in kana, kanji and English and aimed at cross-cultural communication. Has its own website: **www.hiraganatimes.com/**.
- *The Nihongo Journal* (monthly, available with cassette. Website: **www.alc.co.jp/nj/**). Language instruction for learners of all levels with up-to-date information about Japan.
- *Mangajin* (quarterly). Extracts from popular Japanese comics with translation, grammar and cultural explanations in English.

Dictionaries

- *The Oxford Starter Japanese Dictionary*, Jonathan Bunt, Oxford University Press, 2000. Two-way dictionary especially written for students of Japanese, with examples of how the words are used in practice. Entries in script and English.
- *Webster's New World Compact Japanese Dictionary*, 1997. Two-way dictionary, entries in *romaji*, script and English.
- *Pictorial Japanese and English Dictionary*, ed. John Pheby, Oxford University Press, 1997.

Websites

The internet is constantly changing and developing and it is always worth doing searches for new Japanese language sites but some good current ones include:

- *Japanese Writing Tutor Site:* **members.aol.com/writejapan/**. This is an excellent site for learning how to write hiragana and katakana (a 'virtual' calligraphy brush demonstrates the shape and stroke order of each symbol for you to copy) and also includes an introduction to 45 basic kanji.
- *Jim Breen's Japanese Page:* **www.csse.monash.edu.au/~jwb/japanese.html** (or do a search for Jim Breen). This site includes instructions on how to download a freeware Japanese word processing programme (JWPce), a Japanese–English dictionary and links to many other Japanese learning sites and free/share ware.
- Web Resources for Teaching and Learning of Japanese Language (compiled by Anai Sensei, Essex University): **www.eesex.ac.uk/centres/japan/resources/menu.html**.

- A useful kanji tutor site: **www.kanjicards.com**.
- *Write hiragana*: **www.jfet.org.uk/FS1.html**.
- JIN (Japan Information Network): **www.jinjapan.org/ index.html**. various information about Japan with links to Japanese language sites found under *Japan Web Navigator – Education*.
- For information on the Japanese Language Proficiency tests (there are four levels from beginners to advanced): **www.soas.ac.uk/centres/Japan/proficiency.html**.
- **www.about.com** Search for 'Japanese language' on this website and it will bring up a number of activities under titles such as: 'Japanese for beginners', 'Japanese grammar' and 'All about Japan'.
- **www.quia.com/dir/japanese** This site lists a top 20 of Japanese language and culture activities such as food and drink, verb cards, particles and Japanese writing.

Organizations

- Japanese embassies across the world have JICC (Japan Information and Cultural Centres) from which you can borrow books and videos as well as subscribe to a number of magazines and newsletters and find out about Japanese classes, societies and other organizations in your country. Go to **www.embjapan.org** and you will find links to every JICC and Japanese embassy in the world.
- Japan National Tourist Organization (JNTO): **www.jnto.go.jp**
- For information on the JET programme (teaching English in Japan): **www.jetprogramme.org/**

key to the exercises

Unit 1

Practice

1 Order on recording: c, f, a, e, d, b. **a** Konnichiwa **b** Sayōnara
(Ja, mata ne) **c** Konbanwa **d** Oyasumi (nasai) **e** Ohayō (gozaimasu)
f Hajimemashite (Dōzo yoroshiku)   **2 a** Kochira wa Tanaka
Machiko-san desu. Kochira wa Suzuki Fumi-san desu. **b** Kochira
wa Yamamoto Masaki-san desu. Kochira wa Sue Teesdale-san
desu. **c** Kochira wa Yamaguchi Reiko-san desu. Kochira wa An
Jenkinsu-san desu. **d** Kochira wa Kimura Ichirō-san desu. Kochira
wa Hayashi-san desu.   **5 a** 0 **b** 2 **c** 2 **d** 1 **e** 1 **f** 1 **g** 0 **h** 2 **i** 1
6 a X **b** san **c** san **d** san

Test

1 a Ohayō (gozaimasu) **b** Hajimemashite (Dōzo yoroshiku) **c**
Oyasumi (nasai) **d** Sumimasen   **2** Hajimemashite, (*your name*)
desu. Dōzo yoroshiku.   **3** Kochira wa An Jenkinsu-san desu.

Unit 2

Let's talk

a whisky **b** cake **c** ice cream **d** tape recorder **e** stereo **f** computer
g bus (or bath) **h** taxi **i** pants (*trousers*) **j** coat **k** bed **l** restaurant
m pen

Practice

1 All start with 'zero (rei) san no' **a** san ni nana roku no go yon go
san **b** hachi hachi kyū san no san ni ni ichi **c** nana nana roku ni no
ichi ni san yon **d** hachi ni hachi san no yon yon go go   **2** T **b** F **c**
T **d** T **e** F **3 a** March **b** January **c** August **d** November   **5 a** Japan
b Germany **c** Ireland **d** America **e** France **f** Italy

Test

1 a 'Hat' wa nihongo de nan desu ka. **b** Shitsurei shimasu. **c**
Watashi (boku) wa Igirisujin desu. **d** Nihongo no hon desu.   **2**
Crossword   **3 a** yon (shi) = 4 **b** nana (shichi) = 7 **c** san = 3 **d** nana
(shichi) = 7

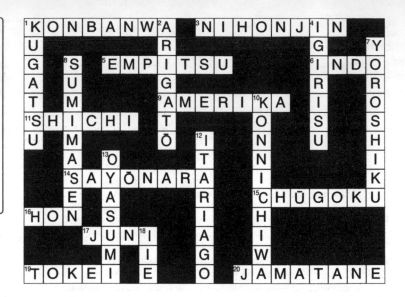

	¹K	O	N	B	A	N	W	²A		³N	I	H	O	N	J	⁴I	N		
	U					R									G		⁷Y	
	G	⁸S		⁵E	M	P	I	T	S	U			⁶I	N	D	O	
	A	U		G		R							R		R	
	T	M		⁹A	M	E	R	I	¹⁰K	A			I		O	
¹¹S	H	I	C	H	I		T		O			S		S	
U	M			Ō		¹²I		N			U		H	
	A	¹³O		T		N			I		
¹⁴S	A	Y	Ō	N	A	R	A			K	
E	A		R		¹⁵C	H	Ū	G	O	K	U
¹⁶H	O	N	S		I		H		I	
¹⁷J	U	N	¹⁸I		A		I	
M		I		G		W	
¹⁹T	O	K	E	I		E		O	²⁰J	A	M	A	T	A	N	E

Unit 3

Let's talk

Sukotto-san wa Amerikajin desu; Han-san wa Chūgokujin desu; Takeshi-kun wa Nihonjin desu; Tani-san wa Furansujin desu; Haidi-san wa Doitsujin desu.

Practice

1 a (Mr) Suzuki, 5, company employee, golf b Yuki, 3, student (pupil) swimming c Hanako Yamada, 4, shop assistant, gardening d Reiko Yamaguchi, 4, housewife, flower arranging 2 All begin with 'Kochira wa *name* desu' a Susan-san wa shufu desu. Shumi wa dansu desu. b Andrew-san wa ten'in desu. Shumi wa sakkā desu. c Peter-san wa isha desu. Shumi wa gorufu desu. d John-san wa kaishain desu. 3 a isha b shufu c ten'in d gakusei 4 a 14 b 40 c 17 d 03-1353-0154 e 03-6637-1289 f 3 g March 5 An-san mo Haidi-san mo gakusei desu. b Tani-san mo Henri-san mo Furansujin desu. c Haha mo chichi mo haisha desu.

Test

1 nana (shichi), jūnana (jūshichi), jūni, nijū, jūyon (jūshi), ni, ku (kyū), jūsan, jūroku, yonjū, gojū, rokujū 2 a Mōichido itte kudasai. b Yukkuri itte kudasai. 3 c 4 Watashi wa sensei dewa (ja) arimasen. Gakusei desu. 5 gonin, yonin, sannin, futari, hitori

Unit 4

Let's talk

1 Kazoku wa rokunin desu.   3 a okāsan b haha; ani c otōto d go-kazoku

Practice

1 a 9 b 11 c 61 d 89 e 20 f 9   2 a 18th, 11th b 20th, 23rd c 14th
d 21st, 31st, 27th   3 Each begins with '(*Name*) no tanjōbi wa …'
a gogatsu jūichi-nichi b hachigatsu nijūichi-nichi c jūichigatsu hatsuka
d kugatsu nijūgo-nichi e ichigatsu jūyokka f shigatsu sanjū-nichi   4 a
Kazoku wa yonin desu. Haha to chichi to otōto to watashi (boku)
desu. b Kazoku wa sannin desu. Haha to ani to watashi desu.
c Kazoku wa yonin desu. Kanai to musume to musuko to watashi
(boku) desu. d Kazoku wa yonin desu. Shūjin to musuko ga futari to
watashi desu.   5 Example: Imōto wa jūnana-sai desu. Watashi wa
nijūni-sai desu. a Chichi wa gojū-sai desu. Otōto wa jūroku-sai desu.
Watashi (boku) wa hatachi desu. b Haha wa yonjūsan-sai desu. Ani
wa sanjūissai desu. c Musume wa jūkyū-sai desu. Musuko wa jūyon-
sai desu.   6 Example: Onēsan wa nijūgo-sai desu. Imōtosan wa
jūnana-sai desu. An-san wa nijūni-sai desu. a Otōsan wa gojū-sai
desu. Otōtosan wa jūroku-sai desu. Sukotto-san wa hatachi desu.
b Okāsan wa yonjūsan-sai desu. Oniisan wa sanjūissai desu. c
Musume-san wa jūkyū-sai desu. Musuko-san wa jūyon-sai desu.
7 a 4 c 1 d 2 e 3

Test

1 a sangatsu nijūku-nichi b hachigatsu jūichi-nichi c jūnigatsu nijūgo-
nichi d ichigatsu jūsan-nichi e Gogatsu sanjūichi-nichi   2 haha = own
mother, ane = own older sister, okāsan = someone else's mother,
kazoku = own family, imōto ga futari = two younger sisters, musuko ga
sannin = three sons, otōsan = someone else's father   3 kyūjukyū,
kyūjūhachi, kyūjūshichi, etc.

Unit 5

Let's talk

1 a san-ji b hachi-ji c jūichi-ji d ichi-ji e jūni-ji   2 tabako o kudasai;
hon o kudasai; sandoitchi o kudasai; kōhī o kudasai.

Practice

1 a 8 o'clock b 11 a.m. c 12 p.m. d 12 (p.m.) e 6 a.m. f 3 a.m.   2 a
iii, b vi, c iv, d ii, e v, f i   3 a Getsuyō kurasu wa gozen jūji kara
jūniji made desu. b Kinyō kurasu wa gogo shichiji kara kuji made
desu. c Doyōkurasu wa gogo niji kara yoji made desu.   4 a Are wa
(Nihon no) tokei desu. b Kore wa empitsu desu. c Sore wa kaban
desu. d Kore wa shimbun desu.   5 Drinks: coffee, milk, beer, iced
coffee, juice. Food: sandwich(es), spaghetti, pizza, ice cream, cake(s).

Menyū o misete kudsasai./*Your choice* o kudasai. (use **to** for *and*)
6 a sore b kore c ano d sore e dono   7 a Sono hon o misete kudasai.
/ Dore desu ka. / Sore desu. b Irasshaimase. / Ano tokei o misete
kudasai. / Dono tokei desu ka. / Are desu. / Hai, dōzo. / Dōmo
arigatō.

Test

1 a Gogo rokuji b Gozen hachiji c Gozen jūji d jūichiji e shichiji han
f yoji han   2 Nihongo wa jūji kara jūichiji made desu. Furansugo wa
jūichiji han kara jūniji han made desu. Eigo wa ichiji han kara niji
han made desu. Tenisu kurabu wa sanji kara yoji made desu.   3 a
Menyū o misete kudasai. b Kore o kudasai. c Sono tokei o misete
kudasai. d Ano tokei o misete kudasai. e Dore desu ka.

Unit 6

Let's talk

2 a yonhyaku gojū b kyūhyaku gojū c gohyaku gojū d nisen nihyaku
e nisen gohyaku f nisen nihyaku gojū

Explanations

9 – fishmonger's; electrical store; bakery; butcher's; chemist's/
pharmacy; ❶: a hanaya, b sakanaya, c denkiya, d ginko, e kusuriya, f
panya, g yūbinkyoku

Practice

1 a 200 yen b 600 yen c 950 yen d 1,000 yen e 1,050 yen f 40,000
yen g 25,000 yen   2 a 2 b 12 c 1 d 6 e 3 f 20 g 6 h 4   3 a Example:
and i hyaku nijū-en ii nihyaku jū-en iii hyaku gojū-en iv hyaku nijū-
en b Name of place + 'made ikura desu ka'.   4 a *price* + 'no kitte o
kudasai.' i kyūjū-en ii hachijū-en iii nihyaku-en iv gohyaku-en v
hyaku-en vi jū-en. b i sanmai ii jūmai iii gomai iv ichimai v yonmai vi
nijūmai   5 All begin with 'Tōkyō kara ...'. b ... Narita made nisen
happyaku kyūjū-en desu. c ... Kyōto made ichiman nisen kyūhyaku
nanajū-en desu. d ... Shin-Ōsaka made ichiman sanzen yonhyaku
hachijū-en desu. e ... Hiroshima made ichiman nanasen nanahyaku-
en desu. f ... Nagasaki made niman sanzen gohyaku jū-en desu. g ...
Sapporo made niman issen sambyaku hachijū-en desu.   6 a Hagaki o
sanmai kudasai. b Bīru o ippon kudasai. c Miruku o futatsu kudasai.
d Pen o roppon kudasai. e Nihyaku-en no kēki o mittsu kudasai.
f Sen-en no kippu o nimai kudasai.   7 a sen kyūhyaku kyūjū roku-
nen b sen rokujū roku-nen c sen kyūhyaku rokujūsan-nen d sen
kyūhyaku hachijū-nen e sen kyūhyaku yonjūgo-nen   8 a Yūbinkyoku
b Yaoya c Sakaya d Sakaya e Sakanaya f Panya

Unit 7

Let's talk

a Sumimasen b ginkō wa doko desu ka c Mōichido itte kudasai
d (Dōmo) arigatō (gozaimasu)

Practice

1 a i Massugu itte kudasai. ii Migi ni magatte kudasai. iii Hidari ni
magatte kudasai. iv (Tsugi no) shingō o massugu itte kudasai. v
(Tsugi no) shingō o migi ni magatte kudasai. vi Kōsaten o massugu
itte kudasai. vii Kōsaten o hidari ni magatte kudasai. viii Nibanme no
shingō o migi ni magatte kudasai. ix Nibanme no kōsaten o hidari ni
magatte kudasai. x Kado o migi ni magatte kudasai. b Massugu itte,
migi ni magatte kudasai, etc. 2 (1) e sūpā, (2) b hanaya, (3) d eki, (4)
c ginkō, (5) a yūbinkyoku 3 a Sumimasen, yūbinkyoku wa doko desu
ka. b Sumimasen, hanaya wa doko desu ka. c Sumimasen, ginkō wa
doko desu ka. d Sumimasen, eki wa doko desu ka. e Sumimasen,
sūpā wa doku desu ka. (To say *the nearest* add 'Ichiban chikai' before
the place as in: a Sumimasen, ichiban chikai yūbinkyoku wa doko
desu ka, etc.) 4 a O b X c X d O e O f X   5 a chikaku b tonari c
tonari d sakanaya e mukaigawa f panya/ sūpā/depāto   7 a

b Ohayō gozaimasu (*good morning*)

Test

1 Check Unit 6, pp. 59–61.   2 b   3 a Ohayō gozaimasu. b Massugu
itte, kōsaten o migi ni magatte kudasai. c Yaoya wa ginkō no
mukaigawa desu. d Kōhī to kēki o kudasai. e Ichiban chikai panya
wa doko desu ka.

Unit 8

Let's talk

1 a rokuji b yoji han c gogo kuji d gozen shichiji han e jūniji f gozen
jūichiji han. 2 a Ginkō wa kuji kara sanji made desu. b Sūpā wa
hachiji kara hachiji made desu c Yūbinkyoku wa kuji kara rokuji
made desu d Panya wa hachiji kara rokuji made desu.

Practice

1 **a** ii, **b** i, **c** ii   2 **a** studies French; afternoon **b** Friday, from 8 p.m. **c** morning; evening **d** all day; eats dinner **e** Monday–Friday; eats lunch 3 **a** vii, **b** iv, **c** i, **d** viii, **e** ii/ vi, **f** iii, **g** v, **h** Sunday   4 All begin with '(Name)-san wa asagohan ni …' **a** … pan o tabemasu. Sore ni kōhī o nomimasu. **b** … tamago o tabemasu. Sore ni kōcha o nomimasu. **c** … gohan o tabemasu. Sore ni ocha o nomimasu. **d** … tōsuto o tabemasu. Sore ni miruku o nomimasu. **e** … kudamono o tabemasu. Sore ni jūsu o nomimasu.   5 Shichiji han goro okimasu. Daitai asagohan ni tamago o tabemasu. Soshite kōcha o nomimasu. Sorekara kuji kara yoji made nihongo o benkyō shimasu. Daitai jūniji han ni hirugohan o tabemasu. Doyōbi ni tenisu o shimasu. Yoru tokidoki terebi o mimasu. Sore ni jūichiji goro nemasu.   6 **a** Nanji ni okimasu ka. **b** Asagohan ni nani o tabemasu ka. **c** Nanyōbi ni kaimono o shimasu ka. **d** Yoru nani o shimasu ka. **e** Itsu benkyō shimasu ka.

Test

1 **a** Kinyōbi **b** Kayōbi **c** Getsuyōbi **d** Mokuyōbi   2 okimasu; asagohan; tabemasu; o nomimasu; kara; ji made; hirugohan; bangohan o; mimasu; ji; nemasu; ni; yomimasu

Unit 9

Let's talk

1 shimashō 2 shimashō 3 tabemashō 4 nomimashō 5 mimashō 6 benkyō shimashō

Practice

1 3rd November f; 7th July c; 15th November d; 3rd March a; 4th May e; 20th July h; 5th May b; 1st October g   2 **a** i Ashita Rondon ni ikimasu. ii Konban konsāto ni ikimasu. iii Kyō Furansu ni ikimasu. iv Mainichi uchi ni kaerimasu. **b** As in **a** but add 'Tani-san wa …' at the start of each sentence. **c** i Ashita doko ni ikimasu ka. ii Konban doko ni ikimasu ka. iii Kyō doko ni ikimasu ka. iv Mainichi doko ni kaerimasu ka.   3 **a** ni **b** X **c** X **d** ni **e** X **f** ni   4 **a** Ashita eiga o mimashō ka. **b** Raishū doraibu ni ikimashō! **c** Kono zasshi o yomimasen ka. **d** Kyō hirugohan o tabemashō ka. **e** Konban watashi no uchi ni kimasen ka. **f** Raishū no doyōbi ni kaimono ni ikimashō! **g** Kōhī o nomimasen ka. **h** Ashita no ban resutoran ni ikimashō ka 5 Konnichi wa./Raishū watashi no uchi ni kimasen ka. (Raishū no) suiyōbi wa dō desu ka./Mokuyōbi wa? (dō desu ka)./Doyōbi wa daijōbu desu. Yoji wa dō desu ka./Ja mata ne, sayōnara!

Test

1 c   2 **a** ikimashō ka **b** kimasen ka **c** mimashō **d** tabemashō ka **e** ikimashō ka **f** mimasen ka   3 **a** Ashita tomodachi to Rondon ni ikimasu. **b** Zannen desu ga nichiyōbi wa chotto … **c** Bīru o nomimasen ka. **d** Mokuyōbi wa dō desu ka. **e** Doyōbi wa daijōbu

desu. Yorokonde. f Watashi no tanjōbi wa hachigatsu yōka desu.
g Doko ni ikimashō ka.

Unit 10

Let's talk

1 nomimashita 2 shimashita 3 mimashita 4 yomimashita 5 ikimashita
6 kaerimashita

Practice

1 i a, ii d, iii b, iv f, v e, vi c, vii d, h   2 a iii, b ii, c iv, d i, e v   3 b
gojikan c yonjuppun d ichijikan e gofun. b Tōkyō kara Kyōto made
shinkansen de gojikan gurai kakarimasu. c Dābī kara Shefirudo made
densha de yonjuppun gurai kakarimasu. d An-san no uchi kara
Sukotto-san no uchi made chikatetsu de ichijikan gurai kakarimasu.
e An-san no uchi kara sūpā made aruite gofun gurai kakarimasu.
4 a iv, b vii, c iii, d vi, e ii, f i, g v 5 a Senshū no doyōbi ni Ginza de
kaimono o shimashita. b Senshū no suiyōbi ni uchi de eigo o benkyō
shimashita. c Ashita tomodachi to resutoran de bangohan o
tabemasu. d Kyonen Kyōto de ryokō o shimashita. e Yūbe eigakan de
eiga o mimashita. f Sengetsu no tōka ni Tōkyō no gekijō de nihon no
odori o mimashita.   6 a Eki made jitensha de gofun kakarimasu.
b Ashita kaimono o shitai desu. c Chichi wa kuruma de kaisha ni
ikimasu. d Kesa no asagohan ni tōsuto o tabemashita. e Kotoshi
Furansu ni ikitai desu. f Rainen no kugatsu ni Nihon ni ikimasu.
g Kayōbi no ban gekijō ni ikimashō ka.

Test

1 a Ohayō gozaimasu b Hajimemashite c Oyasumi nasai d
Sumimasen e (Dōmo) arigatō gozaimasu. f Ja mata ne!   3 a iii, b ii,
c iii   4 a shimashita b no; ni; shi c de; o; shimasu d o
tabemasu/mashita e wa/to; ikimashita f o mimashita g no; ni; mashita;
h kara; made; de; iki

Unit 11

Let's talk

a wakai desu ne b kawaii desu ne c sono tokei wa suteki desu ne
d nihongo ga jōzu desu ne e hayai desu ne f ii desu ne

Practice

1 a Yasui kuruma desu ne. b Omoshiroi eiga desu ne. c Shizukana
resutoran desu ne. d Shinsetsuna hito desu ne. e Oishii aisukurīmu
desu ne. f Ōkii terebi desu ne. g Chiisai terebi desu ne. h Genkina
hito desu ne. 2 a Yasukatta desu. b Omoshirokatta desu ne. c Shizuka
deshita ne.
d Shinsetsu deshita ne. e Oishikatta desu ne. f Ōkikatta desu ne.
g Chiisakatta desu ne. h Genki deshita ne.   3 a Atsui desu. b
Shizukana gakkō desu. c Tanoshii desu. d … ii desu. e … oishii desu.

f ... shinsetsu desu. g Sutekina sētā desu. h ... kawaii desu. 4 a Shizukana hito deshita ga omoshirokatta desu. b Kono aisukurīmu wa oishii desu ga chotto takai desu. c Nihon ni ikitai desu ga takai desu. d Kyonen no haru wa chotto samukatta desu ga kotoshi no haru wa chotto atsui desu. e Kono sētā wa chotto ōkii desu ga sono (ano) sētā wa chotto chiisai desu. 5 a small b hot c convenient d smart e kind f expensive g nice 6 Sapporo: 15°C, a bit cold; Tōkyō 25°C, rain; Ōsaka: 27°C, rain later fine; Hiroshima: 26°C, nice weather; Nagasaki: 33°C, very hot

Test

1 a wakai b tanoshikatta c shizukana d benri e desu 2 a iv, b v, c ii, d i, e iii 3 Senshū nihongo no eiga o mimashita./ Omoshirokatta desu./Ashita no ban eigakan ni ikimashō (ka)/Yorokonde (ii desu ne). 'Rūna' kissaten ni ikimashō ka./Chotto takai desu ga aisukurīmu wa totemo oishii desu.

Unit 12

Let's talk

1 Nomimasen – *I don't drink*; gorufu o shimasen – *I don't play golf*; okimasen – *I don't wake up*; nemasen – *I don't sleep*, yomimasen – *I don't read*; ikimasen – *I don't go* 2 a Ginkō wa yūbinkyoku no tonari desu. b Eki wa eigakan no chikaku desu. c Depāto wa ginkō no mukaigawa desu. d Hanaya wa depāto no mae desu.

Practice

1 Dialogue a Tokei wa tēburu no ue ni arimasu. b Inu wa kuruma no shita ni imasu. c Tamago wa kaban no naka ni arimasu. d Takeshi-kun wa uchi ni imasu. e Yūbinkyoku wa ginkō no mukaigawa desu. f An-san wa Emi-san no tonari ni imasu.

Answers: a maru b batsu c maru d maru e batsu f batsu

2 Dialogue:

Reiko	An-san, Nihon no ryōri wa dō desu ka.
Anne	Totemo suki desu.
Reiko	Yokatta desu ne. Nihon no terebi wa?
Anne	Sō desu ne. Nyūsu wa hotondo wakarimasen no de amari suki dewa arimasen. Demo hōmu dorama wa suki desu. Reiko-san wa?
Reiko	Ē, watashi mo hōmu dorama ga suki desu. Demo Takeshi wa hōmu dorama ga amari suki dewa arimasen.
Takeshi	Kirai desu. Boku wa anime ga suki desu. Soshite supōtsu bangumi mo suki desu ga tenisu wa amari suki dewa arimasen. Mochiron, Emi wa tenisu bangumi ga daisuki desu.

	Anne	**Takeshi**	**Emi**	**Mr Yamaguchi**	**Reiko**
Tennis		×	✓✓		
Japanese cookery	✓✓				
TV news	×			✓	
Soap drama	✓	×			✓
Whisky				✓✓	
Cartoons		✓			

Anne   Yamaguchi-san, donna bangumi ga suki desu ka.
Mr Yamaguchi   Sō desu ne. Nyūsu ga suki desu. Nyūsu o mitari uisukī o nondari suru to rirakkusu dekimasu. Boku wa uisukī ga totemo suki desu.

Answers

3 a imasu; imasu; arimasu **b** arimasu; arimasu; arimasu **c** imasu; imasen; imasu; imasu   **4 a** Yūbinkyoku no tonari desu. **b** Terebi no ue ni arimasu. **c** Kuruma no shita ni imasu. **d** Daidokoro ni imasu. **e** Isu no ushiro desu.   **5** Yamaguchi-san wa Emi-san no ushiro ni imasu. Reiko-san wa Yamaguchi-san no tonari ni imasu. Takeshi-kun wa Reiko-san no tonari ni imasu. Inu wa Takeshi-kun no mae ni imasu. An-san wa inu no tonari ni imasu. Emi-san wa Yamaguchi-san no mae ni imasu.   **6 a** Takeshi-kun wa hyaku mētoru ga jōzu desu. **b** Yamaguchi-san wa gorufu ga totemo jōzu desu. **c** iie, mada mada desu. **d** Watashi wa Furansugo ga tokui desu. **e** Kinō zenzen terebi o mimasen deshita. **f** Amari shimbun o yomimasen.   **7 a** Hai, tokidoki mimasu. **b** Hai, yoku shimasu. **c** Iie, amari yomimasen. **d** Iie, zenzen basu de ikimasen. **e** Iie, amari mimasen. **f** Iie, zenzen kikimasen.

8 Word puzzle

1		a	m	a	r	i	s	u	k	i
2			n	y	ū	s	u	
3			d	o	i	t	s	u	
4		n	i	a	r	i	m	a	s	u
5		y	o	m	i	m	a	s	e	n
6	k	ō	r	a	g	a	s	u	k	i
7			g	a	t	o	k	u	i
8			g	a	j	ō	z	u
9	k	y	ō	s	ō	n	i
10		z	e	n	z	e	n
				u			

Revision test

1 a vi, **b** iv, **c** i, **d** vii, **e** ii, **f** iii, **g** v   **2 a** Kore o kudasai. **b** Ano hon o misete kudasai. **c** Aisukurīmu to kōhī o kudasai. **d** Sumimasen, ima nanji desu ka. **e** Yūbinkyoku wa kuji kara goji han made desu. **f** Kono Eigo no shimbun wa ikura desu ka. **g** Kono tegami wa Igirisu made ikura desu ka. **h** Kitte ga arimasu ka. **i** Bīru o nihon kudasai.   **3 a** Sumimasen, Nihon ginkō wa doko desu ka/doko ni arimasu ka. **b** Chotto itte, shingō o migi ni magatte kudasai. **c** Sumimasen, mōichido itte kudasai. **d** Ginkō wa 'Sōgō' depāto no mukaigawa desu/ni arimasu. **e** (Dōmo) arigatō gozaimasu/mashita. **4 a** Rokuji han ni okimashita. **b** Asagohan ni tamago to tōsuto o tabemashita. **c** Basu de kaisha (shigoto) ni ikimashita. **d** Hachiji han kara jūniji made shigoto o shimashita. **e** Tomodachi to resutoran de hirugohan o tabemashita (or: Resutoran de tomodachi to hirugohan o tabemashita.) **f** Chikatetsu de (uchi ni) kaerimasu. **g** Niji kara yoji made bangohan o tsukurimasu. **h** Bangohan ni toriniku to gohan o tabemasu. **i** Terebi o mimasu. **j** Jūichiji han goro nemasu.   **5 a** Sumimasen, yūbinkyoku wa doko desu ka/ni arimasu ka. **b** 'Book' wa Nihongo de nan desu ka. **c** Doyōbi ni nani o shimasu ka. **d** Nanji ni okimasu ka. **e** Itsu Furansu ni ikimasu ka. **f** Yūbe nani o shimashita ka. **g** Asagohan ni nani o tabemasu ka. **h** Tōkyō kara Ōsaka made shinkansen de dono gurai kakarimasu ka. **6 a** mashō ka **b** mashō **c** tai desu **d** mashō ka **e** masen ka **f** tai desu **g** mashō   **7 a** atsui **b** samukatta **c** shizukana **d** shizuka **e** jōzu **f** tokui

Unit 13

Practice

2 In order from top to bottom f, g, e, a, c, d; Extra kanji = b = Thursday   **3 a** Getsuyōbi desu. **b** Nichiyōbi **c** Kayōbi **d** Doyōbi **e** Kinyōbi **f** Nichiyōbi **g** Suiyōbi   **5** From top to bottom c, f, e, b, a, d   **6** From top to bottom: f, e, a, b, c, d   **7** From top to bottom: **h** 31st **g** 8th **a** 23rd **b** 1st **f** 5th **c** 14th **d** 20th **e** 12th   **8** Saturday 21st October   **9** From top to bottom: e, g, f, b, c, d, a   **10** From top to bottom: salad = f = sarada; cake = e = kēki; milk = g = miruku; ice = b = aisu; cheese = c = chīzu; pizza = d = piza   **11 a** 500 **b** 800 **c** 1,100 **d** Coffee plus pizza/hamburger/cake; iced coffee plus hamburger/cake; cola plus any food on the menu.

12

Test

1 b Saturday June 11th c Tuesday 3rd January d Sunday 25th
September e Monday 7th April f Friday 18th February g 5th May
(Boys' Day) 2 a ii, b i, c iii, d ii, e i

Unit 14

Practice

1 a 9–7 b Yes c They wear very smart uniforms and their Japanese is
very polite. d Ginza 4 a Sumimasen, fujinfuku uriba wa doko desu
ka. b Ikura desu ka. c Motto chiisai no wa arimasu ka. d Ja, chotto
kitemimasu. e Ja, kore o kudasai. f Sore de kekkō desu. g Gosen-en
de onegaishimasu. h Arigatō gozaimashita. Mata okoshi kudasai.   5
Possible answers (shop assistant in brackets): (Irasshaimase.)/Ano
kuroi zubon o misete kudasai./(Hai, dōzo.)/Ikura desu ka./(Sanzen-en
desu.)/Saizu wa?/(Esu desu.)/Motto ōkii no wa arimasu ka./(Hai,
shōshō omachi kudasai.)/Ja, kore o kudasai. Ichiman-en de
onegaishimasu.   6 All answers end with '... ni arimasu'. a A no
nikai. b A no hachikai. c A no nanakai. d A no rokkai. e B no sankai.
f A no chika ikkai (or A no chikai). g B no ikkai.   7 a Niman-en
desu. b Nihon-sei desu. c Takai. d Ichiman gosen-en desu.
e Nana pāsento ni shimashita.   8 Ano rajikase o misete
kudasai./Nihon-sei desu ka./Ikura desu ka./Chotto takai desu ne.
Diskaunto dekimasu ka./Ja, kore o kudasai.   9 All answers end in
'kudasai'. a Yukata o mittsu (sanmai). b Washi o jūmai. c Hashi o
futatsu. d Sensu o nihon. e Chōchin o yottsu. f O-sake o gohon.
10 d, i, c, a, g, j, h, f, b, e

Test

a Chotto ōkii desu. b Saizu wa? c Motto yasui no wa arimasu ka.
d Kamera uriba wa nankai ni arimasu ka (nankai desu ka). e Denki
seihin uriba wa doko desu ka. f Ichiman-en de onegaishimasu. g Ano
kuroi T. shatsu o misete kudasai. h O-hashi o mittsu kudasai.

Unit 15

Practice

1 a the family b A variety from Japanese to western-style cuisine. c
Reiko: pork cutlets and egg on rice; Mr Yamaguchi: beef steak; Emi,
Anne and Takeshi: hamburgers. d Two bottles. e They really like
western food and don't eat Japanese cuisine very much.   2 All end in
'... kudasai'. a Kōhī o futatsu b Sarada o mittsu c Hambāgā o yottsu
d Aisukurīmu o hitotsu to chīzukēki o futatsu e Remon tī o futatsu to
bīru o ippon   3 f, a, p, m, e, d, h, j, o, l, b, g, n, k, c, i   4 a Nanmei-
sama desu ka. Sannin desu. b Menyū o misete kudasai. c O-kimari
desu ka. d Chīzu sandoitchi to sarada ni shimasu. e Supagetti ga
totemo suki desu. f Chīzukēki o tabetai desu. g (Watashi wa) mō
kekko desu.   5 Hitori desu./Menyū o misete kudasai./(*Your choice*) o

kudasai./(*drink*) o kudasai./Oishikatta desu./Mō kekko desu. 6 H = chickenburger, medium chips, medium strawberry shake; T = cheeseburger, large chips, small banana shake; Price = c 1,400 yen 8 All start with 'Sore wa ...'. a sashimi desu. b tempura desu. c soba desu. d yakitori desu. e miso shiru desu. f udon desu. 9 a Nanmei-sama b ni-mei c Menyū d Nihon e shōshō o-machi f Bīru o dōzo g Arigatō gozaimasu h Kampai i wakarimasu ka j sashimi teishoku k miso shiru, gohan to tsukemono l sushi, ni shimasu m O-kimari n hitotsu; onegaishimasu; Nihon 10 a Sushi teishoku wa sushi to miso shiru, gohan to tsukemono desu. b Yakitori teishoku wa yakitori to miso shiru, gohan to tsukemono desu. c Tempura teishoku wa tempura to miso shiru, gohan to tsukemono desu.

Test

a Chīzubāga to furaido poteto ni shimasu. b O-kimari desu ka. c Niku ga taberaremasen. d Oishikatta desu. e Mō kekko desu. f Bīru o sambon kudasai. g Kampai.

Unit 16

Practice

1 a nihyaku-en, sambyaku-en, yonhyaku-en b happyaku-en, roppyaku-en, gohyaku-en c yonhyaku gojū-en, nanahyaku gojū-en, kyūhyaku gojū-en d sen-en, nisen-en, sanzen-en e sen gohyaku-en, sen gojū-en, hassen gojū-en f ichiman-en, yonman-en, yonsen-en g niman gosen-en, niman gohyaku-en, niman gojū-en 3 Bank: 9–3, not open on weekends. Post office: 9–5, 9–12, not open on Sundays.
4 a Toraberāzu chekku o kaetai desu. b Toraberāzu chekku o genkin ni kaetai desu. c Gosen-en satsu de kudasai/onegaishimasu. d Koko ni sain shite kudasai. e Sumimasen, ryōgae-guchi wa doko desu ka.
5 a Over near the cashpoint machine. b 100 pounds. c £1 = 170 yen, 17,000 yen. d 3% e In 5,000 and 1,000 notes. 7 a Hagaki o okuritai desu. b Kono hagaki o okuritai desu. c Tegami o okuritai desu. d Kono kozutsumi o okuritai desu. e Kono kozutsumi o funabin de okuritai desu. f Kono kozutsumi o kōkūbin de okuritai desu. 8 The parcel is 1 kilo. She wants to send it by seamail. A Japanese kimono and various books. 5 × 70 yen stamps. 3,350 yen. Order: d, j, c, g, h, l, k, e, b, i, f, a, m 9 Kono kozutsumi o Igirisu ni okuritai desu./Kōkūbin de onegaishimasu./Nihon no omiyage to tegami desu./Earoguramu wa Igirisu made ikura desu ka./Hagaki no kitte o jūmai kudasai./Gosen-en de onegaishimasu.

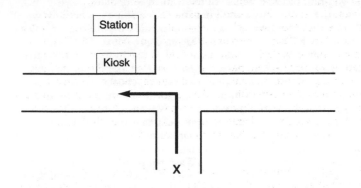

11 Chotto itte, tsugi no shingō o migi ni magatte kudasai. Massugu itte, kōsaten o hidari ni magatte kudasai. Baiten wa ginkō no tonari ni arimasu.

Revision test

1 a iv, b vii, c vi, d ii, e viii, f iii, g i. Extra item: h Yōshoku **2** a ii, b i, c iii, d ii **3** a Chotto chiisai desu. Motto ōkii no wa arimasu ka. b Sen-en de onegaishimasu. c Furaido poteto no esu o onegaishimasu/o kudasai. d Tempura teishoku ni shimasu. e Toraberāzu chekku o kaetai desu. f Jū doru o en ni kaetai desu. g Kono tegami o kōkūbin de okuritai desu.

Unit 17

Practice

1

	Japanese inn	Hotel	Youth hostel
Price/night	From 6,000 yen	From 5,000	From 2,000
Per person?	Y	N	Y
Per room?	N	Y (Twin)	N
Japanese room?	Y	N	N
Western room?	N	Y	Y
Japanese food?	Y	N	N
Western food?	N	Y	Y
Page number (in guide book)	2	3	4

2 **a** Hokkaidō no gaido (kankō annai) ga arimasu ka. **b** Tōkyō no chizu ga arimasu ka. **c** Washitsu to yōshitsu to dochira ga yoroshii desu ka. **d** Tsuin no heya wa ikura desu ka. **e** Shinguru no heya wa ikura desu ka. **f** Watashi no uchi de kono gaido o yomimashō. 3 **a** 3rd February **b** Three nights **c** 2,500 yen **d** Breakfast: 600 yen; evening meal; 1,000 yen **e** His name and phone number 4 Nigatsu muika ni yoyaku o shitai desu./Yonin desu./Nihaku desu./Ippaku ikura desu ka./Shokuji wa haitteimasu ka./Ja, chōshoku to yūshoku o onegaishimasu. 5 **a** Moshi moshi; de gozaimasu **b** Gogatsu tōka **c** Nanmei-sama **d** Futari; ikura desu ka **e** Washitsu; yōshitsu **f** onegaishimasu **g** Yokushitsu; gohyaku-en; hassen-en **h** Shokuji **i** chōshoku; yūshoku **j** hassen-en; onegaishimasu **k** O-namae; O-denwa-bangō 6 Moshi moshi, Ryokan Hanaya desu/de gozaimasu./Nanmei-sama desu ka/Washitsu desu/deshō ka. Yōshitsu desu/deshō ka (or: Washitsu to yōshitsu to dochira ga yoroshii desu ka)./Yokushitsu ga aru heya wa niman-en de/desu/de gozaimasu; yokushitsu ga nai heya wa niman yonsen-en desu/de gozaimasu./Iie, chōshoku wa sen-en de yūshoku wa nisen-en desu/de gozaimasu./O-namae to o-denwa-bangō o onegaishimasu.
7 **a** Iie **b** Hai **c** Iie **d** Iie **e** Hai

Test

1 **a** iii, **b** ii, **c** iii, **d** iii, **e** iii 2 **a** v, **b** vi, **c** ii, **d** vii, **e** i, **f** iii, **g** iv; Per person = **h** Hitori

Unit 18

Practice

1 **a** To Ueno station **b** The kanji (Japanese characters) for Ueno **c** 160 yen **d** 70 yen, because he can pay the rest at the fare adjustment office. 2 **a** Sumimasen, Ueno (eki) made ikura desu ka. **b** Ano chizu o mimashō. **c** Ueno no kanji ga wakarimasu ka. **d** Ueno made 160-en desu. **e** Ueno eki no seisanjo de nokori o haraimasu. 3 Sumimasen, Ginza made ikura desu ka./Sumimasen, mōichido itte kudasai./Hyaku rokujū-en desu ne. Arigatō gozaimashita. 4 **a** iii, **b** i, **c** ii 5 **a** Sumimasen, Ueno ni ikitai desu. **b** Koko kara Asakusa ni itte kudasai. Soshite, Ginza-sen ni norikaete kudasai. **c** Asakusa de norikaemasu ne. **d** Hai, sō desu. Ginza-sen ni norikaemasu. **e** Wakarimashita. Arigatō gozaimashita. 6 **a** T **b** F **c** F **d** F **e** F **f** T **g** T 7 Doko de shinkansen no kippu o kaimasu ka. **b** Kyōto-yuki no kippu o yonmai kudasai. **c** Katamichi desu ka, ōfuku desu ka. **d** Shitei seki o onegaishimasu. **e** Waribiki kippu ga arimasu ka. **f** Pasupōto o misete kudasai. 8 Sumimasen, Hiroshima-yuki no kippu o nimai kudasai./Katamichi o onegaishimasu (kudasai)./ Jiyūseki o onegaishimasu (kudasai). Kodomo no waribiki kippu ga arimasu ka. 9 c, a, d, b, e 10 Sumimasen, Hiroshima-yuki no densha wa nanban-sen desu ka./Tsugi no densha wa nanji desu ka/Yoji desu ne. Arigatō gozaimashita. 11 Anne: Sumimasen, kono densha wa Hiroshima-yuki desu ka. Passer-by: Iie, sono densha wa Ōsaka-yuki desu. Tsugi no densha wa Hiroshma-yuki desu. 12 **a** dono gurai

b Jūjikan han **c** Tōi **d** kaimashō **e** O-cha; ikaga **f** nani ga arimasu ka **g** gozaimasu **h** Eigo de **i** Oishii **j** hitotsu; **o** kudasai **k** kyūhyaku-en **l** otsuri **m** tōchaku shimasu **n** Kuji han **o** ichiji **p** Nani o shimashō ka **13 b 14 a** Takushī de ikimashō. **b** Takushī noriba wa doko desu ka. **c** Sapporo yūsuhosuteru ni ikitai desu. **d** Yūsuhosuteru no chizu ga arimasu ka. **e** Yūsuhosuteru wa asoko desu. Ano resutoran no tonari desu. **15** *Possible answer*: 'Plaza' hoteru ni ikitai desu./(Koko kara) massugu itte kudasai. (Soshite) kōsaten o hidari ni magatte kudasai./Hai, sō desu. (Sorekara) tsugi no shingō o migi ni magatte kudasai./'Plaza' hoteru wa asoko desu. Ano depāto no mukaigawa desu./Arigatō. Sen-en de onegaishimasu.

Test

1 a Shinjuku (eki) made ikura desu ka. **b** Shibuya eki ni ikitai desu. **c** Doko de norikaemasu ka. **d** Doko de shinkansen no kippu o kaimasu ka. **e** Kyōto-yuki no kippu o ichimai kudasai. **f** Tsugi no shingō o hidari ni magatte kudasai. **g** Maebashi-yuki no densha wa nanban-sen desu ka. **2 a** i, **b** ii, **c** iii, **d** ii, **e** i

Unit 19

Practice

1 a 2 **b** 1 **c** 5 **d** 4 **e** 3 **f** 11 a.m.–9 p.m. **g** 11 o'clock **2 a** Sapporo no chizu ga arimasu ka. **b** Yuki Matsuri wa doko desu ka. **c** Sapporo ni omoshiroi hakubutsukan ga arimasu ka. **d** Sapporo no kankō o shitai desu. **e** Yūmeina bīru-en wa doko ni arimasu ka (doko desu ka). **f** Konban disuko ni ikitai desu. **3** Tōkyō no chizu ga arimasu ka./Tōkyō ni omoshiroi hakubutsukan ga arimasu ka./Meiji jingū wa doko desu ka (doko ni arimasu ka.) Nihon no omiyage o kaitai desu./Asakusa wa doko desu ka (doko ni arimasu ka.) Yūmeina Sunshine rokujū biru wa doko desu ka/(doko ni arimasu ka)./Konban kabuki o mitai desu. Kabuki-za wa doko desu ka. (doko ni arimasu ka.) Arigatō gozaimashita. National Museum/Tokyo Art Gallery: Ueno area, 9–4.30; Meiji shrine: in Yoyogi park, 9–4.30; Japanese souvenirs: Asakusa – near Ueno park; Sunshine 60 building; Ikebukuro area; Kabuki theatre: Near Higashi-Ginza, from 7.30. **4 a** Hai, totemo suki desu. **b** Sukī-jō ni ikimashita. **c** Gosen-en desu. **d** Sukī yōgu o karitai desu. **e** Rifuto de ikimashita. **f** Iie, amari shimasen deshita. **g** Iie, jōzu dewa arimasen. **h** Sukotto-san to An-san wa sukī no renshū o shimashita. **5 a** Kyō wa nani o shimashō ka. **b** Sumimasen, nyūjōken wa ikura desu ka. **c** Ichinichi no nyūjōken o yonmai kudasai. **d** Sore ni, sukī yōgu o karitai desu. **e** (Watashi wa) sukī ga amari jōzu dewa arimasen. **6** Ichijikan wa gohyaku-en desu. Ichinichi wa nisen-en desu./Hitori sanbyaku-en desu./Ichijikan wa sen-en desu./Zembu de sen roppyaku-en desu./Yonhyaku-en no otsuri desu. **7 a** Moshi moshi **b** konshū no doyōbi **c** man-in; gogo; seki **d** ikura **e** Ikkai no; nanasen; rokusen; ichiman; Kodomo no seki **f** nanasen; 4; 1 **g** sanman issen gohyaku **h** nanji kara **i** 2; 6; 3 **j** gaido **k** gaido: iyahōn **l** o-namae; o-denwa-bangō **m** 3,844-2,329 **8 a** iv, **b** vii, **c** v, **d** vi, **e** i, **f** iii, **g** ii **9** Doyōbi wa man-in desu ga nichiyōbi wa mada seki ga arimasu./Ikkai no seki wa hachi pondo to jū pondo desu. Nikai no seki wa roku pondo to kyū pondo desu. Kodomo no seki wa hangaku desu./Zembu de nijūyon pondo desu./Shichiji han kara desu./(Sore dewa) o-namae to o-denwa-bangō o onegaishimasu.

Revision test

1

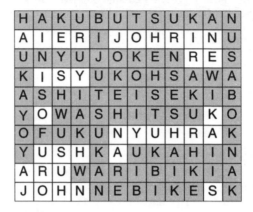

2 **a** arimasu **b** shitai **c** haitteimasu **d** gomai **e** nanban-sen **f** kakarimasu **g** seki **h** ikura **i** onegaishimasu　3 **a** Tōkyō no gaido (kankō annai) ga arimasu ka. **b** Daburu no heya wa ikura desu ka. **c** Konban heya ga arimasu ka. **d** Katamichi (no kippu) o kudasai. **e** Gakusei no waribiki (diskaunto) kippu ga arimasu ka. **f** Kono hen ni bijutsukan ga arimasu ka. **g** Doko de norikaemasu ka.　4 **a** iii, **b** i, **c** ii, **d** iii

Unit 20

Practice

1 **a** vi, **b** iii, **c** iv, **d** viii, **e** v, **f** i, **g** ix, **h** ii. **i** = Oishisō desu ne.　3 **a** Gomen kudasai. **b** and **c** Shitsurei shimasu. **d** Tsumaranai mono desu ga, dōzo. **e** Itadakimasu. **f** Kōhī o onegaishimasu. **g** Mō kekkō desu. **h** Oishikatta desu. **i** Gochisōsama deshita.　5 **a** v, **b** vii, **c** viii, **d** ix, **e** x, **f** ii, **g** i, **h** vi, **i** Kōhī no okawari wa ikaga desu ka. **j** iii, **k** iv.　6 Yoku irasshaimashita; dōzo o-hairi kudasai./Kochira e dōzo; o-kake kudasai./Rondon wa dō deshita ka./Doko ni e ikimashita ka./Dōmo arigatō gozaimasu./Kōcha to kōhī to dochira ga ii desu ka/Sandoitchi wa ikaga desu ka./An-san wa genki desu ka./Kōcha no okawari wa ikaga desu ka/Mata asobi ni kite kudasai./O-ki o tsukete; sayōnara. 7 Name: Mike Robinson; Place of work: Bank of England; Bank of Japan　8 Example: Eikoku Ginkō no (*your name*) desu.　9 **a** batsu **b** batsu **c** maru **d** batsu **e** maru **f** batsu　10 **a** Moshi moshi, Rondon Hoken no Gates desu ga Suzuki-san wa irasshaimasu ka. **b** Sumimasen, ima gaishutsu-chū desu. Go-dengon ga arimasu ka.

c Hai, watashi ni denwa o onegaishimasu. Kaisha no denwa-bangō wa zero ichi nana ichi no roku roku san no ni ichi kyū hachi desu. Goji han made koko ni imasu. d Hai, wakarimashita. e Yoroshiku onegaishimasu. 11 Sunday–Wednesday: business trip to Ōsaka; Thursday: meeting at Mainichi newspaper company; Friday: free (going to Mr Yamaguchi's house); Saturday: returns to England

Test

1 a Gomen kudasai. b Yoku irasshaimashita. c Konnichiwa. d Dōzo, o-hairi kudasai. e Shitsurei shimasu. f Surippa o dōzo. 2 Yamaguchi-san no o-taku desu ka. b Dengon o onegai dekimasu ka. c Mata denwa o shimasu. d Watashi ni denwa o onegaishimasu. e Go-dengon ga arimasu ka. f Sumimasen, ima denwa-chū desu. g Yoroshiku onegaishimasu/shitsurei shimasu.

Japanese–English vocabulary

The unit where each word first appears is given in brackets.

aisu (U13) *ice*
aisukōhī (U5) *iced coffee*
aisukurīmu (U2) *ice cream*
aiteimasu (U14) *is open*
akai (U14) *red*
aki (U11) *Autumn*
amari (U12) *not very*
ame (U11) *rain*
Amerika (U2) *America*
Amerika-jin (U2) *American person*
anata (U18) *you*
ane (U4) (my) *older sister*
ani (U3) (my) *older brother*
annai (U17) *information*
annaijo (U14) *information desk*
annaisho (U17) *information guidebook*
ano... (U1) *a hesitation word, like er, erm*
ano (U5) *that (over there)*
aoi (U14) *blue*
appuru pai (U15) *apple pie*
are! (U4) *expression of surprise*
are (U5) *that one over there (noun)*
arigatō (U1) *thanks*
arimasu (U6) *have, there is*
aru (U17) *have*
aruite (U10) *on foot, walking*
asa (U8) *morning*
asagohan (U8) *breakfast*
ashita (U9) *tomorrow*
asoko (U6) *over there*
atsui (U11) *hot*

bai bai (U1) *goodbye* (casual)
baiten (U16) *kiosk*
ban (U7) *number*
ban (U8) *evening/night*
bangohan (U8) *evening meal*
bangumi (U12) *programme*
banku kādo (U16) *bank card*
basu (U2) *bus*
basu noriba (U19) *bus stop*
beddo (U2) *bed*
benkyō shimasu (U8) *study*
benri(na) (U11) *convenient, handy*
bentō (U18) *packed lunch*
bideo (U2) *video*
bīfu sutēki (U15) *beef steak*
bīru (U5) *beer*
bīru-en (U19) *beer garden*
bijinesu hoteru (U17) *business hotel*
bijutsukan (U19) *art gallery*
biru (U19) *building*
bōifurendo (U3) *boyfriend*
boku (U2) *I* (men)
bōshi (U14) *hat*
burausu (U14) *blouse*

chichi (U3) *father*
chiisai (U5) *small*
chīzu (U13) *cheese*
chīzubāgā (U15) *cheeseburger*
chīzukēki (U15) *cheesecake*
chikai (U14) *basement*
chika ikkai (U14) *first floor of basement*
chikaku (U7) *near (to)*
chikatetsu (U10) *underground (train)*

chikin (U2) *chicken*
chikinbāgā (U15) *chickenburger*
chizu (U17) *map*
chōchin (U14) *paper lantern*
chōdo ii (U5) *just right*
chokoretto (U15) *chocolate*
chōshoku (U17) *breakfast*
chotto (U5) *a little*
chotto matte kudasai (U18) *please wait*
Chūgoku (U2) *China*
Chūgokugo (U2) *Chinese* (language)
Chūgokujin (U2) *Chinese person*
chūmon (U15) *an order*

daburu (U17) *double*
daidokoru (U12) *kitchen*
daigaku (U19) *university*
daisuki (U12) *really like*
daitai (U8) *more or less; usually*
dame (U7) *no good*
dansei (U14) *men's*
dansu (U3) *dancing*
dare (U3) *who*
de gozaimasu (U15) *is* (formal)
dekimasen (U7) *can't*
dekimasu (U7) *can, able to*
demasu (U12) *take part in*
demo (U14) *even; also; but*
dengon (U20) *message*
denki (U6) *lights; electricity*
denki seihin (U14) *electrical goods*
denkiya (U6) *electrical shop*
densha (U10) *train*
denwa (U2) *telephone*
denwa-bangō (U2) *telephone number*
denwa-chū (U20) *on the phone*
denwa o shimasu U8) *make a phone call*
depāto (U5) *department store*
deshita (U3) *was*
deshō (U17) *polite form of* **desu**
desu (U1) *am; is; are*
dewa (U5) *right!*
dewa arimasen (U3) *is not*
dezāto (U15) *dessert*
do (U11) *degrees*
dō (U9) *how?*
dochira (U17) *which one?*
Doitsu (U2) *Germany*
Doitsugo (U2) *German* (language)
Doitsujin (U2) *German person*
doko (U7) *where*

dokusho (U3) *reading*
dokyumentarī (U12) *documentary*
dōmo (U1) *thanks*
dōmo arigatō (gozaimasu) *thank you* (U1) (*very much*)
donata (U3) *who*
dono (U5) *which*
dono gurai (U10) *how long? how much?*
doraibu (U9) *drive*
dorama (U12) *drama*
dore (U5) *which one* (noun)
doru (U16) *dollars*
dōshi (U12) *verbs*
dōshite (U15) *why?*
dōyatte (U10) *how?*
doyōbi (U8) *Saturday*
dōzo (U2) *go ahead; there you are*
dōzo yoroshiku (U1) *pleased to meet you*

e (U11) *picture, drawing*
ē (U4) *yes* (softer than hai)
ē? (U8) *expression of surprise*
earoguramu (U16) *aerogramme*
eiga (U8) *film, movie*
eigakan (U7) *cinema*
Eigo (U2) *English* (language)
Eikoku (U20) *England*
eki (U7) *station*
ekiben (U18) *train lunches*
empitsu (U2) *pencil*
emu (U14) *M* (medium)
en (U6) *yen*
engei (U3) *gardening*
erebētā (U14) *elevator*
eru (U14) *L* (large)
esu (U14) *S* (small)
esukarētā (U14) *escalator*
ē to (U2) *a hesitation word* (er, erm)

firumu (U6) *camera film*
fujinfuku (U14) *women's clothes*
funabin (U16) *sea mail*
fune (U10) *boat, ship*
furaido poteto (U15) *chips*
Furansu (U2) *France*
Furansugo (U2) *French* (language)
Furansujin (U2) *French person*
furo (U11) *a bath*
futari (U3) *two people*
futatsu (U6) *two* (items)

futon (U2) *Japanese-style bed*
futorimasu (U15) *put on weight*
futsuka (U9) *2nd* (of month)
fuyu (U11) *winter*

ga (U11) *but*
gaido (bukku) (U17) *guide* (book)
gaishoku (U15) *eating out*
gaishutsu-chū *out* (of the office) (U20)
gakkō (U5) *school*
gakusei (U3) *student*
gasu (U20) *gas*
gekijō (U10) *theatre*
gendai (U15) *these days*
genkan (U20) *entrance porch*
genki(na) (U11) *well; healthy; lively*
genkin (U16) *cash*
getsuyōbi (U8) *Monday*
ginkō (U7) *bank*
ginkō-in (U16) *bank clerk*
go (U2) *five*
gochisōsama deshita (U20) *said after a meal*
gogatsu (U2) *May*
gogo (U5) *p.m.; afternoon* (U10)
gohan (U8) *rice* (cooked)
go-jūsho (U17) *address* (somebody else's)
go-kazoku (U3) *family* (somebody else's)
gomen kudasai (U20) *excuse me*
goro (U8) *about* (with times)
gorufu (U3) *golf*
gorufu o shimasu (U8) *play golf*
go-shujin (U4) *husband* (somebody else's)
gozaimasu (U17) *have* (formal)
gozen (U5) *am*
gurai (U10) *about*
guramu (U16) *gram*

hachi (U2) *eight*
hachigatsu (U2) *August*
hagaki (U6) *postcard*
haha (U3) *mother*
hai (U1) *yes*
hairimasu (U20) *enter*
haisha (U3) *dentist*
haitteimasu (U17) *is included*
hajimemashite (U1) *how do you do?*

haku (paku) (U17) *counter for nights*
hakubutsukan (U19) *museum*
hambāgā (U13) *hamburger*
han (U5) *half* (past)
hana(ya) (U6) *flower (shop)*
hangaku (U19) *half price*
haraimasu (U18) *pay*
hare (U11) *fine* (weather)
haru (U11) *spring*
hashi (U11) *chopsticks*
hayai (U8) *early*
hayai (U10) *quick, fast*
hayaku (U5) *quickly*
he! (U10) *hey; really!*
hen (U19) *area*
heya (U17) *room*
hidari (U7) *left*
hidarigawa (U7) *left-hand side*
hidoi (U12) *terrible*
hikōki (U10) *aeroplane*
hinzūgo (U2) *Hindi*
hiru (U8) *midday*
hirugohan (U8) *lunch*
hisashiburi (U11) *'long time, no see'*
hisho (U3) *secretary*
hitori (U3) *one person; alone*
hitori ni tsuki (U17) *per person*
hitotsu (U6) *one* (item)
hoken (U20) *insurance*
hokkē (U12) *hockey*
hōmu (U18) *platform*
hōmu dorama (U12) *soap opera*
hon (U2) *book*
hon (bon, pon) (U6) *counter for cylindrical objects*
honbako (U12) *bookcase*
hontō ni (U11) *really; in truth*
hoteru (U17) *hotel*
hyaku (U6) *hundred*

ichi (U2) *one*
ichiban (U7) *number 1; most*
ichigatsu (U2) *January*
ichinichijū (U8) *all day long*
ie (U20) *house*
Igirisu (U2) *England*
Igirisujin (U2) *English person*
ii (U9) *good, fine, nice*
iie (U1) *no*
ijō de... (see page 60)
ikaga (U18) *how about?*
ikebana (U3) *flower arranging*

ikimasu (U9) *go*
ikkai (U14) *ground floor*
ikura (U6) *how much?*
ikura (U18) *salmon roe*
imasu (U12) *is, there is* (animate)
imōto (U4) *younger sister* (own)
imōto-san (U4) *younger sister*
   (somebody else's)
Indo (U2) *India*
Indojin (U2) *Indian person*
inu (U12) *dog*
ippaku (U17) *one night*
irasshaimase (U5) *welcome; may I*
   help you?
irasshaimasu   polite form of (U20)
   imasu
iroiro (na) (U14) *various*
isha (U3) *doctor*
isu (U12) *chair*
itadakimasu (U12) said before eating
Itaria (U2) *Italy*
Itariago (U2) *Italian* (language)
Itariajin (U2) *Italian person*
itsu (U8) *when?*
itsuka (U9) *5th* (of month)
itsutsu (U6) *five* (items)
itte (U3) *speak* (command)
itte (U7) *go* (command)
iyahōn (U19) *earphones*

ja arimasen (U3) *is not*
ja mata ne! (U1) *see you!* (casual)
jazu (U12) *jazz*
ji (U5) *o'clock*
jidō kenbaiki (U18) *automatic*
   ticket machine
jikan (U10) *hour*
jikan-hyō (U5) *timetable*
jitensha (U10) *bicycle*
jiyū seki (U18) *unreserved seat*
jōba (U3) *horse riding*
jōdan (U4) *joke*
josei (U17) *female*
jōzu (U7) *good at*
jū (U2) *ten*
jūgatsu (U2) *October*
jūichigatsu (U2) *November*
jūnigatsu (U2) *December*
jūsho (U17) *address*
jūsu (U5) *juice*

kaban (U5) *bag*
kabuki-za (U19) *Kabuki theatre*

kado (U7) *corner*
kaemasu (U16) *to change*
kaerimasu (U9) *return; go back*
kaetai (U16) *want to change*
kai (U14) *floor*
kaidan (U14) *stairs*
kaigi (U20) *meeting*
kaigi-chū (U20) *in a meeting*
kaimasu (U14) *buy*
kaimono (U8) *shopping*
kaisatsu-guchi (U18) *ticket gate*
kaisha-in (U3) *company worker/*
   employee
kakari-in (U17) *attendant*
kakarimasu (U10) (It) *takes*
kamera (U14) *camera*
kampai (U15) *cheers!*
kan (U10) (length of time)
ka na (U11) *I wonder?* (casual speech)
kanai (U4) (my) *wife*
kane (U6) *money*
kani (U18) *crab*
kanjō (U14) *bill*
kankō (U17) *sightseeing*
Kankoku (U10) *Korea*
kappu nūdoru (U10) *cup noodles*
kara (U2) *from*
karē (U13) *curry*
karimasu (U19) *rent, borrow*
kashikomarimashita (U15) *certainly,*
   sir/madam
katamichi (U18) *one way; single*
katsudon (U15) *pork cutlet dish*
kawaii (U4) *pretty; cute*
kawase rēto (U16) *exchange rate*
kayōbi (U8) *Tuesday*
kazoku (U3) (own) *family*
keiken (U17) *experience*
keiyōshi (U11) *adjective*
kēki (U2) *cake*
kekkō (U14) *enough*
kesa (U10) *this morning*
kimari (U15) *decision*
kimasu (U9) *come*
kimeteimasen (U17) *haven't decided*
kinenkan (U19) *memorial museum*
kinō (U10) *yesterday*
kinyōbi (U8) *Friday*
kippu (U6) *ticket*
kirei (na) (U14) *beautiful*
kiro (U16) *kilo*
kissaten (U11) *coffee shop*

kitte (U6) *stamp*
kiteimasu (U14) *try on* (clothes)
kōcha (U8) *black tea*
kochira (U1) *this person; this way*
kodomo (U19) *child(ren)*
kōen (U19) *park*
kōhī (U5) *coffee*
kōka (U16) *coin*
koko (U6) *here*
kokonoka (U9) *9th* (of month)
kokonotsu (U6) *nine* (items)
kōkūbin (U16) *airmail*
kokuritsu (U19) *national*
komedī (U12) *comedy*
komisshon (U16) *commission*
kompyūta (U2) *computer*
kompyūta gēmu (U2) *computer games*
konban (U9) *this evening*
konbanwa (U1) *good evening*
kongetsu (U9) *this month*
konnichiwa (U1) *hello; good afternoon*
kono (U5) *this*
kono chikaku ni (U12) *near here*
kono hito (U3) *this person*
kono yō (na) (U15) *this type* (of)
konshū (U9) *this week*
kōra (U8) *cola*
kore (U2) *this one* (noun)
kōsaten (U7) *crossroads*
kōshū denwa (U16) *public telephone*
kōto (U2) *coat*
kotoshi (U10) *this year*
kozutsumi (U16) *parcel*
ku (U2) *nine*
kudasai (U5) *please; could I have*
kugatsu (U2) *September*
kurashikku (U12) *classical*
kurejitto kādo (U16) *credit card*
kuriketto (U12) *cricket*
kuroi (U14) *black*
kuruma (U10) *car*
kusuri (U6) *medicine*
kusuriya (U6) *chemist's*
kutsu (U14) *shoes*
kyasshu mashīn (U16) *cashpoint*
kyō (U9) *today*
kyōgijō (U12) *playing field*
kyokuin (U6) *post assistant*
kyonen (U10) *last year*

kyōsō (U12) *a race*
kyū (U2) *nine*
kyūkei (U19) *interval, break*

mada (U7) *not yet*
made (U5) *until*
madoguchi (U18) (ticket) *window*
mae (U7) *in front of*
magatte (U7) *turn* (command)
mai (U6) *counter for flat objects*
mainichi (U9) *every day*
maishū (U9) *every week*
maitsuki (U9) *every month*
man (U6) *10,000*
manga (U8) *comic book; cartoon*
man-in (U19) *full house*
massugu (U7) *straight on*
mata (U10) *again*
mata ashita (U1) *see you tomorrow*
matsuri (U19) *festival*
meishi (U20) *business card*
men (U14) *cotton*
menyū (U5) *menu*
michi (U7) *road; path*
midori (U18) *green*
migi (U7) *right*
migigawa (U7) *right-hand side*
mikka (U9) *3rd* (of month)
mimasu (U8) *see; watch; look*
mina-san (U2) *everybody*
minshuku (U17) *family-run inn*
miruku (U5) *milk*
miruku shēku (U15) *milk shake*
misete (U5) *show me; may I see?*
miso shiru (U15) *miso soup*
mittsu (U6) *three* (items)
mizu (U8) *water*
mo (U3) *also; too*
mō (U11) *already*
mōichido (U3) *once more*
mokuyōbi (U8) *Thursday*
mono (U20) *thing*
mōshimasu (U20) (I am) *called*
moshi moshi (U17) *hello* (on phone)
mō sugu (U5) *soon, shortly*
mottekaerimasu (U15) *take away*
mottekimasu (U12) *bring, get*
motto (U5) *more*
muika (U9) *6th* (of month)
mukaigawa (U7) *opposite side*
musuko (U1) (my) *son*
musuko-san (U4) *son* (someone else's)

musume (U4) (my) *daughter*
musume-san (U4) *daughter* (someone else's)
muttsu (U6) *six* (items)
muzukashii (U19) *difficult*
muzukashisō (U19) *looks difficult*

nai (U17) *don't have*
naka (U12) *inside*
namae (U2) *name*
nan/nani (U2) *what*
nanban (U18) *what number?*
nan de (U10) *how?*
nana (U2) *seven*
nanatsu (U6) *seven* (items)
nanji (U5) *what time?*
nannichi (U8) *what date?*
nannin (U3) *how many people?*
nanoka (U9) *7th* (of month)
nansai (U4) *how old?*
nanyōbi (U8) *what day?*
narimasu (U16) *become*
natsu (U11) *summer*
nemasu (U8) *sleep*
nen (U6) *year*
ni (U2) *two*
ni (U8) *on, at* (with time/dates)
niaimasu (U14) *to suit*
nibanme (U7) *second*
nichi (U4) *day* (date)
nichiyōbi (U8) *Sunday*
nichiyōhin (U14) *everyday goods*
nigatsu (U2) *February*
nihaku (U17) *two nights*
Nihon (U2) *Japan*
Nihongo (U2) *Japanese*
Nihonjin (U2) *Japanese person*
niku (U6) *meat*
nikuya (U6) *butcher's*
nin (U3) *people*
ningyō (U14) *doll*
ni shimasu (U15) *decide on*
nochi (U11) *later*
nodo ga kawaiteimasu (U12) *I'm thirsty*
nokori (U18) *the rest*
nomimasu (U8) *drink* (verb)
nomimono (U8) *drinks* (noun)
noriba (U19) (bus/taxi) *stop*
norikaemasu (U18) *change; transfer*
nyūjōken (U19) *admission ticket*
nyūsu (U12) *news*

ocha (U8) *green tea*
odori (U10) *dance*
ōfuku (U18) *return* (ticket)
o-genki de (U11) *take care*
o-hairi kudasai (U20) *please come in*
ohayō gozaimasu (U1) *good morning*
oishii (U11) *delicious*
oishisō (U15) *looks delicious*
okāsan (U1) *mother*
okagesama de (U11) *I'm fine, thanks*
o-kake kudasai (U20) *please sit down*
o-kane (U6) *money* ōkii (U5) *big*
okimasu (U8) *wake up*
okujō (U14) *rooftop*
okurimasu (U16) *send*
okusan (U4) *wife* (somebody else's)
okyakusan (U5) *customer; guest*
omedetō (gozaimasu) (U18) *congratulations*
o-meshiagari (U15) *to eat in* (formal)
omiyage (U14) *souvenir*
o-mochikaeri (U15) *to take away* (formal)
omoshiroi (U11) *interesting*
o-namae wa? (U2) *what's your name?*
onēsan (U4) *older sister* (somebody else's)
onegaishimasu (U14) *please*
ongaku (U12) *music*
oniisan (U4) *older brother* (somebody else's)
orenji (U15) *orange*
o-tearai (U11) *toilet*
o-tera (U10) *temple*
otona (U19) *adult*
otōsan (U4) *father*
otōto (U3) *younger brother* (own)
otōto-san (U4) *younger brother* (somebody else's)
otsuri (U14) *small change*
owarimasu (U12) *end; finish*
oyasumi nasai (U1) *good night*

pan (U6) *bread*
panfuretto (U17) *pamphlet*
pantsu (U2) *trousers*
panya (U6) *bakery*
pāsento (U14) *per cent*
pasokon (U14) *PC*
pasupōto (U16) *passport*
pātī (U9) *party*

pēji (U17) *page*
pen (U2) *pen*
penshon (U17) *pension* (lodgings)
piza (U5) *pizza*
pondo (U16) *pounds* (sterling)
poppusu (U12) *pop music*
posuto (U12) *postbox*

raigetsu (U9) *next month*
rainen (U10) *next year*
raishū (U9) *next week*
raisu (U14) *rice*
rajikase (U14) *radio cassette*
rajio (U14) *radio*
reji (U14) *cash desk*
remon tī (U15) *lemon tea*
ressun (U19) *lesson*
resutoran (U2) *restaurant*
rifuto (U19) (ski) *lift*
ringo (U6) *apple*
rirakkusu (U8) *relax*
rokku (U12) *rock music*
roku (U2) *six*
rokugatsu (U2) *June*
rusu (U20) *not in* (the house)
ryōgae-guchi (U16) *exchange
    window*
ryokan (U17) *Japanese inn*
ryokō shimasu (U10) *travel; take a
    trip*
ryōri (U10) *cooking, cuisine*

sai (U4) *years old*
saikin (U12) *recently*
sain (U16) *signature*
saisho (U17) *first*
saizu (U14) *size*
sakana (U7) *fish*
sakanaya (U6) *fishmonger's*
sakaya (U6) *wine shop*
sake (U6) *rice alcohol*
sakkā (U3) *football*
sampaku (U17) *three nights*
samui (U11) *cold*
san (U1) *Mr/Mrs/Miss/Ms*
san (U2) *three*
sandoitchi (U5) *sandwich*
sangatsu (U2) *March*
sannin (U3) *three people*
sarada (U13) *salad*
sashimi (U15) *sliced raw fish*
satsu (U16) *note* (money)

sayōnara (U1) *goodbye*
sei (U14) *made in*
seifuku (U14) *uniform*
seisanjō (U18) *fare adjustment
    office*
seito (U3) *pupil*
seki (U18) *seat*
sen (U6) *thousand*
sen (U18) (train) *line*
sengetsu (U10) *last month*
sensei (U3) *teacher; professor*
senshū (U10) *last week*
sensu (U14) *fan*
sētā (U14) *jumper*
shatsu (U14) *shirt*
shi (U2) *four*
shichi (U2) *seven*
shichigatsu (U2) *July*
shigatsu (U2) *April*
shigoto (U3) *work*
shī dī purēyā (U2) *CD player*
shimasu (U8) *do; make; play*
shimbun (U5) *newspaper*
shimpai (U18) *worry*
shingō (U7) *traffic lights*
shinkansen (U10) *bullet train*
shinsetsu(na) (U11) *kind, helpful*
shiroi (U14) *white*
shita (U12) *below, under*
shitei seki (U18) *reserved seat*
shitsurei shimasu *pardon me for
    (U2) interrupting*
shizuka(na) (U11) *quiet*
shōji (U20) *trading*
shokuji (U17) *meal*
shōshō omachi (U5) *please wait a
    moment*
shufu (U3) *housewife*
shūgaku ryokō (U10) *school trip*
shujin (U4) *husband* (own)
shūmatsu (U16) *weekend*
shumi (U3) *hobby*
shutchō-chū (U20) *on a business trip*
soba (U15) *noodles*
sō desu (U1) *that's right*
soko (U6) *there* (that place)
soku (U19) *pair* (counter)
sono (U5) *that*
sore (U5) *that one* (noun)
sorekara (U7) *and then*
sore ni (U8) *and, besides*

sorosoro (U20) *soon, shortly*
soshite (U7) *and*
soto (U12) *outside*
suiei (U3) *swimming*
suiyōbi (U8) *Wednesday*
sukāto (U14) *skirt*
sukēto gutsu (U19) *skates*
suki (U12) *like*
sukī (U3) *skiing*
sukījō (U19) *ski ground*
sukī tsuā (U5) *ski tour*
sukottorando (U2) *Scotland*
sumimasen (U1) *excuse me; sorry*
sūpā (U5) *supermarket*
supagetti (U5) *spaghetti*
supōtsu (U3) *sports*
surippa (U20) *slippers*
surōpu (U19) (ski) *slope*
suteki (na) (U5) *smart, fashionable*
sutēki (U13) *steak*
sutereo (U2) *stereo*
sutoa gaido (U14) *store guide*
sutoroberī (U15) *strawberry*

tabako (U5) *cigarettes*
tabemasu (U8) *eat*
tabemono (U8) *food*
taberaremasu (U15) *can eat*
taishikan (U20) *embassy*
takai (U11) *expensive; high*
takusan (U10) *many*
takushī (U2) *taxi*
takushī noriba (U18) *taxi tank*
tamago (U8) *eggs*
tanjōbi (U4) *birthday*
tanoshii (U11) *pleasant, enjoyable*
tatoeba (U14) *for example*
tēburu (U12) *table*
tegami (U6) *letter*
teinei (U14) *polite*
teishoku (U15) *set meal*
tempura (U15) *Japanese fried food*
ten'in (U3) *shop assistant*
tenisu (U8) *tennis*
tenisu kōto (U12) *tennis court*
tenki (U11) *weather*
tēpu rekōdā (U2) *tape-recorder*
tera (U10) *temple*
terebi (U2) *television*
terehon kādo (U16) *telephone card*
teriyakibāgā (U15) *teriyaki burger*
to (U3) *and*

tōchaku shimasu (U18) *arrive*
tōi (U18) *far*
tōka (U9) *10th* (of month)
tokei (U2) *watch* or *clock*
toki (U12) *time, when*
tōki (U14) *pottery*
tokidoki (U8) *sometimes*
tokoro (U11) *place*
tokui (U12) *good at*
toku ni (U19) *in particular*
tomodachi (U9) *friend*
tonari (U7) *next to*
toraberāzu chekku
    (U16) *travellers' cheques*
toriniku (U2) *chicken, poultry*
tōsuto (U8) *toast*
totemo (U11) *very*
T.shatsu (U14) *T-shirt*
tsugi (U7) *next*
tsuin (U17) *twin* (room)
tsuitachi (U9) *1st* (of month)
tsukemono (U15) *pickles*
tsukue (U12) *desk*
tsumaranai (U20) *boring*

uchi (U8) *house, home*
udon (U15) *noodles*
ue (U12) *above, on top*
uētoresu (U15) *waitress*
uisukī (U2) *whisky*
untenshu (U18) *driver*
uriba (U14) (shop) *department*
ūru (U14) *wool*
ushiro (U12) *behind*
utteimasu (U14) *sell*

wakai (U4) (looks) *young*
wakamono (U15) *young people*
wakarimashita (U7) *I've understood*
wanpīsu (U14) *dress*
wā puro (U2) *word processor*
waribiki (U14) *discount*
warui (U10) *bad*
washi (U14) *Japanese paper*
washitsu (U17) *Japanese-style room*
washoku (U15) *Japanese cuisine*
watashi (U2) *I*
watashitachi (U18) *we*

ya (U19) *and*
yakitori (U15) *grilled meat on
    skewers*
yakyū (U12) *baseball*

yaoya (U6) *greengrocer's*
yasai (U6) *vegetables*
yasui (U11) *cheap*
yasumi (U5) *holiday*
yo (U2) *I tell you; actually*
yōfuku (U14) *clothes*
yōgu (U19) *equipment*
yōka (U9) *8th* (of month)
yokka (U9) *4th* (of month)
yoku (U12) *often*
yokushitsu (U17) *bathroom*
yomimasu (U8) *read*
yonin (U3) *four people*
yorokonde (U9) *I'd love to*
yoroshii (U6) *fine; all right*
yoru (U8) *evening*
yorugohan (U8) *evening meal; dinner*

yōshitsu (U17) *western-style room*
yōshoku (U15) *western cuisine*
yoyaku (U17) *reservation*
yūbinkyoku (U6) *post office*
yukata (U14) *cotton robe*
yuki (U18) *destined for*
yuki (U19) *snow*
yukkuri (U3) *slowly*
yūro (U16) *euro*
yūshoku (U17) *evening meal*
yūsuhosuteru (U17) *youth hostel*

zannen (U9) *shame; pity*
zasshi (U8) *magazine*
zembu de (U3) *altogether*
zenzen (U12) *never*
zubon (U14) *trousers*

Appendix: numbers

0	zero/rei	30	sanjū	6,000	rokusen
1	ichi	40	yonjū	7,000	nanasen
2	ni	50	gojū	8,000	hassen
3	san	60	rokujū	9,000	kyūsen
4	shi/yon	70	nanajū	10,000	ichiman
5	go	80	hachijū	20,000	niman
6	roku	90	kyūjū	30,000	sanman
7	shichi/nana	100	hyaku	1,000,000	hyakuman
8	hachi	200	nihyaku	10,000,000	senman
9	kyū/ku	300	sambyaku	100,000,000	ichioku
10	jū	400	yonhyaku	1000,000,000	jūoku
11	jūichi	500	gohyaku	1000,000,000,000	itchō
12	jūni	600	roppyaku		
13	jūsan	700	nanahyaku		
14	jūshi/jūyon	800	happyaku		
15	jūgo	900	kyūhyaku		
16	jūroku	1,000	sen/issen		
17	jūnana/jūshichi	2,000	nisen		
18	jūhachi	3,000	sanzen		
19	jūkyū/jūku	4,000	yonsen		
20	nijū	5,000	gosen		

index of grammatical structures

(U = Unit; E = Explanation)